Hands-On Deep Learning Architectures with Python

Create deep neural networks to solve computational problems using TensorFlow and Keras

Yuxi (Hayden) Liu
Saransh Mehta

BIRMINGHAM - MUMBAI

Hands-On Deep Learning Architectures with Python

Copyright © 2019 Packt Publishing

Commissioning Editor: Sunith Shetty
Acquisition Editor: Porous Godhaa
Content Development Editor: Karan Thakkar
Technical Editor: Sushmeeta Jena
Copy Editor: Safis Editing
Project Coordinator: Hardik Bhinde
Proofreader: Safis Editing
Indexer: Pratik Shirodkar
Graphics: Jisha Chirayil
Production Coordinator: Arvindkumar Gupta

First published: April 2019

Production reference: 1300419

Published by Packt Publishing Ltd.
Livery Place
35 Livery Street
Birmingham
B3 2PB, UK.

ISBN 978-1-78899-808-6

www.packtpub.com

`mapt.io`

Mapt is an online digital library that gives you full access to over 5,000 books and videos, as well as industry leading tools to help you plan your personal development and advance your career. For more information, please visit our website.

Why subscribe?

- Spend less time learning and more time coding with practical eBooks and Videos from over 4,000 industry professionals

- Improve your learning with Skill Plans built especially for you

- Get a free eBook or video every month

- Mapt is fully searchable

- Copy and paste, print, and bookmark content

Packt.com

Did you know that Packt offers eBook versions of every book published, with PDF and ePub files available? You can upgrade to the eBook version at `www.packt.com` and as a print book customer, you are entitled to a discount on the eBook copy. Get in touch with us at `customercare@packtpub.com` for more details.

At `www.packt.com`, you can also read a collection of free technical articles, sign up for a range of free newsletters, and receive exclusive discounts and offers on Packt books and eBooks.

Contributors

About the authors

Yuxi (Hayden) Liu is an author of a series of machine learning books and an education enthusiast. His first book, the first edition of *Python Machine Learning By Example*, was a #1 bestseller on Amazon India in 2017 and 2018 and his other book *R Deep Learning Projects*, both published by Packt Publishing.

He is an experienced data scientist who is focused on developing machine learning and deep learning models and systems. He has worked in a variety of data-driven domains and has applied his machine learning expertise to computational advertising, recommendations, and network anomaly detection. He published five first-authored IEEE transaction and conference papers during his master's research at the University of Toronto.

Saransh Mehta has cross-domain experience of working with texts, images, and audio using deep learning. He has been building artificial, intelligence-based solutions, including a generative chatbot, an attendee-matching recommendation system, and audio keyword recognition systems for multiple start-ups. He is very familiar with the Python language, and has extensive knowledge of deep learning libraries such as TensorFlow and Keras. He has been in the top 10% of entrants to deep learning challenges hosted by Microsoft and Kaggle.

First and most, I would like to thank my mentor and guide, Ankur Pal, for providing me with opportunities to work with deep learning. I would also like to thank my family and friends, Yash Bonde and Kumar Subham, for being my constant supports in the field of artificial intelligence. This book is the result of the help and support I have been receiving from them.

About the reviewers

Antonio L. Amadeu is a data science consultant and is passionate about data, artificial intelligence, and neural networks, in particular, using machine learning and deep learning algorithms in daily challenges to solve all types of issues in any business field and industry. He has worked for large companies, including Unilever, Lloyds Bank, TE Connectivity, and Microsoft.

As an aspiring astrophysicist, he does some research in relation to the Virtual Observatory group at Sao Paulo University in Brazil, a member of the International Virtual Observatory Alliance (IVOA).

Junho Kim received a BS in mathematics and computer science engineering in 2015, and an MS in computer science engineering in 2017, from Chung-Ang University, Seoul, South Korea. After graduation, he worked as an artificial intelligence research intern at AIRI, Lunit, and Naver Webtoon. Currently, he is working for NCSOFT as an artificial intelligence research scientist.

His research interests include deep learning in computer vision, especially in relation to generative models with GANs, and image-to-image translation. He likes to read papers and implement deep learning in a simple way that others can understand easily. All his works are shared on GitHub (@taki0112). His dream is to make everyone's life more fun using AI.

Packt is searching for authors like you

If you're interested in becoming an author for Packt, please visit authors.packtpub.com and apply today. We have worked with thousands of developers and tech professionals, just like you, to help them share their insight with the global tech community. You can make a general application, apply for a specific hot topic that we are recruiting an author for, or submit your own idea.

Table of Contents

Preface

Deep learning architectures are composed of multilevel nonlinear operations that represent high-level abstractions. This allows you to learn useful feature representations from data. *Hands-On Deep Learning Architectures with Python* gives you a rundown explaining the essential learning algorithms used for deep and shallow architectures. Packed with practical implementations and ideas to build efficient artificial intelligence systems, this book will help you learn how neural networks play a major role in building deep architectures.

You will gain an understanding of various deep learning architectures, such as AlexNet, VGG Net, GoogleNet, and many more, with easy-to-follow code and diagrams. In addition to this, the book will also guide you in building and training various deep architectures, such as the Boltzmann mechanism, autoencoders, **convolutional neural networks (CNNs)**, **recurrent neural networks (RNN)**, **natural language processing (NLP)**, **generative adversarial networks (GANs)**, and others, with practical implementations. This book explains the essential learning algorithms used for deep and shallow architectures.

By the end of this book, you will be able to construct deep models using popular frameworks and datasets with the required design patterns for each architecture. You will be ready to explore the possibilities of deep architectures in today's world.

Who this book is for

If you're a data scientist, machine learning developer/engineer, deep learning practitioner, or are curious about the field of AI and want to upgrade your knowledge of various deep learning architectures, this book will appeal to you. You are expected to have some knowledge of statistics and machine learning algorithms to get the most out of this book.

What this book covers

Chapter 1, *Getting Started with Deep Learning*, covers the evolution of intelligence in machines and artificial intelligence and, eventually, deep learning. We'll then look at some applications of deep learning and set up our environment for coding our way through deep learning models. Completing this chapter, you will learn the following things.

Chapter 2, *Deep Feedforward Networks*, covers the evolution history of deep feedforward networks and their architecture. We will also demonstrate how to bring up and preprocess data for training a deep learning network.

Chapter 3, *Restricted Boltzmann Machines and Autoencoders*, explains the algorithm behind the scenes, called restricted Boltzmann machines (RBMs) and their evolutionary path. We will then dig deeper into the logic behind them and implement RBMs in TensorFlow. We will also apply them to build a movie recommender. We'll then learn about autoencoders and briefly look at their evolutionary path. We will also illustrate a variety of autoencoders, categorized by their architectures or forms of regularization.

Chapter 4, *CNN Architecture*, covers an important class of deep learning network for images, called **convolutional neural networks** (**CNNs**). We will also discuss the benefits of CNNs over deep feedforward networks. We will then learn more about some famous image classification CNNs and then build our first CNN image classifier on the CIFAR-10 dataset. Then, we'll move on to object detection with CNNs and the TensorFlow detection model, zoo.

Chapter 5, *Mobile Neural Networks and CNNs*, discusses the need for mobile neural networks for doing CNN work in a real-time application. We will also talk about the two benchmark MobileNet architectures introduced by Google—MobileNet and MobileNetV2. Later, we'll discuss the successful combination of MobileNet with object detection networks such as SSD to achieve object detection on mobile devices.

Chapter 6, *Recurrent Neural Networks*, explains one of the most important deep learning models, recurrent neural networks (RNNs), its architecture, and the evolutionary path of RNNs. Later, we'll will discuss a variety of architectures categorized by the recurrent layer, including vanilla RNNs, LSTM, GRU, and bidirectional RNNs, and apply the vanilla architecture to write our own *War and Peace* (a bit nonsensical though). We'll also introduce the bidirectional architecture that allows the model to preserve information from both past and future contexts of the sequence.

Chapter 7, *Generative Adversarial Networks*, explains one of the most interesting deep learning models, generative adversarial networks (GANs), and its evolutionary path. We will also illustrate a variety of GAN architectures with an example of image generation. We will also explore four GAN architectures, including vanilla GANs, deep convolutional GANs, conditional GANs, and information-maximizing GANs.

Chapter 8, *New Trends in Deep Learning*, talks about a few deep learning ideas that we have found impactful this year and more prominent in the future. We'll also learn that Bayesian deep learning combines the merits of both Bayesian learning and deep learning.

To get the most out of this book

Readers will require prior knowledge of Python, TensorFlow, and Keras.

Download the example code files

You can download the example code files for this book from your account at
`www.packt.com`. If you purchased this book elsewhere, you can visit
`www.packt.com/support` and register to have the files emailed directly to you.

You can download the code files by following these steps:

1. Log in or register at `www.packt.com`.
2. Select the **SUPPORT** tab.
3. Click on **Code Downloads & Errata**.
4. Enter the name of the book in the **Search** box and follow the onscreen
   instructions.

Once the file is downloaded, please make sure that you unzip or extract the folder using the
latest version of:

- WinRAR/7-Zip for Windows
- Zipeg/iZip/UnRarX for Mac
- 7-Zip/PeaZip for Linux

The code bundle for the book is also hosted on GitHub at `https://github.com/`
`PacktPublishing/Hands-On-Deep-Learning-Architectures-with-Python`. In case there's
an update to the code, it will be updated on the existing GitHub repository.

We also have other code bundles from our rich catalog of books and videos available
at `https://github.com/PacktPublishing/`. Check them out!

Download the color images

We also provide a PDF file that has color images of the screenshots/diagrams used in this
book. You can download it here: `https://www.packtpub.com/sites/default/files/`
`downloads/9781788998086_ColorImages.pdf`.

Conventions used

There are a number of text conventions used throughout this book.

CodeInText: Indicates code words in text, database table names, folder names, filenames, file extensions, pathnames, dummy URLs, user input, and Twitter handles. Here is an example: "Mount the downloaded WebStorm-10*.dmg disk image file as another disk in your system."

A block of code is set as follows:

```
import tensorflow as tf
import numpy as np
import matplotlib.pyplot as plt
from sklearn.model_selection import train_test_split
```

When we wish to draw your attention to a particular part of a code block, the relevant lines or items are set in bold:

```
import tensorflow as tf
import numpy as np
import matplotlib.pyplot as plt
from sklearn.model_selection import train_test_split
```

Any command-line input or output is written as follows:

```
conda activate test_env
conda install tensorflow
```

Bold: Indicates a new term, an important word, or words that you see onscreen. For example, words in menus or dialog boxes appear in the text like this. Here is an example: "Select **System info** from the **Administration** panel."

Warnings or important notes appear like this.

Tips and tricks appear like this.

Get in touch

Feedback from our readers is always welcome.

General feedback: If you have questions about any aspect of this book, mention the book title in the subject of your message and email us at customercare@packtpub.com.

Errata: Although we have taken every care to ensure the accuracy of our content, mistakes do happen. If you have found a mistake in this book, we would be grateful if you would report this to us. Please visit www.packt.com/submit-errata, selecting your book, clicking on the Errata Submission Form link, and entering the details.

Piracy: If you come across any illegal copies of our works in any form on the Internet, we would be grateful if you would provide us with the location address or website name. Please contact us at copyright@packt.com with a link to the material.

If you are interested in becoming an author: If there is a topic that you have expertise in and you are interested in either writing or contributing to a book, please visit authors.packtpub.com.

Reviews

Please leave a review. Once you have read and used this book, why not leave a review on the site that you purchased it from? Potential readers can then see and use your unbiased opinion to make purchase decisions, we at Packt can understand what you think about our products, and our authors can see your feedback on their book. Thank you!

For more information about Packt, please visit packt.com.

Section 1: The Elements of Deep Learning

In this section, you will get an overview of deep learning with Python, and will also learn about the architectures of the deep feedforward network, the Boltzmann machine, and autoencoders. We will also practice examples based on DFN and applications of the Boltzmann machine and autoencoders, with the concrete examples based on the DL frameworks/libraries with Python, along with their benchmarks.

This section consists of the following chapters:

- Chapter 1, *Getting Started with Deep Learning*
- Chapter 2, *Deep Feedforward Networks*
- Chapter 3, *Restricted Boltzmann Machines and Autoencoders*

Getting Started with Deep Learning

Artificial intelligence might work, and if it does, it will be the biggest development in technology ever.

– Sam Altman

Welcome to the *Hands-On Deep Learning Architectures with Python!* If you are completely unfamiliar with deep learning, you can begin your journey right here with this book. And for readers who have an idea about it, we have covered almost every aspect of deep learning. So you are definitely going to learn a lot more about deep learning from this book.

The book is laid out in a cumulative manner; that is, it begins from the basics and builds it over and over to get to advanced levels. In this chapter, we discuss how humans started creating intelligence in machines and how artificial intelligence gradually evolved to machine learning and eventually deep learning. We then see some nice applications of deep learning. Moving back to the fundamentals, we will learn how artificial neurons work and, in the end, set up our environment for coding our way through deep learning models. After completing this chapter, you will have learned about the following things.

- What artificial intelligence is, and how machine learning, deep learning relates to it
- The types of machine learning tasks
- Information about some interesting deep learning applications
- What an artificial neural network is, and how it works
- Setting up TensorFlow and Keras with Python

Let's begin with a short discussion on artificial intelligence and the relationships between artificial intelligence, machine learning, and deep learning.

Artificial intelligence

Ever since the beginning of the computer era, humans have been trying to mimic the brain into the machine. Researchers have been developing methods that would make machines not only compute but also decide like we humans do. This quest of ours gave birth to artificial intelligence around the 1960s. By definition, artificial intelligence means developing systems that are capable of accomplishing tasks without a human explicitly programming every decision. In 1956, the first program for playing checkers was written by Arthur Samuel. Since then, researchers tried to mimic human intelligence by defining sets of handwritten rules that didn't involve any learning. Artificial intelligence programs, which played games such as chess, were nothing but sets of manually defined moves and strategies. In 1959, Arthur Samuel coined the term **machine learning**. Machine learning started using various concepts of probability and bayesian statistics to perform pattern recognition, feature extraction, classification, and so on. In the 1980s, inspired by the neural structure of the human brain, **artificial neural networks** (**ANN**) were introduced. ANN in the 2000s evolved into today's so-called deep learning! The following is a timeline for the evolution of artificial intelligence through machine learning and deep learning:

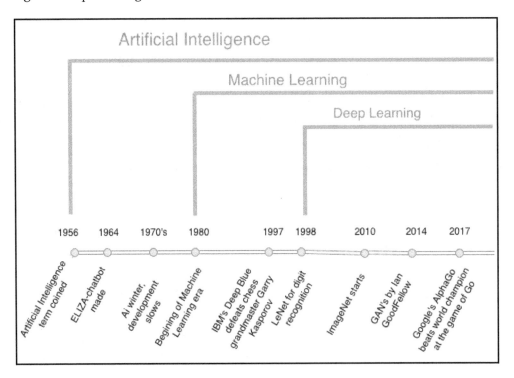

Machine learning

Artificial intelligence prior to machine learning was just about writing rules that the machine used to process the provided data. Machine learning made a transition. Now, just by providing the data and expected output to the machine learning algorithm, the computer returns an optimized set of rules for the task. Machine learning uses historic data to train a system and test it on unknown but similar data, beginning the journey of machines learning how to make decisions without being hard coded. In the early 90s, machine learning emerged as the new face of artificial intelligence. Larger datasets were developed and made public to allow more people to build and train machine learning models. Very soon a huge community of machine learning scientists/engineers developed. Although machine learning algorithms draw inference from statistics, what makes it powerful is the error minimization approach. It tries to minimize the error between expected output provided by the dataset and predicted algorithm output to discover the optimized rules. This is the learning part of machine learning. We won't be covering machine learning algorithms in this book but they are essentially divided into three categories: supervised, unsupervised, and reinforcement. Since deep learning is also a subset of machine learning, these categories apply to deep learning as well.

Supervised learning

In supervised learning, the dataset consists of both the input data point and the expected output, commonly known as the label. The job of the algorithm is to learn a mapping function from inputs to expected outputs. The function could be a linear function such as $y = mx + c$ or non-linear like $y = ax3 + bx2 + cx + d$, where y is the target output and x is the input. All the supervised learning tasks can be categorized into regression and classification.

Regression

Regression deals with learning continuous mapping functions that can predict values provided by various input features. The function can be linear or non-linear. If the function is linear, it is referred to as linear regression, and if it is non-linear, it is commonly called polynomial regression. Predicting values when there are multiple input features (variables), we call multi-variate regression. A very typical example of regression is the house prediction problem. Provided with the various parameters of a house, such as build area, locality, number of rooms, and so on, the accurate selling price of the house can be predicted using historic data.

Classification

When the target output values are categorized instead of raw values, as in regression, it is a classification task. For example, we could classify different species of flowers based on input features, petal length, petal width, sepal length, and sepal width. Output categories are versicolor, setosa, and virginica. Algorithms like logistic regression, decision tree, naive bayes, and so on are classification algorithms. We will be covering details of Classification in Chapter 2.

Unsupervised learning

Unsupervised learning is used when we don't have the corresponding target output values for the input. It is used to understand the data distribution and discover similarity of some kinds between the data points. As there is no target output to learn from, unsupervised algorithms rely on initializers to generate initial decision boundaries and update them as they go through the data. After going through the data multiple times, the algorithms update to optimized decision boundaries, which groups data points based on similarities. This method is known as clustering, and algorithms such as k-means are used for it.

Reinforcement learning

Remember how you learned to ride a bicycle in your childhood? It was a trial and error process, right? You tried to balance yourself, and each time you did something wrong, you tipped off the bicycle. But, you learned from your mistakes, and eventually, you were able to ride without falling. In the same way, Reinforcement learning does the same! An agent is exposed to an environment where it takes action from a list of possible actions, which leads to a change in the state of the agent. A **state** is the current situation of the environment the agent is in. For every action, the agent receives an award. Whenever the received reward is positive, it signifies the agent has taken the correct step, and when the reward is negative, it signifies a mistake. The agent follows a policy, a reinforcement learning algorithm through which the agent determines next actions considering the current state. Reinforcement learning is the true form of artificial intelligence, inspired by a human's way of learning through trial and error. Think of yourself as the agent and the bicycle the environment! Discussing reinforcement learning algorithms here is beyond the scope of this book, so let's shift focus back to deep learning!

Deep learning

Though machine learning has provided computers with the capability to learn decision boundaries, it misses out on the robustness of doing so. Machine learning models have to be very specifically designed for every particular application. People spent hours deciding what features to select for optimal learning. As the data cross folded and non-linearity in data increased, machine learning models struggled to produce accurate results. Scientists soon realized that a much more powerful tool was required to apex this growth. In the 1980s, the concept of ANN was reborn, and with faster computing capabilities, deeper versions of ANN were developed, providing us with the powerful tool we were looking for—deep learning!

Applications of deep learning

The leverage of a technology is decided by the robustness of its applications. Deep learning has created a great amount of commotion in tech as well as the non-tech market, owing to its hefty applications. So, in this section, we discuss some of the amazing applications of deep learning, which will keep you motivated all through the book.

Self-driving cars

This is probably the coolest and most promising application of deep learning. An autonomous vehicle has a number of cameras attached to it. The output video stream is fed into deep learning networks that recognize, as well as segment, different objects present around the car. NVIDIA has introduced an *End to End Learning for Self-Driving Cars*, which is a convolutional neural network that takes in input images from cameras and predicts what actions should be taken in the form of steering angle or acceleration. For training the network, the steering angles and throttle and camera views are stored when a human is driving along, documenting the actions taken by him for the changes occurring around him. The network's parameters are then updated through backpropagating (Backpropagation is discussed in details in `Chapter 2`, *Deep Feedforward Networks*) the error from human input and the network's predictions.

 If you wish to know more about the NVIDIA's *Learning for Self-Driving Cars*, you can refer to the following NVIDIA's paper: `https://arxiv.org/abs/1604.07316`.

Image translation

Generative adversarial networks (**GANs**) are the most notorious deep learning architectures. This is due to their capability to generate outputs from random noise input vectors. GAN has two networks: generator and discriminator. The job of the generator is to take a random vector as input and generate sample output data. The discriminator takes input from both the real data and faked data created by the generator. The job of the discriminator is to determine whether the input is coming from real data or a faked one from the generator. You can visualize the scenario, imagining the discriminator is a bank trying to distinguish between real and fake currency. At the same time, the generator is the fraud trying to pass fake currency to a counterfeit bank; generator and discriminator both learn through their mistakes, and the generator eventually produces results that imitate the real data very precisely.

One of the interesting applications of GANs is image-to-image translation. It is based on conditional GAN (we will be discussing GANs in details under Chapter 7). Given a pair of images holding some relation, say I1 and I2, a conditional GAN learns how to convert I1 into I2. A dedicated software called **pix2pix** is created to demonstrate the applications of this concept. It can be used to fill in colors to black and white images, create maps from satellite images, generate object images from mere sketches, and what not!

The following is the link to the actual paper published by Phillip Isola for *image-to-image translation* and a sample image from pix2pix depicting various applications of image-to-image translation (https://arxiv.org/abs/1611.07004):

Sourced from pix2pix

Machine translation

There are more than 4,000 languages in this world and billions of people communicating through them. You can imagine the scale at which language translation is required. Most of the translations were done with human translators because classical rule-based translations made by machine were quite often meaningless. Deep learning came up with a solution to this. It can learn the language like we do and generate translations that are more natural. This is commonly referred to as **neural machine translation (NMT)**.

Encoder-decoder structure

Neural machine translation models are **Recurrent Neural Networks (RNN)**, arranged in encoder-decoder fashion. The encoder network takes in variable length input sequences through RNN and encodes the sequences into a fixed size vector. The decoder begins with this encoded vector and starts generating translation word by word, until it predicts the *end of sentence*. The whole architecture is trained end-to-end with input sentence and correct output translation. The major advantage of these systems (apart from the capability to handle variable input size) is that they learn the context of a sentence and predict accordingly, rather than making a word-to-word translation. Neural machine translation can be best seen in action on Google translate in the following screenshot:

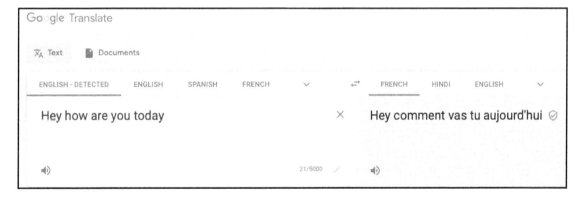

Sourced from Google translate

Chatbots

You might find this is the coolest application! Computers talking to us like humans has been a fascinating desire. It gives us a sense of computers being intelligent. However, most of the chatbot systems built earlier were based on a knowledge base and rules that define which response to pick from it. This made chatbots a very closed domain and they sounded quite unnatural. But with a little tweaking to the encoder-decoder architecture, we saw machine translation can actually make a chatbot generate a response on its own. The encodings learn the context of the input sentences, and, if the whole architecture is trained on sample queries and responses, whenever the system sees a new query, it can generate its response based on the learning. A lot of platforms like IBM Watson, Bottr, and rasa are building deep learning powered tools to build chatbots for business purposes.

Building the fundamentals

This section is where you will begin the journey of being a deep learning architect. Deep learning stands on the pillar of ANNs. Our first step should be to understand how they work. In this section, we describe the biological inspiration behind the artificial neuron and the mathematical model to create an ANN. We have tried keeping the mathematics to a minimum and focused more on concepts. However, we assume you are familiar with basic algebra and calculus.

Biological inspiration

As we mentioned earlier, deep learning is inspired by the human brain. This seems a good idea indeed. To develop the intelligence of the brain inside a machine, you need the machine to mimic the brain! Now, if you are slightly aware of how a human brain learns and memorizes things so fast, you must know that this is possible due to millions of neurons developing an interconnected network, sending signals to each other, which makes up the memory. The neuron has two major components: dendrite and axon. The dendrite acts as a receptor and combines all the signals that the neuron is receiving. The axon is connected to dendrites at the end of other neurons through synapses. Once the incoming signals cross a threshold, they flow through the axon and synapse to pass the signal to the connected neuron. The structure in which the neurons are connected to each other decides the network's capabilities. Following is a diagram of what a biological neuron might look like:

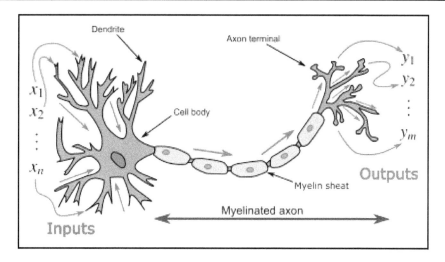

A biological neuron (sourced from Wikimedia)

Hence, the artificial model of neural network should be a parallel network of interconnected nodes, which take in inputs from various other nodes, and pass on the output when activated. This activation phenomenon must be controlled by some sort of mathematical operations. Let's see the operations and equations next!

ANNs

The ANNs is built from two components: nodes and weights. Nodes play the role of a neuron while weights are the learnable parameters, which connect the neurons with each other, and control their activation paths.

So how do we make an artificial neuron or node? Consider x to be a scalar input to the neuron and w to be the scalar weight for the neuron. If you don't know what a scalar and vector are, a scalar is simply a single real number element, while a vector is a list of such elements. The artificial neuron can be represented as the following equation:

$$a = w.x + b$$

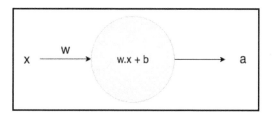

The circle represents the neuron which takes scalar x as input and outputs a after multiplying it with weight w. Here, b is called as bias. Bias is added in the equation to provide the capability of shifting the output for a specific range of inputs. The role of bias will become more clear once we go through the activation functions.

Now, suppose the neuron didn't just take in a single scalar input, but multiple inputs. The inputs can then be called a vector (say P). Then, P could be written as a set of scalar inputs $p_1, p_2, p_3, ..., p_n$ and each input will also have a weight vector (say $W = w_1, w_2, w_3, ..., w_n$), which will be used to activate the neuron. The following matrices represent the P and W vectors:

$$P = \begin{bmatrix} p_1 \\ p_2 \\ p_3 \\ . \\ . \\ p_n \end{bmatrix} \qquad W = \begin{bmatrix} w_1 \\ w_2 \\ w_3 \\ . \\ . \\ w_n \end{bmatrix}$$

So what changes do we need to make in the equation to fit these multiple inputs? Simply sum them up! This changes the basic equation $a = w.x + b$ to the following equation:

$$a = \sum_{i=0}^{n} W_I . P_i + B$$

The artificial neuron taking in multiple inputs would look like the following diagram:

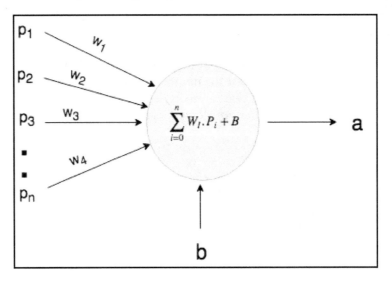

But what would a neuron do alone? Although it can still output values, which can be used to take binary judgements (zero or one), we need a lot of similar neurons arranged in a parallel manner and interconnected just like in the brain in order to go beyond binary decisions. So, what would it look like? Here's the diagram:

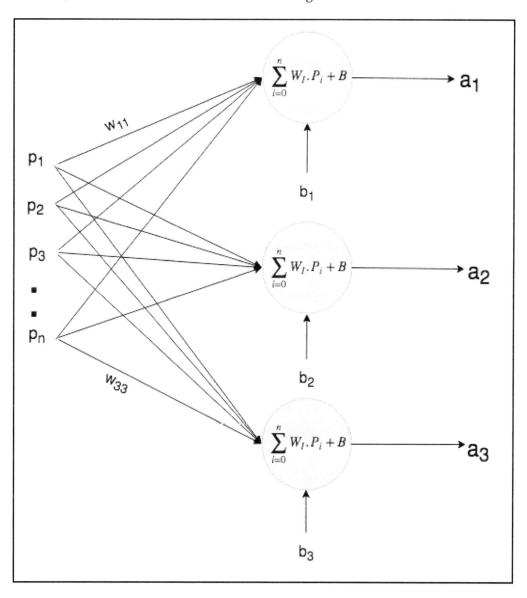

What changes are required in the equation now? Just the dimensions of weight vector and output vector. Now we will have n x m number of weights where n is the number of inputs and m is the number of neurons. Also, we will be having a separate output from each of the neurons. The output, thus, also turns into a vector:

$$P = \begin{bmatrix} p_1 \\ p_2 \\ p_3 \end{bmatrix} \qquad W = \begin{bmatrix} w_{11} & w_{12} & w_{13} \\ w_{21} & x_{22} & w_{23} \\ w_{31} & w_{32} & w_{33} \end{bmatrix} \qquad A = \begin{bmatrix} a_1 \\ a_2 \\ a_3 \end{bmatrix}$$

So far, we have learned the basic structure and mathematical equations modeling the ANNs; next we shall see another important concept called activation functions.

Activation functions

Activation functions are an integral part of any deep learning model. An activation function is a mathematical function that squashes the input values into a certain range. Suppose you feed in a neural network with real number inputs and initialize the weight matrix with random numbers and wish to use the output to classify; that is, you need the output value to be in between zero and one, but your neuron can output any value like -2.2453 or 17854.763. So, there is a need for scaling the output to a specific range. This is what an activation function does:

$$a = f(\sum_{i=0}^{n} W_I . P_i + B), f \rightarrow activation function$$

There are a lot of activation functions depending on the requirements. We will discuss some of the activation functions that are used quite often in deep learning.

Linear activation

This activation is proportional to input. It is used to simply scale the output by certain constant factor c. The following is the plot of output $f(x)$ versus input x to linear activation:

$$f(x) = cx$$

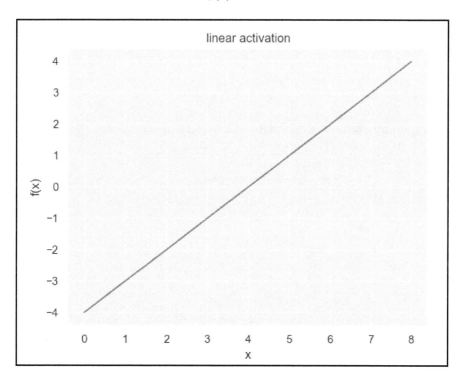

Sigmoid activation

The output range of this function is from zero to one for all real number inputs. This is very important for generating probabilistic scores from neurons. The function is also continuous and non-linear and helps to preserve the non-linearity of outputs. Also, the gradient of curve is steep near the origin and saturates as we start moving away on the x-axis. This means significant change in output will occur for a small change in input around the origin. This characteristic aids in the classification task as it tries to keep the output close to either zero or one. Following is the equation for sigmoid activation against the input x:

$$f(x) = \frac{1}{1+e^{-x}}$$

The following is a plot of the sigmoid activation function:

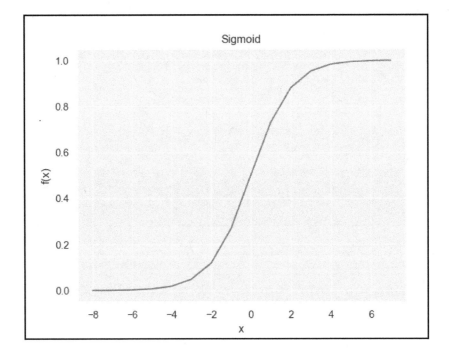

Tanh activation

Tanh or tan hyperbolic function is similar to sigmoid function but just the range of output varies from **-1** to **1** rather than from **0** to **1**. This is generally used in cases where the sign of the output also matters to us. Following, is the plot for tanh activation function:

$$tanh(x) = \frac{2}{1+e^{-2x}} - 1$$

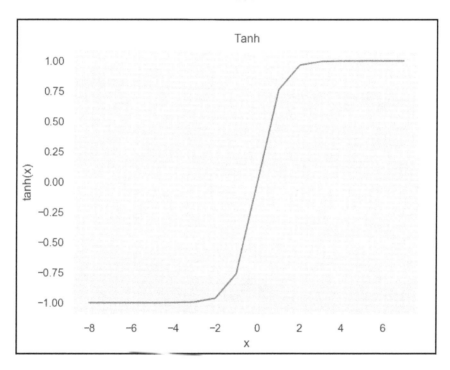

ReLU activation

Rectified linear, or as it is more commonly known, ReLU function is the most widely used activation function in deep learning models. It suppresses the negative values to zero. The reason for ReLU being so widely used is it deactivates the neurons that produce negative values. This kind of behavior is desired in most of the networks containing thousands of neurons. Following, is the plot for the ReLU activation function:

$$f(x) = max(0, x)$$

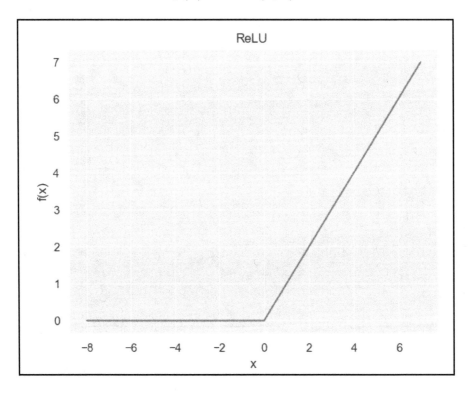

A modified form of ReLU is leaky ReLU. ReLU completely deactivates the neuron with a negative value. Instead of completely deactivating the neuron, leaky ReLU reduces the effect of those neurons by a factor of, say c. The following equation defines the leaky ReLU activation function:

$$f(x) = \left\{ \begin{array}{ll} x, & if\ x > 0, \\ cx, & if\ x < 0 \end{array} \right\}$$

Following, is the plot of output values from ReLU activation function:

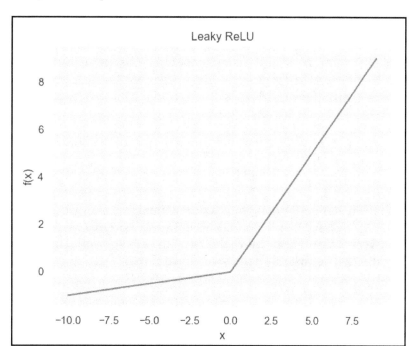

Softmax activation

This is the activation function to go for in most of the classification tasks. Most of the times, the network has to predict the probability of input belonging to that particular class. Softmax activation outputs this probability score, signifying how confident the model is at predicting the classes:

$$f(x_i) = \frac{e^{x_i}}{\sum_{j=0}^{k} e^{x_j}}, \quad for \; i = 0, 1, 2, \ldots, k$$

TensorFlow and Keras

Before proceeding any further, let us quickly set up our coding environment. This book uses Python programming language all throughout the chapters. So, we expect you to have prior knowledge of Python. We will be using two of the most popular deep learning open source frameworks—TensorFlow and Keras. Let's begin with setting up Python first (in case you don't have it installed already).

We highly recommend using a Linux (Ubuntu preferably) or macOS operating system. The reason for this is most of the libraries for deep learning are built to work best with a Linux/Unix operating system. All the setup instructions will be covered for these operating systems.

While installing Python, it is recommended to install version 3.6 rather than the latest 3.7 or beyond. This is to avoid unpredicted conflicts between TensorFlow and Python due to new keywords in Python that are being used as variable names in TensorFlow.

Setting up the environment

It's always a good practice to work on projects in separate environments. An environment is a space that keeps the libraries and dependencies, which are installed inside it, isolated from the global space of the operating system. Suppose you have to work on two projects; one requires an older version of a library and the other uses a newer version. In this situation, installing the newer version globally would overwrite the older version and make the first project unusable. However, you can create two separate environments for the two projects and install the required versions separately. Hopefully, you now get the idea behind working in environments.

We will use Miniconda, which is a small part of open source Python package management and distribution Anaconda. Conda is the package manager in Miniconda that aids in installing and managing packages with Python.

We will follow this step-by-step procedure to set up our working environment with Conda:

1. Download Miniconda for Python 3.7 according to your operating system from `https://conda.io/en/latest/miniconda.html`. Install Miniconda by simply running the downloaded file.

2. You may want to create a separate directory for storing the codes that we will be covering in this book. Let's call it the `deep_learning` directory. Pull up a Terminal and change to the following directory, in case you wish to upgrade to the latest version of Conda and upgrade packages:

```
conda upgrade conda
conda upgrade --all
```

3. Now we will use Conda to create our working environment. Issue the following command into your Terminal window. Name the environment what you want; we name it `test_env` here:

```
conda create -n test_env
```

4. To activate the environment, issue the following command:

```
conda activate test_env
```

5. To deactivate the environment when you are done, issue the following command in the Terminal window:

```
conda deactivate
```

 Inside the environment created with Conda, you can use both `pip` (default package manager for Python) and Conda (package manager for Anaconda) to install libraries.

To view the packages that are installed in your environment, you can use the following command:

```
conda list
```

It will show the packages, irrespective of whether they are installed with `conda` or `pip`.

Introduction to TensorFlow

TensorFlow is an open source library developed by Google Brain team, built specifically to train and run deep learning models. TensorFlow is offered in two versions: a CPU only version and a GPU supported version.

Installing TensorFlow CPU

We mentioned earlier that TensorFlow is not currently stable with Python 3.7. Therefore, we will use Conda to install TensorFlow rather than using `pip`. Conda deals with it in a unique way. As soon as you issue the following command to install TensorFlow, Conda also downloads and installs the other required packages. It also restores Python to the version with which TensorFlow is known to be stable, say Python 3.6.8! Type the following commands into the Terminal window (except the mentioned comments) to install TensorFlow CPU:

```
# go to the deep_learning directory
  cd deep_learning

# activate the environment
  conda activate test_env

# install TensorFlow CPU
  conda install tensorflow
```

After the installation, you can run Python to check whether Conda has restored the version or not.

The commands mentioned are as per the time of publishing this book. You must know that the libraries and repositories keep on changing. In case the commands don't work properly, it is advised to check for the latest updates from the source.

Installing TensorFlow GPU

If you have a TensorFlow supported GPU, you can install TensorFlow GPU version to speed up your training process. TensorFlow provides support for NVIDIA CUDA enabled GPU cards. You can refer to the following link to check whether your GPU card is supported or not: `https://www.tensorflow.org/install/gpu`.

To install TensorFlow GPU version through native `pip`, one has to go through a list of tedious processes:

1. Download and install the CUDA Toolkit for your operating system
2. Download and install cuDNN library (to support deep learning computations in GPU)
3. Add path variables for `CUDA_HOME` and CUDA Toolkit
4. Install TensorFlow GPU through `pip`

Thankfully, however, Anaconda, have compiled everything in a single command—from compatible CUDA Toolkit, cuDNN library, to TensorFlow-GPU. If you already have TensorFlow CPU installed in the current environment, you can deactivate the environment and make a new environment for TensorFlow GPU. You can simply run the following command in your Conda environment and it will download and install everything for you:

```
# deactivate the environment
  conda deactivate

# create new environment
  conda create -n tf_gpu

#activate the environment
  conda activate tf_gpu

# let conda install everything!
  conda install tensorflow-gpu
```

Once you are done installing, it's time to test your installation!

Testing your installation

To test whether you have successfully installed or not, you can run the following snippet in Python. If you have installed the GPU version, import TensorFlow in Python and run the following:

```
>>>import tensorflow as tf
>>>sess = tf.Session(config=tf.ConfigProto(log_device_placement=True))
```

This will return the details about the GPU card and other details that TensorFlow is compiled to use, if you have successfully installed the GPU version.

To check the installation properly (irrespective of CPU or GPU version), we will perform the following simple tensor multiplication operation:

```
>>>t1 = tf.constant([8.0, 4.0, 3.0, 10.0, 9.0, 2.0], shape =
[2,3],name='tensor1')
>>>t2 = tf.constant([12.0, 6.0, 4.0, 5.0, 9.0, 1.0], shape =
[3,2],name='tensor2')
>>>out = tf.matmul(t1, t2)
>>>sess = tf.Session()
>>>print(session.run(out))
```

This code must print the element-wise multiplied output of the two tensors.

Getting to know TensorFlow

Unlike conventional Python libraries, TensorFlow first builds an empty graph containing the structure of model and then uses `Session` to run the graph by feeding in the data. For feeding in the data, TensorFlow uses **tensors**. A tensor is nothing but a multi-dimensional array. Tensor is the fundamental unit of data in TensorFlow. A tensor's dimension is represented by its rank and shape is represented like a `numpy` matrix (`[2, 3]`, for example).

Building a graph

A TensorFlow graph is a series of operations organized in graph. The model architecture is first built in the form of a TensorFlow graph. You need to keep in mind three basic operations:

- `tf.constant`: Holds a constant tensor just like a constant in Python, but unlike Python, it gets activated only during a TensorFlow Session.
- `tf.Variable`: Holds a variable tensor that is learnable during training and updates value.
- `tf.Placeholder`: This is an interesting feature of TensorFlow. At the time of building the graph, we don't provide the input data. But, it is required to lay out the shape and data type of input that the graph will be receiving. Thus, placeholder acts as a container that will allow the flow of input tensors when a Session is activated.

Let's try to add two constants in TensorFlow as follows:

```
>>>import tensorflow as tf
>>>t1 = tf.constant('hey')
>>>t2 = tf.constant('there')
>>sum = t1 + t2
>>>print(sum)
```

This will output something like this: `add:0, shape=(), dtype=string`. You were expecting `heythere`? This doesn't happen because TensorFlow runs the graph only when a Session is activated. By defining the constants, we just made a graph, and that's why the print was trying to tell what the sum would be when the graph is run. So, let's create a Session.

Creating a Session

`tf.Session` object is used to create a Session. It takes the current graph by default, or you can specify which graph to use:

```
>>>sess = tf.Session()
>>>print(sess.run(sum))
```

This will print `heythere` as expected.

Introduction to Keras

Keras is also a popular open source library for deep learning. Keras acts more like a wrapper to ease out building and training models. It uses TensorFlow as its backend. Building complicated deep learning architectures in TensorFlow can get quite tricky due to the complex structure of TensorFlow. Keras provides a very user-friendly coding experience and quick prototyping of models. You can install Keras using Conda:

```
conda install keras
```

Sequential API

The model architecture in Keras can be built simply by stacking the layers one after the other. This is called the sequential approach in Keras and is the most common one:

```
from keras.models import Sequential. # importing the Sequential class
from keras.layers import Dense.       #importing the Deep Learning layers

model = Sequential()                   #making an object of Sequential class

#adding the first Dense layer. You have to mention input dimensions to the
first
#layer of model.
model.add(Dense(units=128, input_dims = 100, activation = 'relu'))
model.add(Dense(units = 4, activation = 'softmax'))
```

When the model architecture is done, Keras uses a `model.compile` method to build the graph with the required loss function and optimizer and `model.fit` to train the model with inputs. If you're not getting what loss function is, don't worry! We will discuss all that in subsequent chapters.

Functional API

This is just another layout for coding the model graph. You can choose the following layout if you are more comfortable with Python style code writing:

```python
from keras.models import Model
from keras.layers import Dense, Input

#defining input placeholder with input shape
inp = Input(shape = 100)

# layers
x = Dense(units = 128, activation = 'relu')
x = Dense(units = 64, activation = 'relu')

# taking output
predict = Dense(units = 4, activation = 'softmax')(x)

# defining model
model = Model(inputs = inp, outputs = predict)
```

Summary

Let's take a quick look at what we learned in this chapter. We began by briefly discussing artificial intelligence and its evolution through machine learning and then deep learning. We then saw details about some interesting applications of deep learning like machine translation, chatbots, and optical character recognition. This being the first chapter of the book, we focus on learning the fundamentals for deep learning.

We learned how ANN works with the help of some mathematics. Also, we saw different types of activation functions used in ANN and deep learning. Finally, we moved to set our coding environment with TensorFlow and Keras for building deep learning models.

In the next chapter, we will see how neural networks evolved into deep feedforward networks and deep learning. We will also code our first deep learning model with TensorFlow and Keras!

Deep Feedforward Networks

2

In this chapter, you will build our first deep learning network—**deep deedforward networks (DFN)**. We will begin by discussing the evolutionary history of deep feedforward networks and then discuss the architecture of DFN. In any classification task, DFN plays an integral role. Apart from supporting the classification tasks, DFN standalone can be used both for regression and classification. Any deep learning network has a lot of elements like loss function, gradients, optimizers, and so on coming together to train the network. In this chapter, we will discuss these essential elements in detail. These elements will be common to all kinds of deep learning networks we are going to see in this book. We will also be demonstrating how to bring up and preprocess the data for training a deep learning network. You may find things a little difficult to understand at first, but eventually, you will get it. So, just hold on to it! After completing this chapter, you will have learned about the following things:

- Architecture of DFN
- Loss function
- Gradient descent
- Backpropagation
- Overfitting and regularization
- Coding your first DFN

Let's start with the evolution history of DFNs!

Evolutionary path to DFNs

Warren McCulloch and Walter Pitts were the first to create a model of artificial neural networks back in 1943. They built the model on something called **threshold logic**. A threshold was calculated by summing up inputs, and the output was binary, zero, or one, according to the threshold. In 1958, another model of a neuron was created by Rosenblatt called **perceptron**. Perceptron is the simplest model of an artificial neuron that can classify inputs into two classes (we discussed this neuron in Chapter 1, *Getting started with Deep Learning*). The concept of training neural networks by backpropagating errors using chain rule was developed by Henry J. Kelley around the early 1960s. However, backpropagation as an algorithm was unstructured and the perceptron model failed to solve that famous XOR problem. In 1986, Geoff Hinton, David Rumelhart, and Ronald Williams demonstrated that neural networks with hidden layers can learn non-linear functions with backpropagation. Further, it was also highlighted that neural networks are capable of learning any function through a universal approximation theorem. But, neural networks didn't scale to solve large problems, and by the '90s, other machine learning algorithms, such as **support vector machine** (**SVM**), dominated the space. Around 2006, Hinton once again came up with the idea of adding layers one over the other and training parameters for new layers. Deeper networks were trained using the strategy and the networks were termed as **deep feedforward networks**. From here, the neural networks got a new name—deep learning!

Next, we will discuss the architectural design of DFN. We will see how the layered structure is built, trained, and what significance the terms *deep* and *feedforward* carry.

Architecture of DFN

In the previous chapter, we saw the architecture of a multi-neuron artificial neural network. But, the architecture consisted of only a single layer of neurons. Now think about the brain: does it have a single layer of neurons or multiple layers? Yes, the brain has multiple layers of neurons where the layers are connected one after the other. The inputs coming to the brain pass through an initial layer to extract low-level features and pass through consecutive layers to extract high-level features. The architecture of DFN is inspired by the layered structure of multiple neurons. The network has various layers stacked consecutively where the neuron outputs from previous layers are fed forward as inputs to the next layers (that's why the network is called feedforward network). Three types of layers are present in the architecture-input layer, hidden layer, and output layer. The layers can be seen in the following diagram:

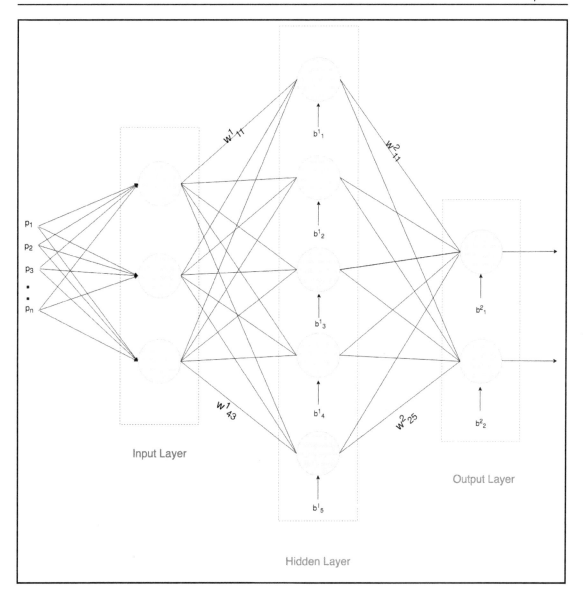

According to universal approximation theorem, a feedforward neural network with a single hidden layer is capable of modeling any real function with a finite number of neurons.

You can read more about the universal approximation theorem at the following link:
`https://en.wikipedia.org/wiki/Universal_approximation_theorem`.

However, the number of neurons grow so far that it becomes practically impossible to make such networks. Instead, increasing the number of layers allows an increasing number of neurons, and helps in the better learning of features. The deeper the network (having a higher number of hidden layers), the better the learning will be. Following, is a diagram showing a typical DFN. For simplicity, the biases and labels are not demonstrated in the diagram, but they work similarly to the feedforward network:

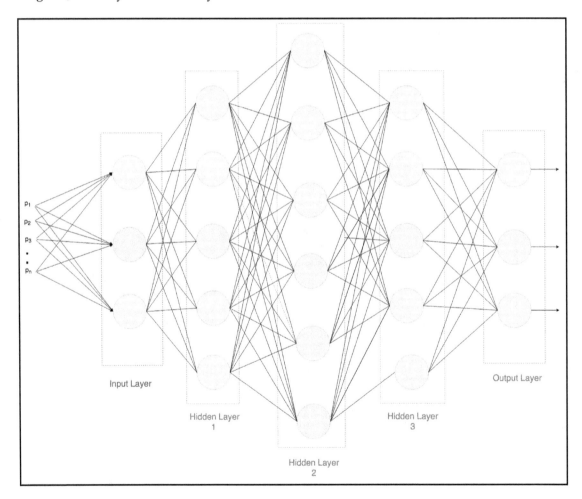

Hopefully, you now understand what *deep* and *feedforward* signify in DFNs. Next, we shall see how these networks are trained to learn through loss function and backpropagation algorithm.

Training

The weight values present in a DFN are responsible for making predictions. Any deep network has so many weights that finding perfect values for weights becomes impossible. Hence, we try to search for a set of weight values that will give us sufficiently good prediction results. Thus, training a network implies learning the optimal weight values starting from an initialized set of weights. Suppose we have a DFN and, initially, we don't know what set of weights will perform well. Hence, we initialize the weight values say with random real numbers. Now, we have to go from initialized weight values to optimal weight values. We can break this task into the following three parts:

- First, we need to know whether the initialized weights are a good fit or not. If not, how much does the predicted output differ from the expected output? This is calculated by loss function.

- Second, comes the concept of **maximum likelihood estimation (MLE)**, which states that, in order to find an optimized set of parameters (in our case weights), we need to maximize the likelihood (probability) of obtaining the expected values. In simple terms, if we try to minimize the loss function by changing the weights (parameters), we are maximizing the probability of predicted output distribution to be as close as the expected distribution.

- From the preceding two points, we can conclude that we need to minimize loss function by updating the weights. When the minimum possible value for loss is reached, we can say the network has learned (trained) the mapping function to predict values close to expected values. In DFNs, updating weights and minimizing loss function is done with a combination of gradient descent and backpropagation algorithm.

In the subsequent sections, we will discuss loss function further, and how it is minimized to train the network with gradient descent and backpropagation.

Loss function

Consider y to be the predicted output from our DFN and $\bar{y}$ to be the expected output (or label). The loss function is a measure of how correct your predictions are! Simplest loss function is defined in terms of the difference between the expected and predicted outputs shown as follows as *L(w)*:

$$L(w) = \bar{y} - y$$

However, this kind of simple equation turns out to be a bad measure, as this loss function tends to give values that could be negative as well as positive. Various loss functions have been developed for regression and classification tasks and we shall see them in the following subsections.

Regression loss

Regression tasks require direct predictions of values and the expected output are direct values too. This allows us to base our loss on the difference between the two values. The first and most common regression loss we shall see is mean squared error loss.

Mean squared error (MSE)

Let us assume we have n samples in our dataset. This means we will be having n prediction values $(y_{1,\dots,}y_{i,\dots,}y_{n})$ and n corresponding expected values $(\bar{y_1}, \cdots, \bar{y_i}, \cdots \bar{y_n})$. The mean squared is defined by the following equation:

$$E = \frac{\sum_{i=1}^{n} (\bar{y_i} - y)^2}{n}$$

As the name suggests, this error function squares the difference between predicted and expected values (error) and then takes the mean. Errors may be positive or negative depending on the values, and summing them up could lead to cancellation of values having opposite signs, leading to improper loss value. Hence, they are squared before summing to make all values positive. This way, each error will just carry the impact of its magnitude only. A further mean is taken to keep the loss normalized and avoid abrupt high loss values. Owing to the squared values, any outlier in the data (a sample that outputs value far away from expected value) will contribute much more to the loss than it should.

So, if there are a lot of outliers in the dataset, then MSE is not the one to go for! But, the ease of computing squares and the function being differentiable, MSE is the most common loss function for regression. Another way of dealing with the problem of errors having different signs is MSE.

Mean absolute error

Mean absolute error, instead of squaring the error, takes the absolute value of error to make everything positive. Taking absolute values instead of squares makes the loss function less sensitive to outliers than MSE. But, calculating absolute values requires computation through linear programming and makes the loss function non-differentiable, which can cause major issues while updating weight values through backpropagation. (We will see backpropagation in coming sections.) The following equation describes the mean absolute error function:

$$E = \frac{\sum_{i=1}^{n} |(\overline{y_i} - y)|}{n}$$

Classification loss

Classification tasks don't have direct values to predict. Rather, they generally have positive integer labels representing categories the inputs belong to. Hence, both the expected and predicted value are just integer representations. Therefore, directly taking the difference won't work for classification as it did for regression. To address this problem, loss functions are developed over probability distributions. One of the most common loss functions for classification is cross entropy.

Cross entropy

A classification problem can be thought of as predicting the probability of an input belonging to each class. The training data will consist of labels as zero or one for each class. The labels can be thought of as probability value too: one represents a sure possibility of input belonging to the class while zero indicates that the input doesn't belong to the class.

To compare the predicted and expected output, we would thus require a method to compare the two probability distributions (probability distribution of prediction and expected labels). Cross entropy does exactly the same! Consider $\overline{y_i}$ to be the expected label for i^{th} training sample and y_i to be the predicted label from our model. Cross entropy loss is then defined by the following equation:

$$H(\overline{y},\, y) = \sum_{i=1}^{n} \left(y_i \, \frac{1}{log \, \overline{y_i}} \right) = -\sum_{i=1}^{n} \left(y_i \, log \, \overline{y_i} \right)$$

Cross entropy is also referred to as *log loss* due to the logarithm it uses. Cross entropy loss will decrease when the two probability distributions are similar, and increase as the distributions diverge from each other.

We already have stated that we need to minimize the loss function. We shall see how gradient descent achieves it.

Gradient descent

Let us consider a cost function **J(w)**, which is a function of weight **w** of the network. A cost function is simply a combination of a loss function with some other parameters related to regularization. (We will discuss overfitting and regularization later. For the time being, consider cost function to be the same as loss function.) We can assume a convex cost function **J(w)** represented by the following diagram:

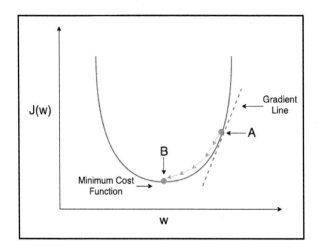

We mentioned earlier that, initially, we choose a random value for weight. Let's say the initial weight is represented by point **A** in the preceding diagram. Our aim is to reach a minimum value of cost function, say $J_{min}(w)$. Assume the cost function in the preceding example has a minimum value at point **B**. You may notice that the slope of cost function at the minimum (point **B**) is zero, while it is non-zero for other points, such as point **A** (our initial point). We can, therefore, exploit the gradient (slope) of cost function to reach the minima.

The gradient or slope is the rate of change of y-axis value with respect to x-axis. At any point on the function, the gradient is obtained by calculating the derivative of that function with respect to x.

The idea is to calculate the gradient of cost function at the initial point and then updating the weights in a way that decreases the gradient until it becomes zero (which will be the minima). This is the reason why the method is called **gradient descent**. So, how are the weights updated then? Different variations of gradient descent use different strategies to update weights. There are three major types of gradient descent: batch gradient descent (vanilla gradient descent), stochastic gradient descent, and mini-batch gradient descent.

Types of gradient descent

Before discussing the types of gradient descent, we should know about an important parameter called learning rate (η). Gradient descent reaches the minima of cost function in steps. Learning rate decides how long the steps will be. As the weights are updated, it is crucial to decide on an appropriate learning rate. If the learning rate is too large, the weight updates may overshoot the minima, which will result in never-ending oscillations around the minima. If the learning rate is too small, the algorithm will take very small steps, which may take a lot of time to converge to a minima.

To have a clearer visualization, both the scenarios are depicted in the following diagram:

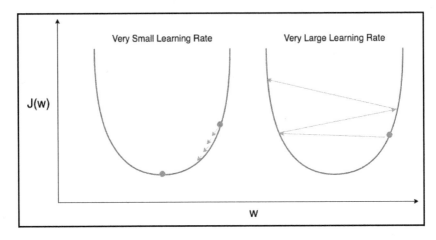

Now we shall see the first and basic variant of gradient descent—batch gradient descent.

Batch gradient descent

Let us say w_{new} is the updated set of weights after one step of batch gradient descent and w is the old set of weights. The weights are updated according to the following rule:

$$w_{new} \leftarrow w - \eta . \frac{\partial J(w)}{\partial w}$$

You can verify yourself by considering a random point on our cost function *J(w)* that the new weight will always be headed towards the minima. Batch gradient descent needs to calculate gradients over an entire dataset to perform one set of updates. Hence, for large datasets, batch gradient descent turns out to be quite slow. For datasets that are processed in parts, batch gradient descent becomes nearly impossible. To overcome this major drawback, another variant of gradient descent was introduced—stochastic gradient descent.

Stochastic gradient descent

Stochastic gradient descent updates the weights after going through every sample in the training set. Let us consider i^{th} training sample x^i and its corresponding label y^i. The weight update rule under stochastic gradient descent then becomes the following:

$$w_{new} \leftarrow w - \eta . \frac{\partial J(w, x^i, y^i)}{\partial w}$$

Updating weights after every sample significantly increases the speed of convergence of gradient descent; however, it makes the update too frequent, leading to fluctuations in cost function. However, the fluctuation addresses an interesting problem of the weights getting stuck at a **Local Minima**. Until now, we have seen a simple cost function with only one **Global Minima**. Imagine a complex cost function with multiple **Local Minima**. The **Global Minima** need not be the same as **Local Minima**. In general, batch gradient descent tends to get stuck at the nearest minima of initialization, which might not be the **Global Minima**. On the other hand, the fluctuations in stochastic gradient descent allow jumping to another **Local Minima,** which might be better. The following diagram shows a complex cost function with multiple minima:

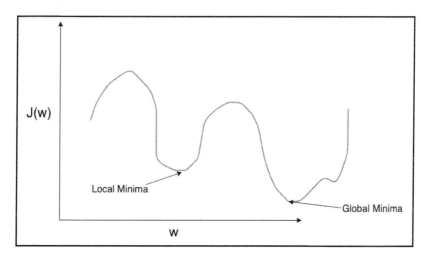

Mini-batch gradient descent

Updating weights after every sample creates a lot of redundant updates, while updating weights after going through the complete dataset is practically impossible too. Mini-batch gradient descent addresses both the issues by updating weights after going through a mini-batch from the data. A mini-batch is a small set of samples from training data; for example, if a dataset has 10,000 training samples, we can break the data into mini-batches of size, say 64. Weight updates will occur after going through every mini-batch. Assuming n to be the size of the mini-batch, the following is the weight update rule:

$$w_{new} \leftarrow w - \eta. \frac{d\, J(w, x^{i:i+n}, y^{i:i+n})}{d\, w}$$

Backpropagation

We have seen how weights are updated with gradient descent, but to perform gradient descent, we need to calculate the gradient (derivative) of cost function with respect to the weights. Say, to calculate the gradient of cost function with respect to weight w, we can use the following equation of derivative, where h is a small positive number:

$$\frac{\partial\, J(w)}{\partial\, w} = \frac{J(w+h) - J(w)}{h}$$

Here, to calculate the gradient for a weight, we need to calculate cost function two times, that is, perform complete forward pass twice. Any deep learning network has millions of weights, and calculating the gradient by the preceding formula would be computationally very expensive. So, what's the solution to this? Backpropagation! The algorithm gained momentum in 1986 when David Rumelhart, Geoffrey Hilton, and Ronald Williams showed gradient can be calculated faster in neural networks using backpropagation. The heart of backpropagation algorithm is chain rule. Chain rule allows you to compute all the required gradients with just one forward and one backward pass.

Chain rule is used to calculate derivatives of composite functions. Consider two function $z = f(y)$ and $y = g(x)$, then the derivative of function $z = f(y)$, with respect to x, can be obtained as the consecutive sum of derivatives of $z = f(y)$, with respect to y and derivative of y, with respect to x. The following equation represents the same:

$$\frac{dz}{dx} = \frac{dz}{dy} \cdot \frac{dy}{dx}$$

Similarly, the chain rule can be extended to n different functions having interdependent variables.

Before jumping to the algorithm, we shall see the notations that we will be using; w_{jk}^{l} will be used to represent the weight connection from k^{th} neuron of $(l\text{-}1)^{th}$ layer to j^{th} neuron of lth layer. For biases, b_{j}^{l} will be used for j^{th} neuron of lth layer. For activation functions, a_{j}^{l} is used to represent activation of jth neuron in l^{th} layer. The notation is simple to understand. Superscript represents the number of layers while subscript represents the neurons of the layer.

For the lth layer, the output can be represented by the following equation where the input to the lth layer is the activated output from $(l\text{-}1)^{th}$ layer, $a^{l-1} = \sigma(z^{l-1})$, σ representing the activation function:

$$z^{l} = w^{l}a^{l-1} + b^{l}$$

Next, considering the jth neuron in l^{th} layer, we define an error δ_{j}^{l} given by the following:

$$\delta_{j}^{l} = \frac{\partial J}{\partial z_{j}^{l}}$$

Using chain rule, we can write the following equation:

$$\delta_{j}^{l} = \frac{\partial J}{\partial z_{j}^{l}} = \frac{\partial J}{\partial a_{j}^{l}} \cdot \frac{\partial a_{j}^{l}}{\partial z_{j}^{l}} = \frac{\partial J}{\partial a_{j}^{l}} \cdot \sigma'(z_{j}^{l})$$

Similarly, we calculate the error for every layer. The error for the last layer is calculated and backpropagated to previous layers through the following relation between errors in $(l+1)^{th}$ layer and the lth layer where $\odot$ represents element-wise multiplication:

$$\delta^l = ((w^{l+1})^T . \delta^{l+1}) \odot \delta'(z^l) \qquad - eq. \ 1$$

Finally, the errors are used to calculate the gradient of cost function with respect to weights of respective layers according to the following equation:

$$\frac{\partial J}{\partial w^l_{jk}} = a^{l-1}_k . \delta^l_j \qquad - eq. \ 2$$

We won't go into mathematical proof of the equations but you can get an idea how the algorithm calculates error from the last layer and backpropagates the error to the previous layers according to *equation one*. The weights of say l^{th} layer j^{th} neuron are thus calculated as a product of error for that layer (δ^l_j) and the activated output from k^{th} neuron from the previous layer to j^{th} neuron of lth layer.

Now we have seen how the gradients required for weight updates are calculated with a single backward pass. We already mentioned the challenge of gradient descent not being able to converge properly due to local minima and complex cost function. Next, we shall see how optimizers address the problem by adjusting the learning rate η.

Optimizers

While descending on the slope of cost function, we need to take smaller steps as we move closer to the required minima. Otherwise, we would overshoot and then oscillate around the minima. This can be done by keeping the learning rate variable during training. Optimizers provide algorithms that adjust the learning rate all through the training to provide better convergence. Optimizers in TensorFlow perform the task of minimizing the loss function (cost function). Two of the most used optimizers are Adam optimizer and RMSProp optimizer. We shall not discuss the mathematics involved in optimizers here.

Train, test, and validation

Usually, we don't use the entire data available for training our model. Doing so would leave us no room to judge the performance of our trained model or keep a check whether the training is going in the right direction or not. We split the data into the following three sets:

- Training set
- Validation set
- Testing set

Training set

The training set contains the data that will be used to train the model. This set is the largest of the three sets and contains the majority of the data (as we don't want to miss a lot of data for training). The model learns the features and patterns from the training set by iterating over it. Although we measure training accuracy during training, it doesn't actually evaluate the model. Training accuracy can reach high values as the model has learned from the training set and is familiar with the data. Thus, high training accuracy need not imply a good model. Real evaluation of the model will happen when the model makes predictions on unseen data.

Validation set

While training the model, the validation set provides frequent and unbiased evaluation for the model. We don't include the validation set in the training set but keep checking accuracy on the validation set after certain iterations during training. The validation set aids in fine-tuning the parameters during training.

At first, it might seem that the validation set is not so important, but you will see the significant role that it plays when we discuss overfitting.

Test set

The purpose of training our model is to make good predictions on unknown data (data that the model hasn't seen). Hence, the real evaluation must be done with data that the model hasn't seen before. The test set is generally reserved from the total available data and never shown to the model while training. The test set allows you to evaluate our model with unknown data. An important thing to understand here is for supervised tasks, the **Test Set** also contains the data and corresponding expected labels like the **Training Set**. The labels are only used when we compare the model predictions with the labels to calculate accuracy. So, how much data should be reserved for the **Validation Set** and the **Test Set**?

Generally, it is a good idea to keep 80% of available data as a **Training Set**, 10% as a **Validation Set,** and the last 10% as a **Test Set**, as in the following diagram:

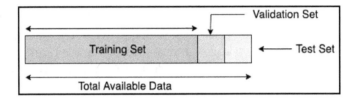

Overfitting and regularization

Any deep learning network (for example DFN) has a lot of learnable parameters (in millions). A network with a large number of parameters can fit any data distribution. However, the point of training is not to completely fit the training data, but to learn the general features and pattern that characterizes the data. A model may learn to predict every sample correctly in the training set, but fails to perform on the test set. This generally happens in networks with a large number of parameters. Free learnable parameters are available to learn every intricacy of a training set. However, when doing so, the network over-learns and becomes very specific to the training data, failing to perform on unfamiliar data. This phenomenon of over-learning is termed as overfitting. You can have a better understanding of the phenomenon with the following picture. An overfitted model learns the decision boundary (in red) very specific to training data, which is not a good decision boundary in general:

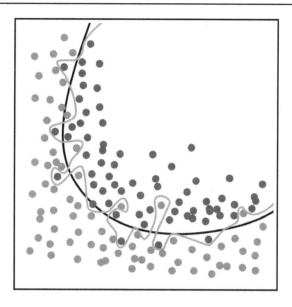

The black line represents a good fit and green line represents overfit—image sourced from Wikipedia

To avoid overfitting, regularization techniques are used in deep learning. What does regularization mean exactly? Regularization restricts the parameters from over-learning by penalizing or bringing randomness in the parameters. Three major regularization techniques are used to avoid overfitting:

- L1 and L2 regularization
- Dropout
- Early stopping

Data augmentation is also considered under regularization. It involves manipulating the input data to create more variants of the same data. For example, an image is shifted and scaled to produce more variants. Data augmentation methods are different for different types of data.

L1 and L2 regularization

Remember we mentioned earlier that the cost function is a combination of the loss function along with regularization parameters. L1 and L2 are the parameters that are added to the loss function to make the cost function. L1 and L2 penalize the loss function by making some weights negligibly small, reducing the free parameters that could potentially lead to over-learning.

L1 regularization adds absolute values of weights as a penalizing coefficient to the loss function as mentioned in the following formula:

$$J(w) = \sum_{i=1}^{n}(y_i - \sum_{j=1}^{m} x_{ij}w_j)^2 + \Lambda \sum_{j=1}^{m} |w_j|$$

The first term in the formula represents the squared loss function in terms of weights and the second term is the L1 regularization coefficient. The Λ is a hyperparameter, which can be manually adjusted for a good fit. L1 regularization is considered robust as it is less sensitive to outliers in data. But L1 regularization sometimes can become computationally expensive and may introduce discontinuity in our loss function. Hence, L1 regularization is generally not used owing to its complexity.

L2 regularization, on the other hand, adds a smooth squared value of weights as penalizing factor to the loss function, as described by the following formula:

$$J(w) = \sum_{i=1}^{n}(y_i - \sum_{j=1}^{m} x_{ij}w_j)^2 + \Lambda \sum_{j=1}^{m} w_j^2$$

The advantage of using L2 regularization is the ease of calculation of the square and assurance of continuity all through the loss function. But this comes at the cost of sensitivity; L2 regularization, due to the square term, magnifies the loss function for outliers and, hence, makes the cost function very sensitive. In the next sub-section, we shall see what dropouts are and how they avoid overfitting.

Dropout

Dropout is a unique way to handle overfitting in neural networks (or deep learning). To bring in randomness in a network, dropout randomly removes few nodes (neurons) by removing the weight connection to and from that node. Dropout happens randomly in every iteration. The following diagram suggests how dropout works in a DFN:

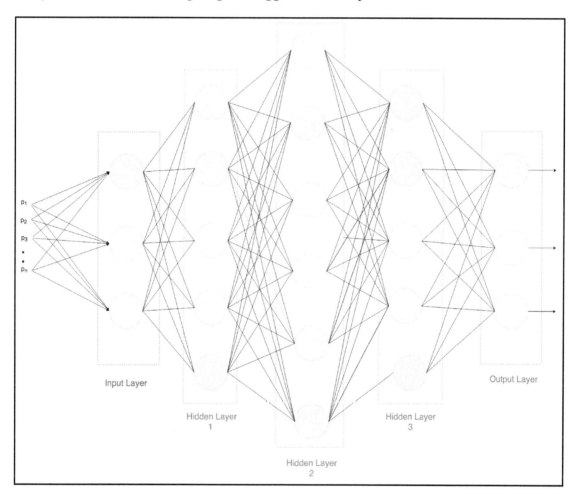

Early stopping

While discussing the validation set, we started to discuss the role of the validation set later in overfitting. During training, we actually don't know how many iterations train the model. This often is a cause for overfitting. Knowing when to stop is an important thing! Having a validation set when training helps us decide when to stop. As the training algorithm minimizes the training loss, the loss will always keep on decreasing irrespective of the model being overfitted. Hence, alongside the training loss, we also monitor loss on the validation set. Both the training and validation losses will keep on decreasing until the optimum point is reached. Thereafter, validation loss will again start increasing due to overfitting. The point where the validation and training loss begins to diverge is the point where we need to stop overtraining and avoid overfitting. You can observe the same in the following diagram:

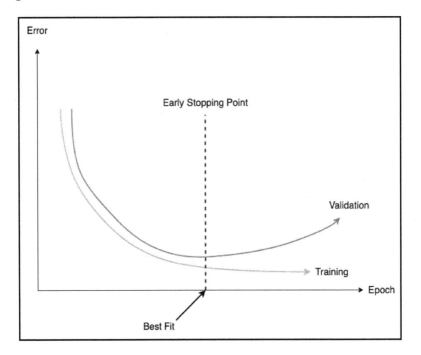

Up until here, we have gathered sufficient information about the essential aspects of deep learning. So let's dive into coding our first DFN with TensorFlow!

Building our first DFN

So far, we have learned how a DFN works, and about the architecture, and aspects involved in training the network. In this section, we shall build our first DFN using TensorFlow. Building any deep learning would more or less involve the following steps:

1. Reading the input data and expected output data (labels)
2. Preparing the data in the required format (preprocessing)
3. Splitting the data into a training, validation, and testing set (a validation set is sometimes optional)
4. Building the model architecture graph along with the loss function and optimizer to update weights
5. Running a TensorFlow Session to iterate over data and train the network
6. Testing the accuracy of the model over test data

MNIST fashion data

MNIST is a dataset of handwritten digits containing 60,000 training samples and 10,000 testing samples of handwritten digits from zero to nine. Each sample is a 28 x 28 single channel (grayscale) image. The dataset is widely used as the starting point into deep learning. However, the dataset is very simple and easy to learn for a deep learning model. Also, the dataset is not a very good example of images in a real-world computer vision task.

Hence, we will build our first model on a MNIST fashion dataset, which is developed in a similar way to the original MNIST. It has 60,000 training and 10,000 testing samples of 10 fashion articles (t-shirt, trouser, pullover, dress, coat, sandal, shirt, sneaker, bag, and ankle boot). Like the original MNIST, the fashion MNIST also has 28 x 28 grayscale images, but the images are more complex to learn. More information on the dataset can be found at https://github.com/zalandoresearch/fashion-mnist.

Getting the data

TensorFlow already has a built-in `keras` class to download and manage the data provided by MNIST fashion. Hence, you don't have to manually download the data, TensorFlow will do it for you! We will start with the following steps:

1. Let's write a Python script to build our first DFN. First, import the dependencies required as follows:

```
import tensorflow as tf
import numpy as np
import matplotlib.pyplot as plt
from sklearn.model_selection import train_test_split

from tensorflow import keras
```

Scikit-learn or sklearn is an important Python library that provides a lot of machine learning models as well as helps in data preparing methods. You can install `scikit` learn with the following command:

`$ conda install scikit-learn.`

2. Make an object of the `keras` class of TensorFlow that has the data loading function as follows:

```
# making object of fashion_mnist class
fashionObj = keras.datasets.fashion_mnist
```

3. The `load_data` method will download the MNIST fashion dataset if not already downloaded on your system:

```
# trainX contains input images and trainY contains corresponding
labels.
# Similarly for test

(trainX, trainY), (testX, testY) = fashionObj.load_data()
print('train data x shape: ', trainX.shape)
print('test data x shape: ', testX.shape)

print('train data y shape: ', trainY.shape)
print('test data y shape: ', testY.shape)
```

4. After loading the data, we print the shape of the training data as well as the test data. The output shapes should be as shown in the following screenshot:

```
train data x shape:  (60000, 28, 28)
test data x shape: (10000, 28, 28)
train data y shape:  (60000,)
test data y shape:  (10000,)
```

The labels contained in data are numeric, from 0 to 9, where each integer represents a class. We shall make a dictionary that will map these integers to their class as mentioned in the MNIST fashion data. You can see the integers and their corresponding classes in the following screenshot:

Labels

Each training and test example is assigned to one of the following labels:

Label	Description
0	T-shirt/top
1	Trouser
2	Pullover
3	Dress
4	Coat
5	Sandal
6	Shirt
7	Sneaker
8	Bag
0	Ankle boot

Code for the preceding output is as follows:

```
# make a label dictionary to map integer labels to classes
classesDict = {0:'T-shirt/top', 1:'Trouser', 2:'Pullover',
3:'Dress',                4:'Coat',5:'Sandal', 6:'Shirt',
7:'Sneaker', 8:'Bag', 9:'Ankle boot'}
```

Visualizing data

Let's look at some images and their corresponding labels from the dataset. We use the `matplotlib` library to plot four sample images from the data as shown in the following code:

```
rows = 2
columns = 2
fig = plt.figure(figsize = (5,5))

for i in range(1, rows*columns +1):
  image = trainX[i]
  label = trainY[i]

  sub = fig.add_subplot(rows, columns, i)
  sub.set_title('Label: ' + classesDict[label])

  plt.imshow(image)
plt.show()
```

The image plot will look like the following screenshot. The title of each subplot conveys the class that image belongs to:

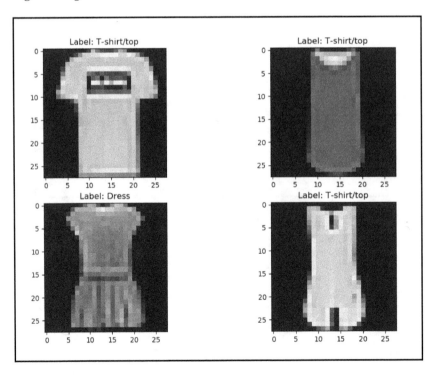

Normalizing and splitting data

Values of pixels in an image range from 0 to 255. It is always advisable computationally to keep the input values between 0 to 1. Hence, we will normalize our data by dividing it with a maximum possible value of 255 to bring everything between 0 to 1. Also, the input images are having dimensions of 28 x 28, but our DFN doesn't take two-dimensional inputs. So we flatten the input training images from (60000, 28, 28) to (60000, 784) and testing input images from (10000, 28, 28) to (10000, 784):

```
trainX = trainX.reshape(trainX.shape[0], 784) / 255.0
testX = testX.reshape(testX.shape[0], 784) / 255.0
```

The dataset already comes in two parts—train data and test data. We, therefore, only need to split the training data into validation and training data. We will do this using sklearn's `train_test_split` method. The method also shuffles the data before splitting to ensure the split data is not biased towards a certain class:

```
trainX, valX, trainY, valY = train_test_split(trainX, trainY, test_size =
0.1, random_state =2)
# random_state is used for randomly shuffling the data.
```

Model parameters

Most of the tasks related to preparing data are now completed. We will now focus on our deep feedforward model. Before building the model graph, we shall decide the following parameters of our model:

- **Number of classes** (CLASS_NUM): In the MNIST fashion dataset, there are 10 classes. Hence, the number of classes we will be classifying is 10.
- **Number of input neurons** (INPUT_UNITS): We attach one neuron in the input layer to one pixel value of the image. We have 784(28 x2 8) neurons in the input layer.
- **Number of neurons in first layer** (HIDDEN_LAYER_1_UNITS): We decide to keep 256 neurons in first hidden layer of the network. You can try changing this number to your choice.
- **Number of neurons in second layer** (HIDDEN_LAYER_2_UNITS): In the second hidden layer, there are 128 neurons kept. Again, you can change this number to be one of your choice.

- **Number of neurons in output layer** (OUTPUT_LAYER_UNITS): As we will be using softmax activation, each neuron in the output layer will output the probability of inputs belonging to that class. So, we need to keep the number of neurons equal to the number of classes.
- **Learning rate for optimizer** (LEARNING_RATE): The default learning rate for the optimizer we are using is 0.001. You can change this and see the effect on training.
- **Batch size** (BATCH_SIZE): We train using mini-batches of data. Divide the entire training data into chunks of size equal to the batch size. For each batch, an update of weights is performed.
- **Iterations** (EPOCHS): The number of times we will go through the entire data.

Let's look into the following code:

```
CLASS_NUM = 10
#number of classes we need to classify

INPUT_UNITS = 784
# no. of neurons in input layer 784, as we have 28x28 = 784 pixels in each
image.
# we connect each pixel to a neuron.

HIDDEN_LAYER_1_UNITS = 256
# no of neurons in first hidden layer

HIDDEN_LAYER_2_UNITS = 128
#no. of neurons in second hidden layer

OUTPUT_LAYER_UNITS = CLASS_NUM
# no. of neurons in output layer = no. of classes we have to classify.
# each neuron will output the probability of input belonging to the class
it represents

LEARNING_RATE = 0.001
# learning rate for gradient descent. Default value is 0.001

BATCH_SIZE = 64
# we will take input data in sets of 64 images at once instead of using
whole data
# for every iteration. Each set is called a batch and batch function is
used to generate
# batches of data.

NUM_BATCHES = int(trainX.shape[0] / BATCH_SIZE)
# number of mini-batches required to cover the train data
```

```
EPOCHS = 10
# number of iterations we will perform to train
```

One-hot encoding

One-hot encoding is a vector of a size equal to the number of classes that contains only binary values (0 and 1). It is used to represent the labels. The vector contains 1 at the index of the class and the rest are all 0s. In our case, we have 10 classes; hence, a one hot encoded vector for label representing third class (pullover) would look like this:

$$[0, 0, 1, 0, 0, 0, 0, 0, 0, 0]$$

The reason for using one-hot encoding instead of integer values is because each neuron in the output layer classifies one class; that is, 1 for belonging to the class and 0 for not belonging. Hence, each neuron needs a value of 0 or 1 in the expected output vector and not an integer. To convert the labels into one-hot vectors, we use the numpy library as shown here:

```
trainY = np.eye(CLASS_NUM)[trainY]
valY = np.eye(CLASS_NUM)[valY]
testY = np.eye(CLASS_NUM)[testY]
```

Building a model graph

We build the TensorFlow graph with different name scopes. Name scopes in TensorFlow allow grouping and distinguishing variables in the graph. It also allows reusing the same name for different variables. For example, all variables related to the input layer are put under the name input_layer scope.

Adding placeholders

The placeholders that will hold the input data *x* and the labels *y* are placed under the name placeholders scope as shown here:

```
with tf.name_scope('placeholders') as scope:

    # making placeholders for inputs (x) and labels (y)
    # the first dimension 'BATCH_SIZE' represents the number of samples
    # in a batch. It can also be kept 'None'. Tensorflow will automatically
    # detect the shape from incoming data.
```

```
  x = tf.placeholder(shape = [BATCH_SIZE, 784], dtype = tf.float32, name =
'inp_x')
  y = tf.placeholder(shape = [BATCH_SIZE, CLASS_NUM], dtype = tf.float32,
name= 'true_y')
```

Adding layers

Next, we will define the input layer that will contain the first set of weights and biases as follows:

```
with tf.name_scope('inp_layer') as scope:

  # the first set of weights will be connecting the inputs layer to first
hidden layer
  # Hence, it will essentially be a matrix of shape [INPUT_UNITS,
#HIDDEN_LAYER_1_UNITS]

  weights1 = tf.get_variable(shape = [INPUT_UNITS, HIDDEN_LAYER_1_UNITS],
dtype = tf.float32, name = 'weights_1')

  biases1 = tf.get_variable(shape = [HIDDEN_LAYER_1_UNITS], dtype =
tf.float32, name = 'bias_1')

  # performing W.x + b, we rather multiply x to W in due to matrix shape
#constraints.
  # otherwise you can also take transpose of W and multiply it to x

  layer1 = tf.nn.relu(tf.add(tf.matmul(x, weights1), biases1), name =
'layer_1')
  # we use the relu activations in the 2 hidden layers
```

Similarly, we will also define the first hidden layer as shown in the following code:

```
with tf.name_scope('hidden_1') as scope:

  # second set of weights between hidden layer 1 and hidden layer 2
  weights2 = tf.get_variable(shape = [HIDDEN_LAYER_1_UNITS,
HIDDEN_LAYER_2_UNITS], dtype = tf.float32, name = 'weights_2')
  biases2 = tf.get_variable(shape = [HIDDEN_LAYER_2_UNITS], dtype =
tf.float32,
          name = 'bias_2')

  # the output of layer 1 will be fed to layer 2 (as this is Feedforward
Network)

  layer2 = tf.nn.relu(tf.add(tf.matmul(layer1, weights2), biases2), name
='layer_2')
```

Finally, we add the output layer as shown here:

```
with tf.name_scope('out_layer') as scope:

  #third set of weights will be from second hidden layer to final output
layer

  weights3 = tf.get_variable(shape = [HIDDEN_LAYER_2_UNITS,
OUTPUT_LAYER_UNITS], dtype = tf.float32, name = 'weights_3')
  biases3 = tf.get_variable(shape = [OUTPUT_LAYER_UNITS], dtype =
tf.float32, name = 'biases_3')

  # In the last layer, we should use the 'softmax' activation function to
get the
  # probabilities. But we won't do so here because we will use the cross
entropy           #loss with softmax which first converts the output to
probabilty with softmax

  layer3 = tf.add(tf.matmul(layer2, weights3), biases3, name = 'out_layer')
```

Adding loss function

We talked earlier about losses. As this is a classification task, cross entropy loss will be suited best. To use cross entropy, the predicted and expected outputs must be probability distributions. This is done by softmax activation. Cross entropy loss function in TensorFlow combines softmax activation and cross entropy loss in single function and we need not apply softmax activation separately in the last layer of the network.

Do not use explicit softmax activation in final the output layer and softmax cross entropy loss together. Doing this will result in an abrupt decrease in training accuracy of the model.

```
# now we shall add the loss function to graph
with tf.name_scope('loss') as scope:
  loss = tf.reduce_mean(tf.nn.softmax_cross_entropy_with_logits(logits =
layer3, labels = y))
```

Adding an optimizer

We use the Adam optimizer to minimize the loss as shown here:

```
# adding optimizer
with tf.name_scope('optimizer') as scope:

  # we will use Adam Optimizer. It is the most widely used optimizer
  optimizer = tf.train.AdamOptimizer(learning_rate = LEARNING_RATE)

  # we will use this optimizer to minimize loss, that is, to train the
network
  train = optimizer.minimize(loss)
```

Calculating accuracy

There are a lot of metrics to measure how well the model is performing. We keep monitoring the training loss value and training accuracy for batches. Accuracy is measured in percentage (how many predictions are correct). The loss value keeps reducing as the accuracy increases. For every iteration, we also check the validation loss and accuracy. As the validation loss starts to increase again after reaching a minimum value, we need to stop training, or else, we will overfit the model:

```
with tf.name_scope('accuracy') as scope:

  # here we will check how many predictions our model is making correct by
comparing               # the labels

  # tf.equal compares the two tensors element wise, where tf.argmax returns
the #index of class which the prediction and label belong to.

  correctPredictions = tf.equal(tf.argmax(layer3, axis=1), tf.argmax(y,
axis = 1))

  # calculating average accuracy
  avgAccuracy = tf.reduce_mean(tf.cast(correctPredictions, tf.float32))
```

Running a session to train

Up until now, we have created the model graph containing the layers, loss, and optimizers. However, to bring the graph to life, we need to run the session! For each iteration, batches of input images and labels are generated. For every call to the run function, data is required to feed into placeholders. The generated batch data is fed into placeholders through a feed_dict argument. Each time the train operation is run, weights are updated according to the loss. The tensors hold their values only under an active session:

```python
# beginning Tensorflow Session to start training
with tf.Session() as sess:

  # initializing Tensorflow variables under session
  sess.run(tf.global_variables_initializer())

  for epoch in range(EPOCHS):

    for i in range(NUM_BATCHES):


      # creating batch of inputs
      batchX = trainX[i*BATCH_SIZE : (i+1)*BATCH_SIZE , :]
      batchY = trainY[i*BATCH_SIZE : (i+1)*BATCH_SIZE , :]

      # running the train operation for updating weights after every mini-
batch
      _, miniBatchLoss, acc = sess.run([train, loss, avgAccuracy],
feed_dict = {x: batchX, y: batchY})

      # printing accuracy and loss for every 4th training batch
      if i % 10 == 0:
        print('Epoch: '+str(epoch)+' Minibatch_Loss:
'+"{:.6f}".format(miniBatchLoss)+' Train_acc: '+"{:.5f}".format(acc)+"\n")

    # calculating loss for validation batches
    for i in range(int(valX.shape[0] / BATCH_SIZE)):

      valBatchX = valX[i*BATCH_SIZE : (i+1)*BATCH_SIZE, :]
      valBatchY = valY[i*BATCH_SIZE: (i+1)*BATCH_SIZE, :]

      valLoss, valAcc = sess.run([loss, avgAccuracy], feed_dict = {x:
valBatchX, y: valBatchY})

      if i % 5 ==0:
        print('Validation Batch: ', i,' Val Loss: ', valLoss, 'val Acc: ',
valAcc)
```

We print the accuracy metric for every eighth training batch, as shown in the following screenshot:

```
Epoch: 0 Minibatch_Loss: 2.477007 Train_acc: 0.06250
Epoch: 0 Minibatch_Loss: 1.174518 Train_acc: 0.59375
Epoch: 0 Minibatch_Loss: 0.533525 Train_acc: 0.81250
Epoch: 0 Minibatch_Loss: 0.804964 Train_acc: 0.68750
Epoch: 0 Minibatch_Loss: 0.868631 Train_acc: 0.67188
Epoch: 0 Minibatch_Loss: 0.626567 Train_acc: 0.71875
Epoch: 0 Minibatch_Loss: 0.804468 Train_acc: 0.71875
Epoch: 0 Minibatch_Loss: 0.847987 Train_acc: 0.68750
Epoch: 0 Minibatch_Loss: 0.812170 Train_acc: 0.67188
Epoch: 0 Minibatch_Loss: 0.578614 Train_acc: 0.81250
Epoch: 0 Minibatch_Loss: 0.594428 Train_acc: 0.78125
Epoch: 0 Minibatch_Loss: 0.702006 Train_acc: 0.79688
Epoch: 0 Minibatch_Loss: 0.836649 Train_acc: 0.70312
Epoch: 0 Minibatch_Loss: 0.504890 Train_acc: 0.84375
Epoch: 0 Minibatch_Loss: 0.524243 Train_acc: 0.81250
Epoch: 0 Minibatch_Loss: 0.717393 Train_acc: 0.79688
Epoch: 0 Minibatch_Loss: 0.662773 Train_acc: 0.78125
Epoch: 0 Minibatch_Loss: 0.696008 Train_acc: 0.75000
Epoch: 0 Minibatch_Loss: 0.512818 Train_acc: 0.79688
Epoch: 0 Minibatch_Loss: 0.391270 Train_acc: 0.87500
Epoch: 0 Minibatch_Loss: 0.389254 Train_acc: 0.85938
```

```
Epoch: 8 Minibatch_Loss: 0.146620 Train_acc: 0.92188
Epoch: 8 Minibatch_Loss: 0.190568 Train_acc: 0.90625
Epoch: 8 Minibatch_Loss: 0.233540 Train_acc: 0.87500
Epoch: 8 Minibatch_Loss: 0.109386 Train_acc: 0.92188
Epoch: 8 Minibatch_Loss: 0.348949 Train_acc: 0.85938
Epoch: 8 Minibatch_Loss: 0.142979 Train_acc: 0.96875
Epoch: 8 Minibatch_Loss: 0.128231 Train_acc: 0.95312
Epoch: 8 Minibatch_Loss: 0.074185 Train_acc: 0.96875
Epoch: 8 Minibatch_Loss: 0.116466 Train_acc: 0.95312
Epoch: 8 Minibatch_Loss: 0.167854 Train_acc: 0.95312
Epoch: 8 Minibatch_Loss: 0.213404 Train_acc: 0.89062
Epoch: 8 Minibatch_Loss: 0.343354 Train_acc: 0.89062
Epoch: 8 Minibatch_Loss: 0.229185 Train_acc: 0.93750
Epoch: 8 Minibatch_Loss: 0.129644 Train_acc: 0.95312
Epoch: 8 Minibatch_Loss: 0.178772 Train_acc: 0.93750
Epoch: 8 Minibatch_Loss: 0.204266 Train_acc: 0.89062
Epoch: 8 Minibatch_Loss: 0.144129 Train_acc: 0.93750
Epoch: 8 Minibatch_Loss: 0.219204 Train_acc: 0.92188
Epoch: 8 Minibatch_Loss: 0.202214 Train_acc: 0.93750
Epoch: 8 Minibatch_Loss: 0.182245 Train_acc: 0.92188
```

Also, we print validation accuracy for every fifth `Validation` Batch, as shown in the following screenshot:

```
Validation Batch:    0   Val Loss:   0.4653142 val Acc:    0.828125
Validation Batch:    5   Val Loss:   0.38405138 val Acc:   0.859375
Validation Batch:   10   Val Loss:   0.29501903 val Acc:   0.859375
Validation Batch:   15   Val Loss:   0.32584494 val Acc:   0.875
Validation Batch:   20   Val Loss:   0.43639016 val Acc:   0.859375
Validation Batch:   25   Val Loss:   0.29149333 val Acc:   0.875
Validation Batch:   30   Val Loss:   0.47251868 val Acc:   0.828125
Validation Batch:   35   Val Loss:   0.44480062 val Acc:   0.84375
Validation Batch:   40   Val Loss:   0.34775206 val Acc:   0.875
Validation Batch:   45   Val Loss:   0.39910126 val Acc:   0.875
Validation Batch:   50   Val Loss:   0.4770884 val Acc:    0.8125
Validation Batch:   55   Val Loss:   0.33082402 val Acc:   0.890625
Validation Batch:   60   Val Loss:   0.4064049 val Acc:    0.84375
Validation Batch:   65   Val Loss:   0.50343746 val Acc:   0.875
Validation Batch:   70   Val Loss:   0.32819054 val Acc:   0.875
Validation Batch:   75   Val Loss:   0.589856 val Acc:     0.828125
Validation Batch:   80   Val Loss:   0.115529224 val Acc:  0.984375
Validation Batch:   85   Val Loss:   0.32357603 val Acc:   0.875
Validation Batch:   90   Val Loss:   0.2779477 val Acc:    0.84375
```

You may notice that, after epoch eight, the validation accuracy starts dropping. This is a sign that the model has learned sufficiently and going beyond this point will overfit the model.

Once the training is complete, we test the performance on the test data. The same operation used for evaluating training and validation accuracy will be used, but the data will be changed to test data as shown in the following code:

```
# after training, testing performance on test batch

for i in range(int(testX.shape[0] / BATCH_SIZE)):

    testBatchX = testX[i*BATCH_SIZE : (i+1)*BATCH_SIZE, :]
    testBatchY = testY[i*BATCH_SIZE: (i+1)*BATCH_SIZE, :]

    testLoss, testAcc = sess.run([loss, avgAccuracy], feed_dict = {x:
testBatchX, y: testBatchY})

    if i % 5 ==0:
      print('Test Batch: ', i,' Test Loss: ', testLoss, 'Test Acc: ',
testAcc)
```

We print the test accuracy for every fifth `Test Batch`, as shown in the following screenshot:

```
Test Batch:  0   Test Loss:  0.5370658 Test Acc:  0.875
Test Batch:  5   Test Loss:  0.4764716 Test Acc:  0.875
Test Batch:  10  Test Loss:  0.6213647 Test Acc:  0.84375
Test Batch:  15  Test Loss:  0.62183535 Test Acc:  0.8125
Test Batch:  20  Test Loss:  0.4803137 Test Acc:  0.84375
Test Batch:  25  Test Loss:  0.60847616 Test Acc:  0.859375
Test Batch:  30  Test Loss:  0.44178692 Test Acc:  0.890625
Test Batch:  35  Test Loss:  0.31912494 Test Acc:  0.875
Test Batch:  40  Test Loss:  0.79027236 Test Acc:  0.859375
Test Batch:  45  Test Loss:  1.2294483 Test Acc:  0.78125
Test Batch:  50  Test Loss:  0.8225608 Test Acc:  0.8125
Test Batch:  55  Test Loss:  0.7792479 Test Acc:  0.828125
Test Batch:  60  Test Loss:  0.51798975 Test Acc:  0.875
Test Batch:  65  Test Loss:  0.23841673 Test Acc:  0.90625
Test Batch:  70  Test Loss:  0.29975313 Test Acc:  0.859375
Test Batch:  75  Test Loss:  0.61564505 Test Acc:  0.859375
Test Batch:  80  Test Loss:  0.56033397 Test Acc:  0.859375
Test Batch:  85  Test Loss:  0.5941291 Test Acc:  0.828125
Test Batch:  90  Test Loss:  0.28267285 Test Acc:  0.90625
Test Batch:  95  Test Loss:  0.50023687 Test Acc:  0.890625
Test Batch:  100  Test Loss:  0.4542423 Test Acc:  0.859375
Test Batch:  105  Test Loss:  0.2554974 Test Acc:  0.890625
Test Batch:  110  Test Loss:  0.29643798 Test Acc:  0.84375
Test Batch:  115  Test Loss:  0.34353817 Test Acc:  0.9375
Test Batch:  120  Test Loss:  0.3945712 Test Acc:  0.859375
Test Batch:  125  Test Loss:  0.37727326 Test Acc:  0.890625
Test Batch:  130  Test Loss:  0.4266193 Test Acc:  0.921875
Test Batch:  135  Test Loss:  0.44261783 Test Acc:  0.921875
Test Batch:  140  Test Loss:  0.2516768 Test Acc:  0.90625
Test Batch:  145  Test Loss:  0.31523055 Test Acc:  0.890625
Test Batch:  150  Test Loss:  0.375046 Test Acc:  0.890625
Test Batch:  155  Test Loss:  0.47178626 Test Acc:  0.828125
```

If you are finding it difficult to follow up the structure and flow of the code snippets, we provide the whole code for the model here:

```
'''
MNIST Fashion Deep Feedforward example
'''
import os

# use following command if you are getting error with MacOS
os.environ['KMP_DUPLICATE_LIB_OK']='True'

import tensorflow as tf
import numpy as np
```

```
import matplotlib.pyplot as plt
from sklearn.model_selection import train_test_split

from tensorflow import keras

fashionObj = keras.datasets.fashion_mnist

(trainX, trainY), (testX, testY) = fashionObj.load_data()
print('train data x shape: ', trainX.shape)
print('test data x shape:', testX.shape)

print('train data y shape: ', trainY.shape)
print('test data y shape: ', testY.shape)

classesDict = {0:'T-shirt/top', 1:'Trouser', 2:'Pullover', 3:'Dress',
4:'Coat', 5:'Sandal', 6:'Shirt', 7:'Sneaker', 8:'Bag', 9:'Ankle boot'}

rows = 2
columns = 2
fig = plt.figure(figsize = (5,5))

for i in range(1, rows*columns +1):
  image = trainX[i]
  label = trainY[i]

  sub = fig.add_subplot(rows, columns, i)
  sub.set_title('Label: ' + classesDict[label])

  plt.imshow(image)
plt.show()

trainX = trainX.reshape(trainX.shape[0], 784) / 255.0
testX = testX.reshape(testX.shape[0], 784) / 255.0

trainX, valX, trainY, valY = train_test_split(trainX, trainY, test_size =
0.1, random_state =2)


CLASS_NUM = 10
#number of classes we need to classify

INPUT_UNITS = 784
# no. of neurons in input layer 784, as we have 28x28 = 784 pixels in each
image.
# we connect each pixel to a neuron.

HIDDEN_LAYER_1_UNITS = 256
```

```
HIDDEN_LAYER_2_UNITS = 128

OUTPUT_LAYER_UNITS = CLASS_NUM

LEARNING_RATE = 0.001

BATCH_SIZE = 64
NUM_BATCHES = int(trainX.shape[0] / BATCH_SIZE)

EPOCHS = 20


trainY = np.eye(CLASS_NUM)[trainY]
valY = np.eye(CLASS_NUM)[valY]
testY = np.eye(CLASS_NUM)[testY]

with tf.name_scope('placeholders') as scope:

  # making placeholders for inputs (x) and labels (y)
  x = tf.placeholder(shape = [BATCH_SIZE, 784], dtype = tf.float32, name =
'inp_x')
  y = tf.placeholder(shape = [BATCH_SIZE, CLASS_NUM], dtype = tf.float32,
name = 'true_y')

with tf.name_scope('inp_layer') as scope:

  weights1 = tf.get_variable(shape = [INPUT_UNITS, HIDDEN_LAYER_1_UNITS],
dtype = tf.float32, name = 'weights_1')

  biases1 = tf.get_variable(shape = [HIDDEN_LAYER_1_UNITS], dtype =
tf.float32,
name = 'bias_1')


with tf.name_scope('hidden_1') as scope:

  weights2 = tf.get_variable(shape = [HIDDEN_LAYER_1_UNITS,
HIDDEN_LAYER_2_UNITS], dtype = tf.float32, name = 'weights_2')
  biases2 = tf.get_variable(shape = [HIDDEN_LAYER_2_UNITS], dtype =
tf.float32,
name = 'bias_2')


  layer2 = tf.nn.relu(tf.add(tf.matmul(layer1, weights2), biases2), name =
'layer_2')

with tf.name_scope('out_layer') as scope:
```

```
    weights3 = tf.get_variable(shape = [HIDDEN_LAYER_2_UNITS,
OUTPUT_LAYER_UNITS], dtype = tf.float32, name = 'weights_3')
    biases3 = tf.get_variable(shape = [OUTPUT_LAYER_UNITS], dtype =
tf.float32,
                name = 'biases_3')

    layer3 = tf.add(tf.matmul(layer2, weights3), biases3, name = 'out_layer')


with tf.name_scope('loss') as scope:
    loss = tf.reduce_mean(tf.nn.softmax_cross_entropy_with_logits(logits =
layer3, labels = y))

with tf.name_scope('optimizer') as scope:

    optimizer = tf.train.AdamOptimizer(learning_rate = LEARNING_RATE)

    train = optimizer.minimize(loss)

with tf.name_scope('accuracy') as scope:

    correctPredictions = tf.equal(tf.argmax(layer3, axis=1), tf.argmax(y,
axis = 1))

    avgAccuracy = tf.reduce_mean(tf.cast(correctPredictions, tf.float32))


with tf.Session() as sess:

    sess.run(tf.global_variables_initializer())

    for epoch in range(EPOCHS):

        for i in range(NUM_BATCHES):

            batchX = trainX[i*BATCH_SIZE : (i+1)*BATCH_SIZE , :]
            batchY = trainY[i*BATCH_SIZE : (i+1)*BATCH_SIZE , :]

            _, miniBatchLoss, acc = sess.run([train, loss, avgAccuracy],
feed_dict = {x: batchX, y: batchY})

            if i % 10 == 0:
                print('Epoch: '+str(epoch)+' Minibatch_Loss:
'+"{:.6f}".format(miniBatchLoss)+' Train_acc: '+"{:.5f}".format(acc)+"\n")

        for i in range(int(valX.shape[0] / BATCH_SIZE)):

            valBatchX = valX[i*BATCH_SIZE : (i+1)*BATCH_SIZE, :]
```

```
        valBatchY = valY[i*BATCH_SIZE: (i+1)*BATCH_SIZE, :]

        valLoss, valAcc = sess.run([loss, avgAccuracy], feed_dict = {x:
valBatchX, y: valBatchY})

        if i % 5 ==0:
            print('Validation Batch: ', i,' Val Loss: ', valLoss, 'val Acc: ',
valAcc)

    for i in range(int(testX.shape[0] / BATCH_SIZE)):

        testBatchX = testX[i*BATCH_SIZE : (i+1)*BATCH_SIZE, :]
        testBatchY = testY[i*BATCH_SIZE: (i+1)*BATCH_SIZE, :]

        testLoss, testAcc = sess.run([loss, avgAccuracy], feed_dict = {x:
testBatchX, y: testBatchY})

        if i % 5 ==0:
            print('Test Batch: ', i,' Test Loss: ', testLoss, 'Test Acc: ',
testAcc)
```

The easy way

Writing all the preceding code just for a simple DFN might seem tedious. Hence,
TensorFlow has high-level modules that make it easier for us to build our model. Keras
takes care of the major coding structure by providing functions to the build layer, allowing
us to focus us on the model architecture. Let's build a small DFN with Keras as follows:

```
import keras
# importing the sequential method in Keras

from keras.models import Sequential

# Importing the dense layer which creates a layer of deep feedforward
network
from keras.layers import Dense, Activation, Flatten, Dropout

# getting the data as we did earlier
fashionObj = keras.datasets.fashion_mnist

(trainX, trainY), (testX, testY) = fashionObj.load_data()
print('train data x shape: ', trainX.shape)
print('test data x shape:', testX.shape)

print('train data y shape: ', trainY.shape)
print('test data y shape: ', testY.shape)
```

```
# Now we can directly jump to building model, we build in Sequential manner
as discussed in Chapter 1
model = Sequential()

# the first layer we will use is to flatten the 2-d image input from
(28,28) to 784
model.add(Flatten(input_shape = (28, 28)))

# adding first hidden layer with 512 units
model.add(Dense(512))

#adding activation to the output
model.add(Activation('relu'))

#using Dropout for Regularization
model.add(Dropout(0.2))

# adding our final output layer
model.add(Dense(10))

#softmax activation at the end
model.add(Activation('softmax'))

# normalizing input data before feeding
trainX = trainX / 255
testX = testX / 255

# compiling model with optimizer and loss
model.compile(optimizer= 'Adam', loss = 'sparse_categorical_crossentropy',
metrics = ['accuracy'])

# training the model
model.fit(trainX, trainY, epochs = 5, batch_size = 64)

# evaluating the model on test data
model.evaluate(testX, testY)
print('Test Set average Accuracy: ', evalu[1])
```

The preceding code will output the following:

```
60000/60000 [==============================] - 19s 323us/step - loss: 0.5032 - acc: 0.8215
Epoch 2/10
60000/60000 [==============================] - 19s 318us/step - loss: 0.3823 - acc: 0.8604
Epoch 3/10
60000/60000 [==============================] - 21s 348us/step - loss: 0.3452 - acc: 0.8734
Epoch 4/10
60000/60000 [==============================] - 19s 314us/step - loss: 0.3241 - acc: 0.8816
Epoch 5/10
60000/60000 [==============================] - 19s 320us/step - loss: 0.3094 - acc: 0.8844
Epoch 6/10
60000/60000 [==============================] - 19s 309us/step - loss: 0.2964 - acc: 0.8903
Epoch 7/10
60000/60000 [==============================] - 18s 307us/step - loss: 0.2840 - acc: 0.8952
Epoch 8/10
60000/60000 [==============================] - 19s 312us/step - loss: 0.2733 - acc: 0.8974
Epoch 9/10
60000/60000 [==============================] - 19s 320us/step - loss: 0.2674 - acc: 0.8992
Epoch 10/10
60000/60000 [==============================] - 19s 310us/step - loss: 0.2579 - acc: 0.9033
10000/10000 [==============================] - 1s 69us/step
Test Set average Accuracy:   0.8871
```

Summary

We began the chapter with the evolutionary history of DFN and deep learning. We learned about the layered architecture of DFN and various aspects involved in training, such as loss function, gradient descent, backpropagation, optimizers, and regularization. Then we coded our way through our first DFN with TensorFlow as well as Keras. We began with the open source fashion MNIST data and learned the step-by-step process of building a network, right from handling data to training our model.

In the next chapter, we shall see the architectures of Boltzmann machines and autoencoders.

3
Restricted Boltzmann Machines and Autoencoders

When you are shopping online or surfing movies, you may wonder how the *products you may also like* or *movies that may also interest you* works. In this chapter, we will explain the algorithm behind the scene, called the **restricted boltzmann machine** (**RBM**). We will start with reviewing RBMs and their evolution path. We will then dig deeper into the logic behind them and implement RBMs in TensorFlow. We will also apply them to build a movie recommender. Beyond a shallow architecture, we will move on with a stacked version of RBMs called **deep belief networks** (**DBNs**) and use it to classify images, of course, with our implementation in TensorFlow from scratch.

RBMs find a latent representation of the input by attempting to reconstruct the input data. In this chapter, we will also discuss the autoencoders as another type of network that shares a similar idea. In the second half of this chapter, we will continue with what autoencoders are and brief their evolution path. We will illustrate a variety of autoencoders categorized by their architectures or forms of regularization. We will also employ autoencoders of different types to detect credit card fraud. It will be an interesting project, and what's more intriguing is that you will see how these varieties of autoencoders strive to learn more robust representation with certain architectures or forms of imposed constraints.

We will get into the details of the following topics:

- What are RBMs?
- The evolution path of RBMs
- Implementation of RBMs in TensorFlow
- RBMs for movie recommendation
- DBNs
- Implementation of DBNs in TensorFlow
- DBNs for image classification
- What are autoencoders?

- The evolution path of autoencoders
- Vanilla autoencoders
- Deep autoencoders
- Sparse autoencoders
- Denoising autoencoders
- Contractive autoencoders
- Autoencoders for credit card fraud detection

What are RBMs?

RBM is a generative stochastic neural network. By saying generative, it indicates that the network models the probability distribution over its set of inputs. And being stochastic means neurons have random behavior when activated. A general diagram of RBMs is depicted as follows:

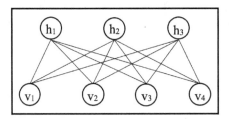

In general, an RBM is composed of one input layer that is more commonly called the visible layer (v_1, **v2**, **v3**, **v4** in the diagram), and one hidden layer ($\mathbf{h_1}$, **h2**, **h3**, **h4**, for example). An RBM model consists of weights $W = \{ w_{i,j}, 1 \leq i \leq |V|, 1 \leq j \leq |H| \}$ that are associated with the connection between the visible layer and the hidden layer, as well as bias $a = \{ a_i, 1 \leq i \leq |V| \}$ for the visible layer, and bias $b = \{ b_j, 1 \leq j \leq |H| \}$ for the hidden layer.

There is obviously no output layer in RBMs, and hence the learning is very different from that in feedforward networks, as outlined here:

- Instead of reducing the loss function, which describes the discrepancy between the ground truth and the output layer, it tries to minimize the energy function, which is defined as follows:

$$E(v, h) = - \int_i a_i v_i - \int_j b_j h_j - \int_{i,j} v_i h_j w_{ij}$$

For those who are not familiar with the energy function, the term **energy** is from physics and is used to quantify the gravity a massive object has toward another object. The energy function in physics measures the compatibility of two objects, or two variables in machine learning. The lower the energy, the better the compatibility between variables, and the higher the quality of the model.

- As opposed to producing outputs, it assigns probabilities over its set of visible and hidden units, and each unit is in a binary state of **0** (off) or **1** (activated) at a point in time. Given a visible layer v, the probability for a hidden unit being activated is computed as follows:

$$P(h_j = 1|v) = sigmoid(b_j + \sum_i v_i w_{ij})$$

Similarly, given a hidden layer h, we can compute the probability for a visible unit being activated as follows:

$$P(v_i = 1|h) = sigmoid(a_i + \sum_j h_j w_{ij})$$

Since the states of h and v are randomly assigned to 0 or 1 based on one another, convergence can be obtained by repeating a few sampling procedures. This process is demonstrated in the following diagram:

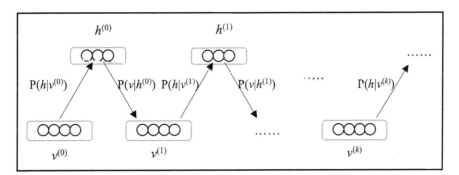

Starting from an initial state of visible layer $v^{(0)}$, $P(h|v^{(0)})$ is computed; hidden layer $h^{(0)}$ is sampled with $P(h|v^{(0)})$, followed by the computation of $P(v|h^{(0)})$. Next, state $v^{(1)}$ is sampled based on $P(v|h^{(0)})$, and $h^{(1)}$ is based on $P(h|v^{(1)})$, and so on and so forth. This process is called Gibbs sampling. It can also be viewed as reconstructing the visible layer.

- The gradients (derived from the energy function) are calculated based on the initial state $v^{(0)}$ and the state $v^{(k)}$ after k Gibbs steps, where $\otimes$ denotes the outer product:

$$\triangle W = v_0 \otimes P(h|v^{(0)}) - v_k \otimes P(h|v^{(k)})$$

$$\triangle a = v_0 - v_k$$

$$\triangle b = P(h|v^{(0)}) - P(h|v^{(k)})$$

These gradients are called contrastive divergence.

I hope you are equipped with the theory behind RBMs by now. You will enhance your understandings of RBMs in the hands-on section, right after a brief overview of their evolution path, which we will cover in the following section.

The evolution path of RBMs

As the name implies, RBMs originated from Boltzmann machines. Invented by Geoffrey Hinton and Paul Smolensky in 1983, Boltzmann machines are a type of network where all units (visible and hidden) are in a binary state and are connected together. Despite their theoretical capability of learning intriguing representations, there are many practical issues for them, including training time, which grows exponentially with the model size (as all units are connected). A general diagram of Boltzmann machines is depicted as follows:

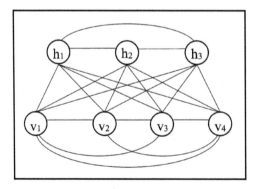

To make it easier to learn a Boltzmann machine model, a connectivity restricted version called Harmonium was initially invented in 1986 by Paul Smolensky. In mid-2000, Geoffrey Hinton and other researchers invented a much more efficient architecture, which contains only one hidden layer and does not allow any internal connections between hidden units. Since then, RBMs have been applied in various supervised learning tasks, including the following:

- Image classification, (*Classification using discriminative restricted Boltzmann machines*, by H. Larochelle and Y. Bengio, proceedings of the 25th International Conference on Machine Learning 2008: 536-543)
- Speech recognition (*Learning a better representation of speech sound waves using restricted Boltzmann machines*, by N. Jaitly and G. Hinton, proceedings of International Conference on Acoustics, Speech, and Signal Processing 2011: 5884-5887)

They have also been applied on unsupervised learning tasks, including the following:

- Dimensionality reduction (*Reducing the Dimensionality of Data with Neural Networks*, by G. Hinton and R. Salakhutdinov, Science, 2006 July: 504-507)
- Feature learning (*An analysis of single-layer networks in unsupervised feature learning*, by A.Coates et al, International Conference on Artificial Intelligence and Statistics 2011: 215-223) and of course collaborative filtering and recommendation systems, which we will work on right after this section

You may notice that RBMs are a bit *shallow*, with only one hidden layer. A *deep* version of RBMs called DBNs were introduced by Geoffrey Hinton in 2006. A DBN can be viewed as a set of RBMs stacked together, where the hidden layer of one RBM is the visible layer of the next RBM. Hidden layers act as hierarchical feature detectors. A general diagram of DBNs is depicted as follows:

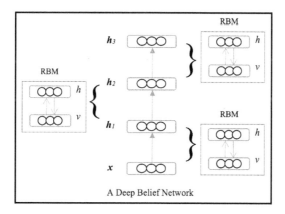

A Deep Belief Network

There are also many interesting applications of DBNs, for example:

- Phone recognition (*Deep belief networks for phone recognition*, by A. Mohamed et al, in proceedings of the NIPS workshop on deep learning for speech recognition and related applications, 2009)
- EEG signals (*Deep Belief Networks for Electroencephalography: A Review of Recent Contributions and Future Outlooks*, by F. Movahedi et al, in IEEE Journal of Biomedical and Health Informatics, May 2018; 22(3): 642-652)
- Natural language understanding (*Application of Deep Belief Networks for Natural Language Understanding*, by R. Sarikaya et al, in IEEE/ACM Transactions on Audio, Speech, and Language Processing, April 2014; 22(4): 778-784)

As promised, we will now study RBMs and their deep version, DBNs in detail, and then apply them to real-world problems.

RBM architectures and applications

We will start with RBMs and their implementation, as well as their application in recommendation systems, and then move on to DBNs and utilizing them to classify images.

RBM and their implementation in TensorFlow

Let's begin with initializing the parameters for the RBM model. Recall that an RMB model consists of weights W associated with the connection between the visible layer and the hidden layer, bias a for the visible layer, and bias b for the hidden layer. An RBM object is configured by weights W, bias a and b, number of visible units and number of hidden units, number of Gibbs steps to take, besides regular neural network hyperparameters including batch size, learning rate, and number of epochs:

```
>>> import numpy as np
>>> import tensorflow as tf
>>> class RBM(object):
...     def __init__(self, num_v, num_h, batch_size, learning_rate,
                     num_epoch, k=2):
...         self.num_v = num_v
...         self.num_h = num_h
...         self.batch_size = batch_size
...         self.learning_rate = learning_rate
...         self.num_epoch = num_epoch
...         self.k = k
...         self.W, self.a, self.b = self._init_parameter()
```

After the initialization of attributes, we define the _init_ parameter method as follows:

```
>>> def _init_parameter(self):
...     """ Initializing the model parameters including weights
            and bias
        """
...     abs_val = np.sqrt(2.0 / (self.num_h + self.num_v))
...     W = tf.get_variable('weights', shape=(self.num_v, self.num_h),
                initializer=tf.random_uniform_initializer(
                    minval=-abs_val, maxval=abs_val))
...     a = tf.get_variable('visible_bias', shape=(self.num_v),
                initializer=tf.zeros_initializer())
...     b = tf.get_variable('hidden_bias', shape=(self.num_h),
                initializer=tf.zeros_initializer())
...     return W, a, b
```

Intuitively, we can safely initialize all biases to 0. When it comes to weights, it is good practice to use a heuristic to initialize them. Commonly used heuristics include the following:

- $\sqrt{\dfrac{2}{size\ of\ previous\ layer}}$

- $\sqrt{\dfrac{1}{size\ of\ previous\ layer}}$, also called **xavier initialization**

- $\sqrt{\dfrac{2}{size\ of\ previous\ layer + size\ of\ current\ layer}}$

These heuristics help prevent slow convergence and are, in general, good starting points for weight initialization.

As we mentioned previously, training an RBM model is a process of searching for parameters that can best reconstruct input vectors via Gibbs sampling. Let's implement the Gibbs sampling method, as follows:

```
>>> def _gibbs_sampling(self, v):
...     """
...     Gibbs sampling
...     @param v: visible layer
...     @return: visible vector before Gibbs sampling,
                conditional probability P(h|v) before Gibbs sampling,
                visible vector after Gibbs sampling,
                conditional probability P(h|v) after Gibbs sampling
...     """
...     v0 = v
```

```
...         prob_h_v0 = self._prob_h_given_v(v0)
...         vk = v
...         prob_h_vk = prob_h_v0
...         for _ in range(self.k):
...             hk = self._bernoulli_sampling(prob_h_vk)
...             prob_v_hk = self._prob_v_given_h(hk)
...             vk = self._bernoulli_sampling(prob_v_hk)
...             prob_h_vk = self._prob_h_given_v(vk)
...         return v0, prob_h_v0, vk, prob_h_vk
```

Gibbs sampling starts with computing $P(h|v)$, given input vector vk. Gibbs steps are then performed. In each Gibbs step, the hidden layer h is obtained by Bernoulli sampling based on $P(h|v)$; the conditional probability $P(v|h)$ is calculated and used to generate the reconstructed version of visible vector v; and the conditional probability $P(h|v)$ is updated based on the latest visible vector. Finally, it returns the visible vector before and after Gibbs sampling, as well as the conditional probability $P(h|v)$ before and after Gibbs sampling.

Now, we realize the computation for conditional probability $P(v|h)$ and $P(h|v)$, as well as Bernoulli sampling:

$$P(v_i = 1|h) = sigmoid(a_i + \sum_j h_j w_{ij})$$

- Computing is as follows:

```
>>> def _prob_v_given_h(self, h):
...         """
...         Computing conditional probability P(v|h)
...         @param h: hidden layer
...         @return: P(v|h)
...         """
...         return tf.sigmoid(
                tf.add(self.a, tf.matmul(h, tf.transpose(self.W))))
```

$$P(h_j = 1|v) = sigmoid(b_j + \sum_i v_i w_{ij})$$

- Calculating is as follows:

```
>>> def _prob_h_given_v(self, v):
...         """
...         Computing conditional probability P(h|v)
...         @param v: visible layer
...         @return: P(h|v)
...         """
...         return tf.sigmoid(tf.add(self.b, tf.matmul(v, self.W)))
```

- Now, we will calculate Bernoulli sampling, like so:

```
>>> def _bernoulli_sampling(self, prob):
...         """ Bernoulli sampling based on input probability """
```

```
...          distribution = tf.distributions.Bernoulli(
                                    probs=prob, dtype=tf.float32)
...          return tf.cast(distribution.sample(), tf.float32)
```

Now that we are able to compute visible input and conditional probability $P(h|v)$ before and after Gibbs sampling, we can calculate the gradients, including $\triangle W = v_o \otimes P(h|v^{(0)}) - P(h|v^{(k)})$, $\Delta a = v_0 - v_k$, and $\Delta b = P(h|v^{(0)}) - P(h|v^{(k)})$, as follows:

```
>>> def _compute_gradients(self, v0, prob_h_v0, vk, prob_h_vk):
...          """
...          Computing gradients of weights and bias
...          @param v0: visible vector before Gibbs sampling
...          @param prob_h_v0: conditional probability P(h|v)
...                                    before Gibbs sampling
...          @param vk: visible vector after Gibbs sampling
...          @param prob_h_vk: conditional probability P(h|v)
...                                    after Gibbs sampling
...          @return: gradients of weights, gradients of visible bias,
...                    gradients of hidden bias
...          """
...          outer_product0 = tf.matmul(tf.transpose(v0), prob_h_v0)
...          outer_productk = tf.matmul(tf.transpose(vk), prob_h_vk)
...          W_grad = tf.reduce_mean(outer_product0 - outer_productk, axis=0)
...          a_grad = tf.reduce_mean(v0 - vk, axis=0)
...          b_grad = tf.reduce_mean(prob_h_v0 - prob_h_vk, axis=0)
...          return W_grad, a_grad, b_grad
```

With Gibbs sampling and gradients, we can put together an epoch-wise parameter update, as shown here:

```
>>> def _optimize(self, v):
...          """
...          Optimizing RBM model parameters
...          @param v: input visible layer
...          @return: updated parameters, mean squared error of reconstructing v
...          """
...          v0, prob_h_v0, vk, prob_h_vk = self._gibbs_sampling(v)
...          W_grad, a_grad, b_grad = self._compute_gradients(v0, prob_h_v0, vk,
                                                              prob_h_vk)
...          para_update=[tf.assign(self.W,
                              tf.add(self.W, self.learning_rate*W_grad)),
...                      tf.assign(self.a,
                              tf.add(self.a, self.learning_rate*a_grad)),
...                      tf.assign(self.b,
                              tf.add(self.b, self.learning_rate*b_grad))]
...          error = tf.metrics.mean_squared_error(v0, vk)[1]
...          return para_update, error
```

Besides updating weights $W := W + lr * \Delta W$, bias $a := a + lr * \Delta a$, and bias $b := b + lr * \Delta b$, we also compute the mean squared error of reconstructing the visible layer.

So far, we have the necessary components ready for training an RBM model, so the next thing is putting them together to form the train method, as shown in the following code:

```
>>> def train(self, X_train):
...     """
...     Model training
...     @param X_train: input data for training
...     """
...     X_train_plac = tf.placeholder(tf.float32, [None, self.num_v])
...     para_update, error = self._optimize(X_train_plac)
...     init = tf.group(tf.global_variables_initializer(),
                        tf.local_variables_initializer())
        with tf.Session() as sess:
            sess.run(init)
            epochs_err = []
            n_batch = int(X_train.shape[0] / self.batch_size)
            for epoch in range(1, self.num_epoch + 1):
                epoch_err_sum = 0
                for batch_number in range(n_batch):
                    batch = X_train[batch_number * self.batch_size:
                                    (batch_number + 1) * self.batch_size]
...                 _, batch_err = sess.run((para_update, error),
                                    feed_dict={X_train_plac: batch})
                    epoch_err_sum += batch_err
                epochs_err.append(epoch_err_sum / n_batch)
                if epoch % 10 == 0:
                    print("Training error at epoch %s: %s" %
                                    (epoch, epochs_err[-1]))
```

Note that we employ mini-batch gradient descent in training, and record training errors at each epoch. The whole training process relies on the _optimize method, which fits the model on each data batch. It also outputs a training error every 10 epochs for quality assurance purposes.

We have just finished implementing the RBM algorithm. In the next section, we will apply it to movie recommendation.

RBMs for movie recommendation

It is commonly known that e-commerce sites recommend products to users based on their purchase and browsing history. The same logic applies for movie recommendation. For example, Netflix predicts what movies a user will like based on the feedback (such as ratings) that the user provided on their watched movies. RBM is one of the most popular solutions to recommendation systems. Let's look at how RBMs for recommendation works.

Given a trained RBM model, an input composed of a set of movies a user likes, dislikes, and has not watched goes to the hidden layer from the visible layer, and then comes back to the visible layer, resulting in a reconstructed version of input. Besides movies the user interacted with, the reconstructed input contains information of those not rated before. It serves as prediction of whether those movies will be liked. A general diagram is depicted as follows:

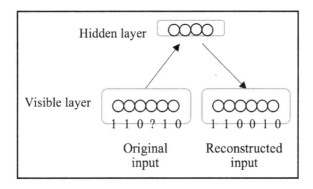

In this example, the input consists of six movies, three of which are liked (denoted by **1**), two are disliked (denoted by **0**), and one not rated (denoted by **?**). The model takes in the input and reconstructs it, including the *missing* movie.

So, how does the model know that the missing unit should be **0** (or **1**)? Recall that each hidden unit is connected to all visible units. During training, a hidden unit attempts to uncover a latent factor that can explain an attribute in the data, or all movies in our case. For example, a binary hidden unit could learn whether a movie genre is comedy or not, whether it is about justice or not, and whether the theme is revenge, or anything else that it catches. In the reconstruction stage, an input is assigned a new value that's calculated based on the hidden units that are representing all these latent factors.

Sounds magical? Let's kick-start building our RBM-based movie recommender.

We will use movie rating datasets from MovieLens (https://movielens.org). It is a non-commercial website for collecting users' moving ratings and providing personalized recommendations and is run by GroupLens, a research lab at the University of Minnesota.

First, we will look at the 1M benchmark dataset in https://grouplens.org/datasets/movielens/1m/. It contains approximately one million ratings from 6,040 users on 3,706 movies. We can download the dataset via http://files.grouplens.org/datasets/movielens/ml-1m.zip and unzip the downloaded file. The ratings are contained in the ratings.dat file, and each line is one rating in the following format:

```
UserID::MovieID::Rating::Timestamp
```

The rating records look like the following:

```
1::1193::5::978300760
2::1357::5::978298709
10::1022::5::979775689
```

There are a few things to note:

- UserIDs range between 1 and 6,040
- MovieIDs range between 1 and 3,952, but not each movie is rated
- The rating is one of {1, 2, 3, 4, 5}
- Each user rates a few movies

We can build an RBM model to recommend movies that a user has not watched based on his/her and others' movie ratings.

You may notice that the input ratings are not binary. How can we feed them to the RBM model? The simplest workaround is binarization, for example, converting ratings greater than three into 1 (like), otherwise 0 (dislike). However, this may result in information loss. Alternatively, in our solution, we scale the original ratings to the range [0, 1] and consider each rescaled rating as the probability of getting 1. That is, $v = P(v = 1|h)$ and Bernoulli sampling is not needed.

Now, let's load the dataset and construct the training dataset. Don't forget to keep track of the rated movies as not all movies are rated:

```
>>> import numpy as np
>>> data_path = 'ml-1m/ratings.dat'
>>> num_users = 6040
>>> num_movies = 3706
>>> data = np.zeros([num_users, num_movies], dtype=np.float32)
>>> movie_dict = {}
>>> with open(data_path, 'r') as file:
```

```
...     for line in file.readlines()[1:]:
...         user_id, movie_id, rating, _ = line.split("::")
...         user_id = int(user_id) - 1
...         if movie_id not in movie_dict:
...             movie_dict[movie_id] = len(movie_dict)
...         rating = float(rating) / 5
...         data[user_id, movie_dict[movie_id]] = rating
>>> data = np.reshape(data, [data.shape[0], -1])
>>> print(data.shape) (6040, 3706)
```

The training dataset is of the size 6,040 x 3,706, with each row consisting of 3706 scaled ratings, including 0.0, meaning not rated. It can be presented as the following table (dummy) for a more visual view:

	movie_0	movie_1	movie_2	...	...	movie_n
user_0	0.0	0.2	0.8	0.0	1.0	0.0
user_1	0.8	0.0	0.6	1.0	0.0	0.0
user_2	0.0	0.0	1.0	1.0	0.8	0.0
...	...	...	...	...	...	...
user_m	0.0	0.6	0.0	0.8	0.0	0.8

Take a look at their distribution, as shown here:

```
>>> values, counts = np.unique(data, return_counts=True)
>>> for value, count in zip(values, counts):
...         print('Number of {:2.1f} ratings: {}'.format(value, count))
Number of 0.0 ratings: 21384032
Number of 0.2 ratings: 56174
Number of 0.4 ratings: 107557
Number of 0.6 ratings: 261197
Number of 0.8 ratings: 348971
Number of 1.0 ratings: 226309
```

We can see that the matrix is pretty sparse. Again, those 0s represent movies that are not rated by corresponding users, not a zero probability of getting 1. Hence, we should keep the rating of an unrated movie as zero throughout the entire training process, which means we should revert them to 0 after each Gibbs step. Otherwise, their reconstructed values will be included in the computation of hidden layer and gradients, and as a result, the model will be largely miss-optimized.

Accordingly, we modify the _gibbs_sampling and _optimize methods, as follows:

```
>>> def _gibbs_sampling(self, v):
...     """
...     Gibbs sampling (visible units with value 0 are unchanged)
...     @param v: visible layer
```

```
...            @return: visible vector before Gibbs sampling,
                        conditional probability P(h|v) before Gibbs sampling,
...                     visible vector after Gibbs sampling,
                        conditional probability P(h|v) after Gibbs sampling
...            """
...            v0 = v
...            prob_h_v0 = self._prob_h_given_v(v0)
...            vk = v
...            prob_h_vk = prob_h_v0
...            for _ in range(self.k):
...                hk = self._bernoulli_sampling(prob_h_vk)
...                prob_v_hk = self._prob_v_given_h(hk)
...                vk_tmp = prob_v_hk
...                vk = tf.where(tf.equal(v0, 0.0), v0, vk_tmp)
...                prob_h_vk = self._prob_h_given_v(vk)
...            return v0, prob_h_v0, vk, prob_h_vk
```

We adopt $v = P(v = 1|h)$ and revert ratings with 0, as follows:

```
>>> def _optimize(self, v):
...            """
...            Optimizing RBM model parameters
...            @param v: input visible layer
...            @return: updated parameters, mean squared error of reconstructing v
...            """
...            v0, prob_h_v0, vk, prob_h_vk = self._gibbs_sampling(v)
...            W_grad, a_grad, b_grad = self._compute_gradients(
                                    v0, prob_h_v0, vk, prob_h_vk)
...            para_update=[tf.assign(self.W,
                              tf.add(self.W, self.learning_rate*W_grad)),
...                     tf.assign(self.a,
                              tf.add(self.a, self.learning_rate*a_grad)),
...                     tf.assign(self.b, tf.add(self.b,
                              self.learning_rate*b_grad))]
...            bool_mask = tf.cast(tf.where(tf.equal(v0, 0.0),
                              x=tf.zeros_like(v0), y=tf.ones_like(v0)),
                              dtype=tf.bool)
...            v0_mask = tf.boolean_mask(v0, bool_mask)
...            vk_mask = tf.boolean_mask(vk, bool_mask)
...            error = tf.metrics.mean_squared_error(v0_mask, vk_mask)[1]
...            return para_update, error
```

We only consider those rated movies when calculating the training error, otherwise it will become incredibly small. With these changes, we can now safely fit an RBM model on the training set, as shown in the following code:

```
>>> rbm = RBM(num_v=num_movies, num_h=80, batch_size=64,
              num_epoch=100, learning_rate=0.1, k=5)
```

We initialize a model with 80 hidden units, a batch size of 64, 100 epochs, a learning rate of 0.1, and 5 Gibbs steps, like so:

```
>>> rbm.train(data)
Training error at epoch 10: 0.043496965727907545
Training error at epoch 20: 0.041566036522705505
Training error at epoch 30: 0.040718327296224044
Training error at epoch 40: 0.04024859795227964
Training error at epoch 50: 0.03992816338196714
Training error at epoch 60: 0.039701666445174116
Training error at epoch 70: 0.03954154300562879
Training error at epoch 80: 0.03940619274656823
Training error at epoch 90: 0.03930238915726225
Training error at epoch 100: 0.03921664716239939
```

The training error decreases to 0.039 and we can use the trained model to recommend movies. To do so, we need to return the optimized parameters and add a prediction method using those parameters.

In the training method we defined before, we keep the updated parameters by changing the following line:

```
... _, batch_err = sess.run(
                (para_update, error),feed_dict={X_train_plac: batch})
```

We need to replace the previous lines with the following:

```
... parameters, batch_err = sess.run((para_update, error),
                            feed_dict={X_train_plac: batch})
```

Then, we need to return the last updated parameters at the end of the method, as follows:

```
... return parameters
```

The prediction method that takes in the trained model and reconstructs the input data is defined as follows:

```
>>> def predict(self, v, parameters):
...     W, a, b = parameters
...     prob_h_v = 1 / (1 + np.exp(-(b + np.matmul(v, W))))
...     h = np.random.binomial(1, p=prob_h_v)
...     prob_v_h = 1 /
                (1 + np.exp(-(a + np.matmul(h, np.transpose(W)))))
...     return prob_v_h
```

We can now obtain the prediction of input data, like so:

```
>>> parameters_trained = rbm.train(data)
>>> prediction = rbm.predict(data, parameters_trained)
```

Take one user as an example, we compare movies with a five-star rating and movies that are not rated, but are predicted to have a rating that's higher than 0.9. This is all shown in the following code:

```
>>> sample, sample_pred = data[0], prediction[0]
>>> five_star_index = np.where(sample == 1.0)[0]
>>> high_index = np.where(sample_pred >= 0.9)[0]
>>> index_movie = {value: key for key, value in movie_dict.items()}
>>> print('Movies with five-star rating:', ',
        '.join(index_movie[index] for index in five_star_index))
Movies with five-star rating: 2918, 1035, 3105, 1097, 1022, 1246, 3257,
265, 1957, 1968, 1079, 39, 1704, 1923, 1101, 597, 1088, 1380, 300, 1777,
1307, 62, 543, 249, 440, 2145, 3526, 2248, 1013, 2671, 2059, 381, 3429,
1172, 2690
>>> print('Movies with high prediction:',
        ', '.join(index_movie[index] for index in high_index if index not
        in five_star_index))
Movies with high prediction: 527, 745, 318, 50, 1148, 858, 2019, 922, 787,
2905, 3245, 2503, 53
```

We can look up the corresponding movies in the `movies.dat` file. For example, it makes sense that this user likes `3257::The Bodyguard` and `1101::Top Gun`, so he/she will also like `50::The Usual Suspects`, `858::The Godfather`, and `527::Schindler's List`. However, because of the unsupervised nature of RBMs, it is difficult to gauge how well the model performs unless we consult each user. We need to develop a simulation approach to measure prediction accuracy.

We randomly select 20% of the existing ratings for each user and make them temporarily unknown when fed into the trained RBM model. Then, we compare the prediction and the actual value of those chosen simulation ratings.

First, let's split the users into 90% training and 10% testing set, whose ratings will be used to train the model and perform simulation, respectively. This is shown in the following code:

```
>>> np.random.seed(1)
>>> np.random.shuffle(data)
>>> data_train, data_test = data[:num_train, :], data[num_train:, :]
```

Second, on the testing set, we randomly select 20% of the existing ratings from each user for simulation, like so:

```
>>> sim_index = np.zeros_like(data_test, dtype=bool)
>>> perc_sim = 0.2
>>> for i, user_test in enumerate(data_test):
...     exist_index = np.where(user_test > 0.0)[0]
...     sim_index[i, np.random.choice(exist_index,
                    int(len(exist_index)*perc_sim))] = True
```

The selected ratings become temporarily unknown, as shown here:

```
>>> data_test_sim = np.copy(data_test)
>>> data_test_sim[sim_index] = 0.0
```

Next, we train the model on the training set and predict on the simulated testing set, as follows:

```
>>> rbm = RBM(num_v=num_movies, num_h=80, batch_size=64,
              num_epoch=100, learning_rate=1, k=5)
>>> parameters_trained = rbm.train(data_train)
Training error at epoch 10: 0.039383551327600366
Training error at epoch 20: 0.03883369417772407
Training error at epoch 30: 0.038669846597171965
Training error at epoch 40: 0.038585483273934754
Training error at epoch 50: 0.03852854181258451
Training error at epoch 60: 0.03849853335746697
Training error at epoch 70: 0.03846755987476735
Training error at epoch 80: 0.03844876645044202
Training error at epoch 90: 0.03843735127399365
Training error at epoch 100: 0.038423490045326095
>>> prediction = rbm.predict(data_test_sim, parameters_trained)
```

Finally, we can evaluate the prediction accuracy by computing the MSE between the prediction and the actual value of those chosen ratings, as follows:

```
>>> from sklearn.metrics import mean_squared_error
>>> print(mean_squared_error(
            data_test[sim_index],prediction[sim_index]))
0.037987366148405505
```

An MSE of 0.038 is achieved by our RBM-based movie recommender. If you are interested, there are larger datasets to play with, such as the 10 million ratings dataset at https://grouplens.org/datasets/movielens/10m/, and the 26 million ratings dataset at https://grouplens.org/datasets/movielens/latest/.

We have gained more knowledge about RBM through its implementation and application. As promised, let's look at a stacked architecture of RBMs—the DBN—in the next section.

DBNs and their implementation in TensorFlow

A DBN is nothing but a set of RBMs stacked up together where the hidden layer of one RBM is the visible layer of the next RBM. During the training of the parameters of a layer, the parameters of the previous layer remain unchanged. In other words, a DBN model is trained layer by layer in a sequential manner. With each layer added on top, we are able to extract features out of the previously extracted ones. This is where the *deep* architecture comes from and what makes DBNs hierarchical feature detectors.

To implement DBN, we need to reuse most of the code from the RBM class since a DBN is composed of a series of RBMs. Therefore, we should explicitly define a variable scope for parameters of each RBM model. Otherwise, we will refer to the same set of variables for more than one RBM class, which is not allowed in TensorFlow. Accordingly, we add an attribute ID and use it to differentiate parameters of different RBM models:

```
>>> class RBM(object):
...     def __init__(self, num_v, id, num_h, batch_size,
                        learning_rate, num_epoch, k=2):
...         self.num_v = num_v
...         self.num_h = num_h
...         self.batch_size = batch_size
...         self.learning_rate = learning_rate
...         self.num_epoch = num_epoch
...         self.k = k
...         self.W, self.a, self.b = self._init_parameter(id)
...
>>> def _init_parameter(self, id):
...     """ Initializing parameters the the id-th model
                including weights and bias """
...     abs_val = np.sqrt(2.0 / (self.num_h + self.num_v))
...     with tf.variable_scope('rbm{}_parameter'.format(id)):
...         W = tf.get_variable('weights', shape=(self.num_v,
                self.num_h), initializer=tf.random_uniform_initializer(
                minval=-abs_val, maxval=abs_val))
...         a = tf.get_variable('visible_bias', shape=(self.num_v),
                            initializer=tf.zeros_initializer())
...         b = tf.get_variable('hidden_bias', shape=(self.num_h),
                            initializer=tf.zeros_initializer())
...     return W, a, b
```

Also, hidden vectors of a trained RBM are used as the input vectors of the next RBM. So, we define an additional method to facilitate this like so:

```
>>> def hidden_layer(self, v, parameters):
...         """
...         Computing hidden vectors
...         @param v: input vectors
...         @param parameters: trained RBM parameters
...         """
...         W, a, b = parameters
...         h = 1 / (1 + np.exp(-(b + np.matmul(v, W))))
...         return h
```

The rest of the RBM class is identical to the one we previously implemented. We can now work on the DBN, as shown here:

```
>>> class DBN(object):
...     def __init__(self, layer_sizes, batch_size,
...                  learning_rates, num_epoch, k=2):
...         self.rbms = []
...         for i in range(1, len(layer_sizes)):
...             rbm = RBM(num_v=layer_sizes[i-1], id=i,
...                       num_h=layer_sizes[i], batch_size=batch_size,
...                       learning_rate=learning_rates[i-1],
...                       num_epoch=num_epoch, k=k)
...             self.rbms.append(rbm)
```

The DBN class takes in parameters including `layer_sizes` (number of units for each layer, starting with the first input layer), `batch_size`, `learning_rates` (list of learning rates for each RBM unit), `num_epoch`, and Gibbs steps `k`.

The train method is defined as follows, where the parameters of a hidden layer are trained on the original input data or the outputs of the previous hidden layer:

```
...     def train(self, X_train):
...         """
...         Model training
...         @param X_train: input data for training
...         """
...         self.rbms_para = []
...         input_data = None
...         for rbm in self.rbms:
...             if input_data is None:
...                 input_data = X_train.copy()
...             parameters = rbm.train(input_data)
...             self.rbms_para.append(parameters)
...             input_data = rbm.hidden_layer(input_data, parameters)
```

With the trained parameters, the `predict` method computes the outputs of the last layer, as follows:

```
...       def predict(self, X):
...           """
...           Computing the output of the last layer
...           @param X: input data for training
...           """
...           data = None
...           for rbm, parameters in zip(self.rbms, self.rbms_para):
...               if data is None:
...                   data = X.copy()
...               data = rbm.hidden_layer(data, parameters)
...           return data
```

The outputs of the last layer are the extracted features, which are used for a downstream task, for example, classification, regression, or clustering. In the next section, we will be demonstrating how to apply DBNs to image classification.

DBNs for image classification

The dataset we will use is made up of 1797 10-class handwritten digit images. Each image is 8 x 8 in size, with each pixel value ranging from 0 to 16. Let's read the dataset and scale the data to a range of 0 to 1, and split it into training and testing sets, as follows:

```
>>> from sklearn import datasets
>>> data = datasets.load_digits()
>>> X = data.data
>>> Y = data.target
>>> print(X.shape)
(1797, 64)
>>> X = X / 16.0
>>> np.random.seed(1)
>>> from sklearn.model_selection import train_test_split
>>> X_train, X_test, Y_train, Y_test =
                train_test_split(X, Y, test_size = 0.2)
```

We employ a DBN with two hidden layers of 256 and 512 hidden units, respectively, and train it on the training set, as shown here:

```
>>> dbn = DBN([X_train.shape[1], 256, 512], 10, [0.05, 0.05], 20, k=2)
>>> dbn.train(X_train)
Training error at epoch 10: 0.0816881338824759
Training error at epoch 20: 0.07888000140656957
Training error at epoch 10: 0.005190357937106303
Training error at epoch 20: 0.003952089745968164
```

With the trained DBN, we produce output vectors of the last hidden layer for both the training and testing sets, as shown in the following code:

```
>>> feature_train = dbn.predict(X_train)
>>> feature_test = dbn.predict(X_test)
>>> print(feature_train.shape)
(1437, 512)
>>> print(feature_test.shape)
(360, 512)
```

We then feed the extracted 512-dimension features into a logistic regression model to complete the digit classification task, like so:

```
>>> from sklearn.linear_model import LogisticRegression
>>> lr = LogisticRegression(C=10000)
>>> lr.fit(feature_train, Y_train)
```

The flow of the whole algorithm is depicted as follows:

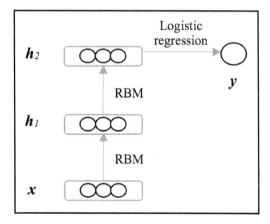

Finally, we use the trained logistic regression model to predict the extracted features from the testing set, as follows:

```
>>> print(lr.score(feature_test, Y_test))
0.9777777777777777
```

A classification accuracy of 97.8% is achieved with this approach.

What are autoencoders?

We just learned and gained practical experience with RBM and its variant, DBN, in the previous sections. Recall that an RBM is composed of an input layer and a hidden layer, which attempts to reconstruct the input data by finding a latent representation of the input. The neural network model **autoencoders** (**AEs**) that we will learn about, starting from this section, share a similar idea. A basic AE is made up of three layers: the input, hidden, and output layers. The output layer is a reconstruction of the input through the hidden layer. A general diagram of AE is depicted as follows:

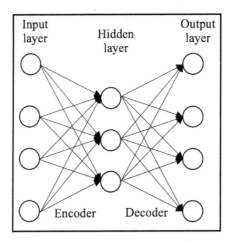

As we can see, when the autoencoder takes in data, it first encodes it to fit the hidden layer, and then it tries to reconstruct it back to the original input data. Meanwhile, the hidden layer can extract a latent representation of the input data. Because of this structure, the first half of the network is called the **encoder**, which compresses the input data into a latent representation. The second half, on the contrary, is a **decoder** that decompresses the extracted representation.

Both AE and RBM aim to minimize reconstruction error, but AE differs from RBM in the following ways:

- AE learns about the hidden representation in a discriminative way without considering the probability distribution of input data
- RBMs find the hidden representation in a stochastic way by sampling from the hidden layer and input layer alternatively

Now, let's quickly go through the evolution path of AE before we apply them to real-world problems.

The evolution path of autoencoders

Autoencoders were first introduced as a method for unsupervised pre-training in *Modular Learning in Neural Networks* (D. Ballard, AAAI proceedings, 1987). They were then used for dimensionality reduction, such as in *Auto-Association by Multilayer Perceptrons and Singular Value Decomposition* (H. Bourlard and Y. Kamp, biological cybernetics, 1988; 59:291-294) and non-linear feature learning, for example, *Autoencoders, Minimum Description Length, and Helmholtz Free Energy* (G. Hinton and R. Zemel, Advances In Neural Information Processing Systems, 1994).

Autoencoders have evolved over time and there have been several variants proposed in the past decade. In 2008, P. Vincent et al. introduced **denoising autoencoders (DAEs)** in *Extracting and Composing Robust Features with Denoising Autoencoders* (proceedings of the 25th International Conference on Machine Learning, 1096-1103), where the networks are forced to reconstruct input data from a corrupted version of it so that they can learn more robust features.

I. Goodfellow et al. in 2009 developed **sparse autoencoders**, which enlarges the hidden representation by introducing a sparsity constraint. Details can be found in *Measuring Invariances In Deep Networks* (Advances in Neural Information Processing Systems 22, NIPS 2009, 646-654).

Contractive autoencoders were proposed by S. Rifai in *Contractive Auto-Encoders: Explicit Invariance During Feature Extraction* (Proceedings of the 28th International Conference on Machine Learning, 2011; 833-840). A penalty term is added to the cost function so that the networks are able to extract representations that are less sensitive toward small changes around input data.

In 2013, a special type called **variational autoencoders** (**VAEs**) was proposed in *Auto-Encoding Variational Bayes* (by D. Kingma and M. Welling, Proceedings of the second International Conference on Learning Representations), which considers the probability distribution of latent variables.

We are going to implement several variants of AE in Keras and use them to solve a credit card fraud detection problem.

Autoencoders architectures and applications

We will start with the basic, vanilla AE, then the deep version, followed by sparse autoencoders, denoising autoencoders, and wrap up with contractive autoencoders.

Throughout this entire section, we will use the credit card fraud dataset as an example to demonstrate how to apply autoencoders of various architectures.

Vanilla autoencoders

This is the most basic three-layer architecture, and is perfect to kick-start implementing autoencoders. Let's prepare the dataset. The dataset we are using is from a Kaggle competition and can be downloaded from the `Data` page in `https://www.kaggle.com/mlg-ulb/creditcardfraud`. Each row contains 31 fields, as follows:

- `Time`: Number of seconds since the first row in the dataset
- `V1, V2, ..., V28`: The principal components obtained with PCA on the original features
- `Amount`: The transaction amount
- `Class`: 1 for fraudulent transactions, 0 otherwise

We load the data in a pandas dataframe and drop the `Time` field since it provides little information, as shown here:

```
>>> import pandas as pd
>>> data = pd.read_csv("creditcard.csv").drop(['Time'], axis=1)
>>> print(data.shape)
(284807, 30)
```

The dataset contains 284,000 samples but is highly imbalanced, with very few fraudulent samples, as shown here:

```
>>> print('Number of fraud samples: ', sum(data.Class == 1))
Number of fraud samples: 492
>>> print('Number of normal samples: ', sum(data.Class == 0))
Number of normal samples: 284315
```

As we can see from the feature visualization panel in the `Data` page in `https://www.kaggle.com/mlg-ulb/creditcardfraud`, V1 to V28 are in Gaussian standard distribution, while `Amount` is not. Therefore, we need to normalize the `Amount` feature, as shown in the following code:

```
>>> from sklearn.preprocessing import StandardScaler
>>> scaler = StandardScaler()
>>> data['Amount'] =
        scaler.fit_transform(data['Amount'].values.reshape(-1, 1))
```

After preprocessing, we split the data into 80% training and 20% testing, like so:

```
>>> import numpy as np
>>> np.random.seed(1)
>>> data_train, data_test = train_test_split(data, test_size=0.2)
```

As we figured the fraudulent class only takes up 0.17% of the entire population, traditional supervised learning algorithms might have difficulties picking up enough of a pattern from the minority class. Therefore, we resorted to an AE-based unsupervised learning solution. A well-trained autoencoder can perfectly reconstruct the input data. If we fit an autoencoder only on normal samples, the model will become a normal data reconstructor that is only good at reproducing non-anomalous data. However, if we feed this model an anomalous input, there will be a relatively large discrepancy between the reconstruction output and the input. Therefore, we can detect anomalies by measuring the reconstruction error with AE.

Accordingly, we reorganize the training and testing set as only normal samples are needed to fit the model, as follows:

```
>>> data_test = data_test.append(data_train[data_train.Class == 1],
                                  ignore_index=True)
>>> data_train = data_train[data_train.Class == 0]
```

We don't need the targets for the training set as our approach is unsupervised. Therefore, we just take the features from the training set, as follows:

```
>>> X_train = data_train.drop(['Class'], axis=1).values
>>> X_test = data_test.drop(['Class'], axis=1).values
>>> Y_test = data_test['Class']
```

The data is now ready to use; it is time to build the vanilla autoencoder in Keras. Now, let's start by importing the necessary modules, like so:

```
>>> from keras.models import Model
>>> from keras.layers import Input, Dense
>>> from keras.callbacks import ModelCheckpoint, TensorBoard
>>> from keras import optimizers
```

There's the first layer, the input layer, with 29 units (input data is 29-dimension), as shown here:

```
>>> input_size = 29
>>> input_layer = Input(shape=(input_size,))
```

There's the second layer, the hidden layer, with 40 units, encodes the input data, as shown here:

```
>>> hidden_size = 40
>>> encoder = Dense(hidden_size, activation="relu")(input_layer)
```

Finally, there's the last layer, the output layer, with the same size as the input one, which decodes the hidden representation, as follows:

```
>>> decoder = Dense(input_size)(encoder)
```

Connect them together with the following code:

```
>>> ae = Model(inputs=input_layer, outputs=decoder)
>>> print(ae.summary())
```

```
Layer (type)                 Output Shape              Param #
=================================================================
input_1 (InputLayer)         (None, 29)                0
_____
dense_1 (Dense)              (None, 40)                1200
_____
dense_2 (Dense)              (None, 29)                1189
=================================================================
Total params: 2,389
Trainable params: 2,389
Non-trainable params: 0
```

We then compile the model with Adam (learning rate 0.0001) as the optimizer, as follows:

```
>>> optimizer = optimizers.Adam(lr=0.0001)
>>> ae.compile(optimizer=optimizer, loss='mean_squared_error')
```

We also use TensorBoard as the callback function besides model checkpoint. TensorBoard is a performance visualization tool from TensorFlow, and provides dynamic graphs of training and validation metrics, for example:

```
>>> tensorboard = TensorBoard(log_dir='./logs/run1/',
                    write_graph=True, write_images=False)
>>> model_file = "model_ae.h5"
>>> checkpoint = ModelCheckpoint(model_file, monitor='loss',
                    verbose=1, save_best_only=True, mode='min')
```

Finally, we fit the model with data (X_train, X_train) and validate with data (X_test, X_test) as autoencoders and try to produce an output that's the same as the input:

```
>>> num_epoch = 30
>>> batch_size = 64
>>> ae.fit(X_train, X_train, epochs=num_epoch, batch_size=batch_size,
            shuffle=True, validation_data=(X_test, X_test),
            verbose=1, callbacks=[checkpoint, tensorboard])
```

The following are the results from the first and last 3 epochs:

```
Train on 227440 samples, validate on 57367 samples
Epoch 1/30
227440/227440 [==============================] - 4s 17us/step - loss:
0.6690 - val_loss: 0.4297
Epoch 00001: loss improved from inf to 0.66903, saving model to model_ae.h5
Epoch 2/30
227440/227440 [==============================] - 4s 18us/step   loss:
0.1667 - val_loss: 0.2057
Epoch 00002: loss improved from 0.66903 to 0.16668, saving model to
model_ae.h5
Epoch 3/30
227440/227440 [==============================] - 4s 17us/step - loss:
0.0582 - val_loss: 0.1124
......
......
Epoch 28/30
227440/227440 [==============================] - 3s 15us/step - loss:
1.4541e-05 - val_loss: 0.0011
Epoch 00028: loss improved from 0.00001 to 0.00001, saving model to
model_ae.h5
```

```
Epoch 29/30
227440/227440 [==============================] - 4s 15us/step - loss:
1.2951e-05 - val_loss: 0.0011
Epoch 00029: loss improved from 0.00001 to 0.00001, saving model to
model_ae.h5
Epoch 30/30
227440/227440 [==============================] - 4s 16us/step - loss:
1.9115e-05 - val_loss: 0.0010
Epoch 00030: loss did not improve from 0.00001
```

We can check out TensorBoard by typing the following command in the Terminal:

```
tensorboard --logdir=logs
```

It returns the following:

```
Starting TensorBoard b'41' on port 6006
(You can navigate to http://192.168.0.12:6006)
```

By going to http://192.168.0.12:6006 (the host may be different, depending on your environment), we can see the training losses and validation losses over time.

Training losses with smoothing = 0 (no exponential smoothing) is shown in the following graph:

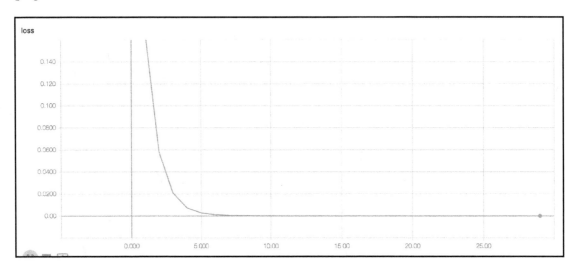

Validation losses with smoothing = 0 (no exponential smoothing) is shown here:

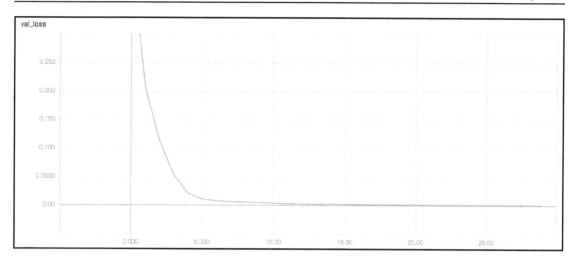

Now, we can feed the testing set to the well-trained model and compute the reconstruction error that's measured by mean squared error like so:

```
>>> recon = ae.predict(X_test)
>>> recon_error = np.mean(np.power(X_test - recon, 2), axis=1)
```

Normally, we would calculate the area under the ROC curve to evaluate the binary classification performance on imbalanced data, as follows:

```
>>> from sklearn.metrics import (roc_auc_score,
                      precision_recall_curve, auc, confusion_matrix)
>>> roc_auc = roc_auc_score(Y_test, recon_error)
>>> print('Area under ROC curve:', roc_auc)
Area under ROC curve: 0.9548928080050032
```

An AUC of ROC `0.95` is achieved. However, it does not necessarily indicate good performance in this case, since the minority class occurs rarely (around 0.87% in the testing set). The AUC of ROC can be easily above `0.9` without any intelligent model. Instead, we should measure performance by the area under the precision-recall curve, which is plotted as follows:

```
>>> import matplotlib.pyplot as plt
>>> precision, recall, th =
              precision_recall_curve(Y_test, recon_error)
>>> plt.plot(recall, precision, 'b')
>>> plt.title('Precision-Recall Curve')
>>> plt.xlabel('Recall')
>>> plt.ylabel('Precision')
>>> plt.show()
```

Refer to the following plot for the resulting precision-recall curve:

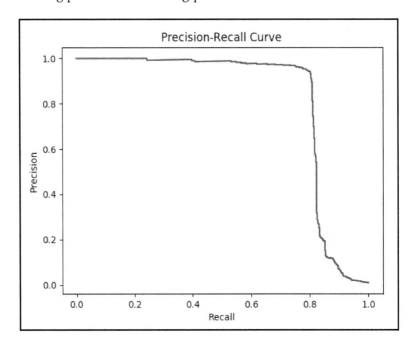

The area under the precision-recall curve is computed as follows:

```
>>> area = auc(recall, precision)
>>> print('Area under precision-recall curve:', area)
Area under precision-recall curve: 0.8217824584439969
```

The area under the precision-recall curve of 0.82 is achieved. We can also plot precisions and recalls under various decision thresholds, like so:

```
>>> plt.plot(th, precision[1:], 'k')
>>> plt.plot(th, recall[1:], 'b', label='Threshold-Recall curve')
>>> plt.title('Precision (black) and recall (blue) for different
              threshold values')
>>> plt.xlabel('Threshold of reconstruction error')
>>> plt.ylabel('Precision or recall')
>>> plt.show()
```

Refer to the following plot for the expected outcome:

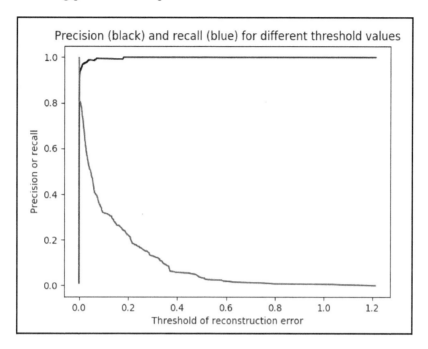

It is observed that the higher the threshold we set, the higher the precision, but lower recall is obtained. We will pick `0.000001` as the decision threshold and compute the confusion matrix, as follows:

```
>>> threshold = 0.000001
>>> Y_pred = [1 if e > threshold else 0 for e in recon_error]
>>> conf_matrix = confusion_matrix(Y_test, Y_pred)
>>> print(conf_matrix)
[[55070 1797]
 [ 73 419]]
```

The AE-based anomaly detector successfully catches most fraudulent transactions, and only falsely declines a few normal ones. You may consider other decision thresholds depending on particular trade-offs.

Deep autoencoders

Besides one hidden layer, the output layer can be a reconstruction of the input through several hidden layers. For example, the following is a model with three hidden layers of 80, 40, and 80 units, respectively:

```
>>> hidden_sizes = [80, 40, 80]
>>> input_layer = Input(shape=(input_size,))
>>> encoder = Dense(hidden_sizes[0], activation="relu")(input_layer)
>>> encoder = Dense(hidden_sizes[1], activation="relu")(encoder)
>>> decoder = Dense(hidden_sizes[2], activation='relu')(encoder)
>>> decoder = Dense(input_size)(decoder)
>>> deep_ae = Model(inputs=input_layer, outputs=decoder)
>>> print(deep_ae.summary())
```

Layer (type)	Output Shape	Param #
input_1 (InputLayer)	(None, 29)	0
dense_1 (Dense)	(None, 80)	2400
dense_2 (Dense)	(None, 40)	3240
dense_3 (Dense)	(None, 80)	3280
dense_4 (Dense)	(None, 29)	2349

```
Total params: 11,269
Trainable params: 11,269
Non-trainable params: 0
```

As there are more parameters to train, we lower the learning rate to 0.00005 and increase the number of epochs, as shown here:

```
>>> optimizer = optimizers.Adam(lr=0.00005)
>>> num_epoch = 50
```

The rest of the codes are identical to the vanilla solution, which we won't repeat here. But here are the results for the first and last two epochs:

```
Epoch 1/50
227440/227440 [==============================] - 6s 25us/step - loss:
0.5392 - val_loss: 0.3506
Epoch 00001: loss improved from inf to 0.53922, saving model to
model_deep_ae.h5
......
```

```
......
Epoch 49/50
227440/227440 [==============================] - 6s 26us/step - loss:
3.3581e-05 - val_loss: 0.0045
Epoch 00049: loss improved from 0.00004 to 0.00003, saving model to
model_deep_ae.h5
Epoch 50/50
227440/227440 [==============================] - 6s 25us/step - loss:
3.4013e-05 - val_loss: 0.0047
Epoch 00050: loss did not improve from 0.00003
```

Again, we measure the performance by the area under the precision-recall curve, and `0.83` is accomplished this time, which is slightly better than the vanilla version:

```
>>> print('Area under precision-recall curve:', area)
Area under precision-recall curve: 0.8279249913991501
```

Sparse autoencoders

When training a neural network, we usually impose constraints in the loss objective function in order to control the capacity of the network and prevent overfitting. Autoencoders are no exception. We can add an L1 norm regularization term in the loss function of an autoencoder, which introduces a sparsity constraint. Autoencoders of this kind are called sparse autoencoders.

When there are a large number of training samples, such as more than 220,000 in our case, it is not easy to tell the impact of sparsity. So, let's only use 5% of the data for training, as follows:

```
>>> data_train, data_test = train_test_split(data, test_size=0.95)
```

We will quickly run through a normal autoencoder for benchmark, as follows:

```
>>> hidden_sizes = [80, 40, 80]
>>> input_layer = Input(shape=(input_size,))
>>> encoder = Dense(hidden_sizes[0], activation="relu")(input_layer)
>>> encoder = Dense(hidden_sizes[1], activation="relu")(encoder)
>>> decoder = Dense(hidden_sizes[2], activation='relu')(encoder)
>>> decoder = Dense(input_size)(decoder)
>>> ae = Model(inputs=input_layer, outputs=decoder)
```

Except for a learning rate of `0.0008` and `30` epochs, the rest of the codes are the same as the last section:

```
>>> optimizer = optimizers.Adam(lr=0.0008)
>>> num_epoch = 30
```

Here are the results for the first and last two epochs:

```
Train on 14222 samples, validate on 270585 samples
Epoch 1/30
14222/14222 [==============================] - 3s 204us/step - loss: 0.5800
- val_loss: 0.2497
Epoch 00001: loss improved from inf to 0.57999, saving model to model_ae.h5
Epoch 2/30
14222/14222 [==============================] - 3s 194us/step - loss: 0.1422
- val_loss: 0.1175
Epoch 00002: loss improved from 0.57999 to 0.14224, saving model to
model_ae.h5
......

......
Epoch 29/30
14222/14222 [==============================] - 3s 196us/step - loss: 0.0016
- val_loss: 0.0054
Epoch 00029: loss did not improve from 0.00148
Epoch 30/30
14222/14222 [==============================] - 3s 195us/step - loss: 0.0013
- val_loss: 0.0079
Epoch 00030: loss improved from 0.00148 to 0.00132, saving model to
model_ae.h5
>>> print('Area under precision-recall curve:', area)
Area under precision-recall curve: 0.6628715223813105
```

We got area under the precision-recall curve of 0.66.

Now, let's work on the sparse version with an L1 regularization factor of 0.00003, like so:

```
>>> from keras import regularizers
>>> input_layer = Input(shape=(input_size,))
>>> encoder = Dense(hidden_sizes[0], activation="relu",
            activity_regularizer=regularizers.l1(3e-5))(input_layer)
>>> encoder = Dense(hidden_sizes[1], activation="relu")(encoder)
>>> decoder = Dense(hidden_sizes[2], activation='relu')(encoder)
>>> decoder = Dense(input_size)(decoder)
>>> sparse_ae = Model(inputs=input_layer, outputs=decoder)
```

The results for the first and last two epochs are as follows:

```
Epoch 1/30
14222/14222 [==============================] - 3s 208us/step - loss: 0.6295
- val_loss: 0.3061
Epoch 00001: loss improved from inf to 0.62952, saving model to
model_sparse_ae.h5
Epoch 2/30
14222/14222 [==============================] - 3s 197us/step - loss: 0.1959
```

```
- val_loss: 0.1697
Epoch 00002: loss improved from 0.62952 to 0.19588, saving model to
model_sparse_ae.h5
......
......
Epoch 29/30
14222/14222 [==============================] - 3s 209us/step - loss: 0.0168
- val_loss: 0.0277
Epoch 00029: loss improved from 0.01801 to 0.01681, saving model to
model_sparse_ae.h5
Epoch 30/30
14222/14222 [==============================] - 3s 213us/step - loss: 0.0220
- val_loss: 0.0496
Epoch 00030: loss did not improve from 0.01681
```

Higher area under the precision-recall curve, 0.70, is achieved with the sparsity autoencoder, which learns sparse and enlarged representations of the input data:

```
>>> print('Area under precision-recall curve:', area)
Area under precision-recall curve: 0.6955808468297678
```

Denoising autoencoders

Denoising autoencoders (**DAEs**) is another regularized version of autoencoders, but the regularization is added on the input data, instead of the loss function. The autoencoders are forced to reconstruct original data from corrupted input data with the hope that more robust features will be learned.

For each input sample, a subset of features are randomly selected for alteration. The corruption rate is suggested to be 30% to 50%. In general, the more training samples, the lower the corruption rate; the less samples, the higher the corruption rate.

There are two typical ways to generate corrupted data:

- Assigning zero to the selected data
- Adding Gaussian noise to the selected data

The following diagram demonstrates how DAEs work:

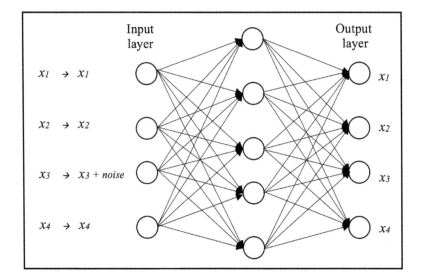

DAEs are frequently used for neural network pre-training, where the extracted robust representation is employed as input features for downstream supervised learning. Hence, they are not perfectly applicable to our unsupervised solution. You may go through the image classification example in `https://blog.keras.io/building-autoencoders-in-keras.html` for further study.

Contractive autoencoders

The last type of autoencoders we will learn about are contractive autoencoders. They are similar to their sparse sibling in that they add a penalty term in order to learn more robust representations. However, the penalty term is more complicated and can be derived as the following, where h_j is the jth unit of the output of hidden layer, and W is the weights of the encoder, W_{ij} is the one connecting the ith input unit, and the jth hidden unit:

$$J_c = \sum_j [h_j(1 - h_j)]^2 \sum_j (W_{ij}^T)^2$$

We add the contractive term on top of the vanilla autoencoder we defined in previous section, as shown here:

```
>>> hidden_size = 40
>>> input_layer = Input(shape=(input_size,))
>>> encoder = Dense(hidden_size, activation="relu")(input_layer)
>>> decoder = Dense(input_size)(encoder)
>>> contractive_ae = Model(inputs=input_layer, outputs=decoder)
```

The loss function now becomes the following:

```
>>> factor = 1e-5
>>> def contractive_loss(y_pred, y_true):
...     mse = K.mean(K.square(y_true - y_pred), axis=1)
...     W = K.variable(
                value=contractive_ae.layers[1].get_weights()[0])
...     W_T = K.transpose(W)
...     W_T_sq_sum = K.sum(W_T ** 2, axis=1)
...     h = contractive_ae.layers[1].output
...     contractive = factor *
                K.sum((h * (1 - h)) ** 2 * W_T_sq_sum, axis=1)
...     return mse + contractive
```

We compile the model with this contractive loss, like so:

```
>>> contractive_ae.compile(optimizer=optimizer, loss=contractive_loss)
```

The remaining codes are unchanged, but the learning rate of 0.0003 (optimizer = optimizers.Adam(lr=0.0003)) is used this time.

We herein present the results for the first and last two epochs:

```
Train on 227440 samples, validate on 57367 samples
Epoch 1/30
227440/227440 [==============================] - 6s 27us/step - loss:
0.3298 - val_loss: 0.1680
Epoch 00001: loss improved from inf to 0.32978, saving model to
model_contractive_ae.h5
Epoch 2/30
227440/227440 [==============================] - 5s 24us/step - loss:
0.0421 - val_loss: 0.0465
Epoch 00002: loss improved from 0.32978 to 0.04207, saving model to
model_contractive_ae.h5
......
......
Epoch 29/30
227440/227440 [==============================] - 5s 23us/step - loss:
3.8961e-04 - val_loss: 0.0045
```

```
Epoch 00029: loss did not improve from 0.00037
Epoch 30/30
227440/227440 [==============================] - 5s 22us/step - loss:
4.7208e-04 - val_loss: 0.0057
Epoch 00030: loss did not improve from 0.00037
```

The model outperforms the vanilla one with an area under precision-recall curve of 0.83 achieved:

```
>>> print('Area under precision-recall curve:', area)
Area under precision-recall curve: 0.8311662962345293
```

So far, we have looked at five different types of autoencoders, including basic vanilla, deep, sparse, denoising, and contractive ones. The speciality of each type of autoencoder comes from either certain architectures or different forms of imposed constraints. Despite the variation of architectures or penalties, they share the same goal, which is to learn more robust representations.

Summary

We just accomplished an important learning journey of DL architectures with restricted Boltzmann machines and autoencoders! Throughout this chapter, we got more familiar with RBMs and their variants. We started with what RBMs are, the evolution paths of RBMs, and how they become the state-of-the-art solutions to recommendation systems. We implemented RBMs in TensorFlow from scratch and built an RBM-based movie recommender. Beyond a shallow architecture, we explored a stacked version of RBMs called deep belief networks and employed it in image classification, which was implemented in TensorFlow from scratch.

Learning autoencoders is the second half of the journey, as they share similar ideas of finding latent representation of the input by input data reconstruction. After discussing what autoencoders are and talking about their evolution path, we illustrated a variety of autoencoders, categorized by their architectures or forms of regularization. We also applied autoencoders of different types in credit card fraud detection. Each type of autoencoder intends to extract more robust representation, with certain architectures or forms of imposed constraints.

Exercise

Can you build a movie recommender using autoencoders?

Acknowledgements

Thanks to Shyong Lam and Jon Herlocker for cleaning up and generating the MovieLens dataset:

F. Maxwell Harper and Joseph A. Konstan. 2015. *The MovieLens Datasets: History and Context. ACM Transactions on Interactive Intelligent Systems* (TiiS) 5, 4, Article 19 (December 2015), 19 pages. DOI=http://dx.doi.org/10.1145/2827872

Section 2: Convolutional Neural Networks

In this section, we will be learning about a class of deep learning network, known as the **convolutional neural network** (**CNN**), for images, and why CNNs are better than deep feedforward networks. We will then look at how we can reduce the computation cost required by deep learning networks, and see that mobile neural networks are nothing but CNNs that have been modified to have fewer parameters and consume less memory.

The following chapters will be covered in this section:

- Chapter 4, *CNN Architecture*
- Chapter 5, *Mobile Neural Network and CNN*

CNN Architecture 4

In this chapter, we will discuss an important class of deep learning network for images called **convolutional neural networks** (**CNNs**). The majority of the deep learning models built for image-related tasks, such as image recognition, classification, object detection, and so on, involve CNNs as their primary network. CNNs allow us to process the incoming data in a three-dimensional volume rather than a single dimension vector. Although CNNs are a class of neural networks (made up of weights, layers, and loss function), there are a lot of architectural differences to deep feedforward networks, which we will explain in this chapter. Just to give you an idea of how powerful CNNs can be, the ResNet CNN architecture achieved a top-error rate of 3.57% at the world famous image classification challenge—ILSVRC. This performance beats the human vision perception on the robust dataset of ImageNet. We will discuss ImageNet and ILSVRC later in this chapter. The following are the topics that you will be learning about in this chapter:

- The problem with deep feedforward networks and the need for CNNs
- Evolution path to CNNs
- Architecture of CNNs
- Different layers of CNNs and their roles
- Image classification with CNNs
- Some famous image classification CNN architectures
- Your first CNN image classifier with the CIFAR-10 dataset
- Object detection with CNNs
- Famous object detectors with CNNs
- Your first object detector with TensorFlow

Problem with deep feedforward networks

In `Chapter 2`, *Deep Feedforward Networks*, we learned to identify (classify) images of fashion items using deep feedforward networks. The size of each image was 28 x 28 and we connected one neuron to each pixel. This way, we have 28 x 28 = 784 neurons in the first layer itself. But in the real world, images are barely this small. Let's consider a medium-sized image of size 500 x 500. So, now, in the first layer, we will need to have 250,000 neurons. That's a huge number of neurons in the first layer for an image of this size. Hence, the network becomes computationally too expensive for the task. So, how do we solve this problem? Again, a biological inspiration comes to the rescue! Let's look at the details about the evolution of CNNs in the next section.

Evolution path to CNNs

In the 1960s, it was discovered that the visual cortex in animals doesn't act in a way deep feedforward networks do with images. Rather, a single neuron in the visual cortex is connected to a small region (and not a single pixel), which is called a receptive field. Any activity in the receptive field triggers the corresponding neuron.

Inspired by the receptive field in the visual cortex, scientists came up with the idea of local connectivity to reduce the number of artificial neurons required to process images. This modified version of deep feedforward networks was termed CNN (all through this book, CNN refers to convolutional neural network). In 1989, Yann LeCun developed a trainable CNN that was able to recognize handwritten digits. In 1998, again, Yann LeCun's LeNet-5 model successfully used seven stacked layers of convolution (like layers in deep feedforward networks) to classify digits of size 32 x 32. Increasing the input image dimensions beyond that was restricted by the lack of processing power available at the time. But in the early 2000s, GPUs significantly reduced the processing time required for deep learning networks, as they were able to perform parallel computation. The development of deeper CNNs started by the virtue of GPUs. Before diving deeper into the details, we will introduce you to ImageNet. It is an open source dataset containing more than 15 million labelled images of around 22,000 different objects. ImageNet was set up with the aim of aiding development under the object recognition field with manually labelled images to train models on. Every year, a competition is held called **ImageNet Large-Scale visual Recognition challenge** (ILSVRC), which uses a subset of the ImageNet dataset, with the challenge to produce more accurate methods for object recognition, more commonly known as **image classification**. For more details, refer to the ImageNet website at `http://www.image-net.org/`.

There are a lot of new aspects in CNNs, such as weight sharing, operation on volumes, and local connectivity. We will discuss all of these, along with the architecture, in the next section.

Architecture of CNNs

CNNs are, of course, neural networks like deep feedforward networks. CNNs are built layer by layer with learnable weights and are trained like any typical deep learning network: by minimizing the cost function and backpropagating errors. The difference lies in the way the neurons are connected. CNNs are built to work with images. Image data has two unique features that are exploited by CNNs to reduce the number of neurons, as well as to achieve a better learning:

- Images are three-dimensional volumes—width, height, and channel (channel is sometimes referred to as depth). Hence, convolutional layers take input and output in three-dimensional volumes rather than single dimension vectors.
- The pixels in a neighborhood have values that are relatable to each other. This is called spatial relation. CNNs use this feature through filters to provide local connectivity to a neuron with pixels in a neighborhood.

In the following subsections, we will look at the layers involved in a CNN, along with the unique features of each layer.

The input layer

The input layer is made of 3D arrays rather than a single dimension vector. The layer holds the pixels in the way they are in an image. Thus, the input layer has a shape (batch size, width, height, and channel). For example, if we have images of dimensions 32 x 32 and three channels for RGB with the batch size as 64, then the shape of the input layer would be (64, 32, 32, 3). This can be observed in the following diagram:

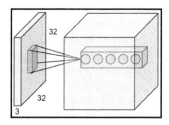

The shape of the input layer is represented by the cube in pink (Image sourced from Wikipedia, part of CS231n course)

An important point to note here is that the input layer serves the purpose of holding the structure in three-dimensional volumes. We shall see how the convolutional layer utilizes this three-dimensional volume in the next subsection.

The convolutional layer

The first thing we are going to discuss here are filters. Filters can be thought of as smaller versions of the image that are made up of learnable weight values. Just like we have weight connections from one neuron to another in deep feedforward networks, the weights are also present in the convolutional layer, except that weights are in the form of filters connecting the spatial region that's covered by the filter to a neuron. Let's consider an example of a filter of size 5 x 5 (width and height). The filter will extend to the third dimension (channel) of the image as well. For a three-channeled image, the filter dimension would be 5 x 5 x 3 and for a single-channeled image, it would be 5 x 5 x 1. The following diagram shows a 5 x 5 x 1 filter:

1	-1	0.5	1	0.8
1	0.3	1	0.7	0.5
-1	1	0.4	1	0.4
0.8	0.6	1	0.9	0.3
0.7	0.8	0.7	0.1	0.1

So, what does a filter do in the convolutional layer? Filters perform two very important tasks in the convolution layer—local connectivity and parameter sharing. Earlier, we talked about receptive fields in CNNs, which meant connecting a neuron only to it's neighborhood image pixels. This neighborhood is defined by the filter. We slide the filter over the image, and each weight in the filter is connected to a particular neuron for a particular slide. The neuron then computes the convolution output using the weights and values of the image pixels covered by the filter at that location. In other words, we can say that each neuron in the convolution layer is locally connected to a local region of the image defined by the filter. This is referred to as local connectivity. The local connectivity is visualized in the following diagram:

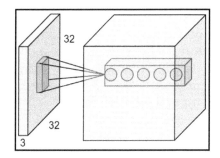

Observe how a receptive field (dark pink patch in the input layer) is connected to a single neuron of the next layer

How does a neuron calculate the output from a filter through convolution? To understand this, let's consider the scenario of the first slide of a 3 x 3 x 1 filter over a 6 x 6 x 1 image. The dot product of each weight value in the filter with the pixel value at the corresponding location is calculated. The dot products are summed over for all weight values at a position, and this calculated sum is the output of the convolution. The activation functions, such as ReLU, are used in the output of the neuron.

Next, we will see how the filter slides over the image to generate convolution outputs. For every slide of the filter, a new neuron is connected to the filter output. Thus, the parameters involved in sliding also tend to control the output dimensions of the convolutional layer. Three important parameters are involved in the sliding of filters—stride, zero-padding, and depth:

- Stride decides the number of pixel(s) the filter will jump while sliding from one position to another. Typically, the stride value is kept to 1. The filter jumps one pixel in every slide. To stride more than 1 is also possible, but generally not used.
- Typically, if the filter starts sliding from the top left of an image, the final generated output from all the slides tends to have a lower dimension. But, generally, we want the output of the convolution layer to have the same width and height as the input image. Zero-padding adds an extra padding of 0s on the boundary of the image, providing extra space for the filter to slide in such a way that the final output has same dimension as the input. As we are adding 0s, this doesn't effect the value of our convolution operation.

- Usually, a CNN doesn't use single filter in a layer. We use a set of filters (say, 12 filters). This is done because each filter with a different set of weights tends to capture different features of the image. The response from each filter is stacked one after another, and each response is called an **activation map**. For example, if we use a 32 x 32 x 1 image and four filters of size 3 x 3 x 1 with stride 2 and padding 1, the output dimension from the convolution layer would be (16 x 16 x 4). Here, the last dimension would be equal to the number of activation maps, which will be equal to the number of filters. The width and height of the output can be calculated using the following formula:

$$(W - F + 2P)/S) + 1$$

Here, W is the input size ($W=32$), F is the filter size ($F=3$), P is padding ($P=1$), and S is the stride ($S=1$).

You may have observed that we are making the same filter slide over the whole image. This means the same of weight is used in the slides instead of creating different sets of weights for each slide. Making the convolution slides share the weights produces good results, as the pixel values in different positions in an image are highly related. If a filter proves useful at a location in the image, the filter will be useful for different locations as well. The sharing of filter weights across the image is called **parameter sharing,** reducing the number of required parameters in the network significantly.

The next layer is called the maxpooling layer. The maxpooling layer is used to reduce the size of activation maps.

The maxpooling layer

The overall idea behind CNNs is to keep extracting features through the filters and increasing the depth of activation maps while reducing the width and height dimensions so that in the end, we are left with a highly compressed feature vector. For reducing the dimensions of the activation maps, CNNs use the maxpooling layer in-between consecutive convolutional layers.

The maxpooling layer has two major parameters—kernel size and stride. Maxpooling also slides a window over the activation maps of the previous layer it is connected to. The window is commonly referred to as a kernel. The job of the kernel at any slide is to compare the values covered by the kernel and *keep only the maximum value* as the output at that position. The most commonly used kernel size is 2 x 2. Using a kernel size beyond this would lead to major loss of information between the layers. Stride, again, is the parameter that decides how many pixels the kernel has to jump in slides. The following diagram demonstrates the kernel performing maxpooling on a 4 x 4 activation map with a kernel of size 2 x 2 and a stride of 2:

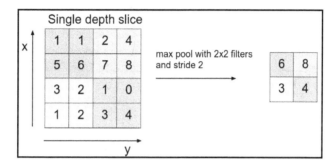

image sourced from the CS231n

The following diagram shows how the maxpooling layer is used to reduce the size of image and feature maps:

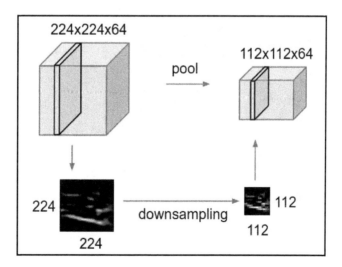

image sourced from the course, CS231n course

The fully connected layer

At the end of a convolutional network, we need to classify the image and train the network. This has to be done using softmax probabilities and cross-entropy loss. Until now, the features have been extracted with the convolution layers. The idea here is to squeeze the 4D tensor output from the last convolution or maxpooling layer into a 2D tensor, where the first dimension will still represent the batch size and the second dimension will contain all the output values from the last layer squeezed like an array. This squeezing operation is often referred to as the **flatten** operation. The purpose of flattening is that we can now add feedforward layers ahead, connect them to all values after flattening, and then train the network using softmax probabilities and cross-entropy loss like we did in with deep feedforward networks. The layer is the same as the feedforward layer, but is referred to as the fully connected layer because, unlike the convolution layer, because it only has local connectivity, the layer is connected to every value coming from the last layer. In general, we can add a series of fully connected layers if the number of parameters after flattening are quite large.

Now that we have seen the architecture and layers in a convolutional network, we will use a convolutional network for image classification in the next section.

Image classification with CNNs

In this section, we will look at some of the most successful CNN architectures for image classification tasks, such as VGGNet, InceptionNet, and ResNet. These networks are also used as feature extractors in object detection models, owing to their great feature extracting capabilities. We will discuss the networks in brief in the following subsection.

VGGNet

VGGNet was developed by K. Simonyan and A. Zisserman, from the University of Oxford. The network was the runner-up at ILSVRC 2014. VGGNet is an improvement over AlexNet, replacing the higher convolution size of 11 and 5 by smaller 3 x 3 convolutions, consistent over multiple stacked layers. Although VGGNet was not the winner of ILSVRC, the simple, easy-to- implement architecture and its powerful feature extraction capability has kept VGGNet as a wise choice for base networks in object detection or segmentation tasks.

VGGNet has a lot of variants based on the number of stacked layers. VGG16 and VGG19, with 16 and 19 layers, respectively, are the most used architectures. The following diagram demonstrates the VGG16 architecture with the 3 x 3 convolution layers, maxpooling, and fully connected layers:

If you wish to refer to the original paper for VGGNet, it is available at the following link: https://arxiv.org/pdf/1409.1556.pdf.

Next, we will discuss the winning architecture of ILSVRC 2014—InceptionNet.

InceptionNet

GoogLeNet, more commonly known as **InceptionNet**, was the winner of the ILSVRC 2014 competition. Let's discuss this in the following points:

- Choosing the right kernel size for convolution is always a big deal in CNNs. The same object can come in various sizes in different images. To capture the features of different sizes, we, of course, need to have kernel sizes accordingly. Bigger kernels are generally good when the object of interest covers most of the area and smaller kernels are suitable for objects that are locally situated.

- The deeper the network, the better it is! But stacking a lot of layers makes the gradient flow difficult and leads to overfitting. In short, the depth of a network is somewhat restricted to a certain limit. Beyond this limit, the network doesn't train anymore; it just overfits.

- While building a network, we need to keep a check on its size. Building extremely big networks requires enormous computational power, which is quite expensive. A lot of the expense of building the network might not meet the trade-off between cost and utility.

The researchers at Google, in order to counter these problems, engineered a complex layer, which they called the Inception module.

The idea is to use different sizes for convolution kernels in parallel rather than using a single kernel size in a layer. This way, the network now has options in kernel sizes and the network can now learn features through the kernel that's best suited to the job. Arranging kernels parallel to each other also makes the architecture sparse, which helps to ease the training for deeper networks.

The typical InceptionNet uses three convolution kernels of sizes 1 x 1, 3 x 3, and 5 x 5 simultaneously. The results from all these three kernels are concatenated to form a single output vector, which acts as the input for the next layer. The inception layer also adds 1 x 1 convolutions before the 3 x 3 and 5 x 5 kernels in order to reduce the size. The Inception module is shown in the following diagram:

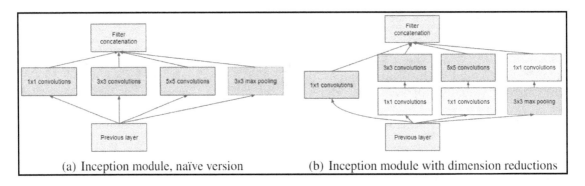

(a) Inception module, naïve version   (b) Inception module with dimension reductions

Image sourced from the original paper Going Deeper with Convolution

The link for the original paper, *Going Deeper with Convolution,* can be found at https://arxiv.org/pdf/1409.4842.pdf.

Next, we will look at an architecture that claims to be even better than human perception in classifying images, called ResNet.

ResNet

ResNet was the winning architecture at ILSVRC 2015. The most amazing fact about ResNet is that it achieved a top-five error rate of 3.57% at ILSVRC, which beats human vision perception!

ResNet exposes a problem that has been restricting the training of very deep networks. During the training of deep networks, the accuracy saturates to a certain limit and thereafter degrades rapidly. This phenomenon has been restricting the accuracy to a certain threshold, no matter how deep the architecture goes. ResNet was introduced by Microsoft research in a paper called, *Deep Residual Learning for Image Recognition*, which can be found at https://arxiv.org/pdf/1512.03385.pdf.

Throughout the paper, the researchers claimed that instead of making the network learn the mapping from x to y directly with a function (say $H(x)$), it uses a residual function $F(x) = H(x) - x$. The function $F(x)$ can be thought of as representing the layer of the network and can be rewritten as $H(x) = F(x) + x$. The authors claim that it is easier to optimize the indirect residual function ($F(x)$) than it is to reach a direct optimized mapping $H(x)$ from x to y.

Here, considering x as the input to the layer, $H(x)$ as the output from the layer, and $F(x)$ as the layer function, we can easily observe that the input x is to be added to the output from the layer in order to make the final output $H(x) = F(x) + x$. This kind of creates a connection from the input to the output of the layer, which is called the **residual connection** or **skip connection**. The following diagram shows the building block of ResNet with the skip connection:

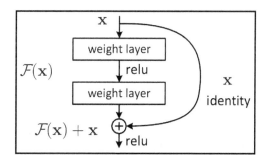

Image sourced from the paper, Deep Residual Learning for Image Recognition

The addition of the skip connection solves the problem of saturation and degradation of accuracy in deep networks, enabling the architectures to have far more layers without saturation. The architecture consists of 34 layers, mostly with 3 x 3 convolution filters. For reducing the width and height of feature maps, stride 2 convolutions are used. At the end, a global average pooling, followed by a 1,000 unit fully connected layer, is used. In the following diagram, you can observe the ResNet architecture in comparison to the typical **VGG-19** and the architecture without residual connections:

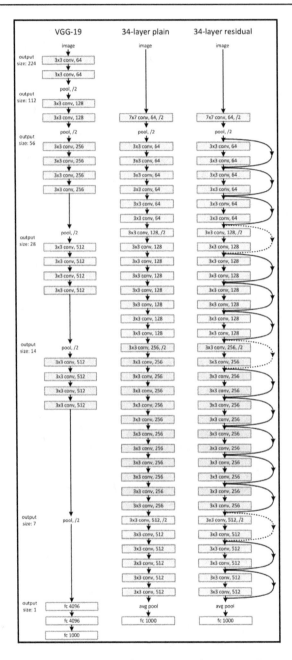

Image sourced from the paper, Deep Residual Learning for Image Recognition

Now it's time to build our own CNN network for image classification.

Building our first CNN

Here, we are going to use the famous CIFAR-10 dataset to demonstrate classification using CNNs. If you are not aware of the CIFAR dataset, the following subsection offers a brief description.

CIFAR

The CIFAR dataset contains nearly 80 million images. The dataset is open sourced and was collated by Alex Krizhevsky, Vinod Nair, and Geoffrey Hinton. The dataset is divided into two subsets—CIFFAR-10 and CIFAR-100. The CIFAR-10 dataset has images belonging to 10 classes—airplane, automobile, bird, horse, cat, dog, deer, frog, ship, and truck. CIFAR-10 has 6,000 images in each class. That means it has a total of 60,000 images. 50,000 images are for training and 10,000 are for testing. The dimension of each image is 32 x 32 x 3, and every image is RGB-colored. The CIFAR-100 dataset is similar to CIFAR-10, except that there are 100 classes rather than 10. We will be using the CIFAR-10 dataset here as it has a fewer number of classes. You can download the CIFAR-10 Python version from the CIFAR website at `https://www.cs.toronto.edu/~kriz/cifar.html`.

Once the data has been downloaded and extracted, you will find the following files in the extracted folder:

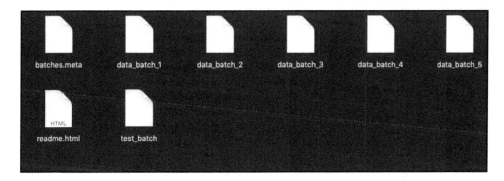

Since the dataset is large, it is broken into five batches—`data_batch_1`, `data_batch_2`, `data_batch_3`, `data_batch_4`, and `data_batch_5`—so that we don't need to load the complete dataset into memory. The data inside each file is dumped using the `pickle` module in Python. To retrieve the data from the file, we can use the load method from the pickle module in Python. Each batch file contains 10,000 images. The dump vector, thus, has the dimensions (10,000 x 3,072). The RGB channeled images are flattened into single dimensions. (32 x 32 x 3 = 3,072). We will need to reshape the data in our required form. Next, we will see how we can load and pre-process the data for our use.

Data loading and pre-processing

Let's begin by writing our function to load a data batch and reshape it into three-dimensional images. We will load the data using the pickle operations, which are mentioned in the original CIFAR website as well. Let's create a class named data, which will hold functions related to data loading and pre-processing. We will also define a function named load_data_batch for loading a data batch into memory. In the class attributes, we will make a dictionary named labelsDicti, which will map the numeric labels to their actual classes. An inverse dictionary, inverseLabelsDicti, is also created to map the actual classes to numeric labels. This will help us during the prediction:

```python
# first import some essential modules
import numpy as np
import pickle
import matplotlib.pyplot as plt
import os
import sys

import tensorflow as tf
from sklearn.utils import shuffle


# define the path to the directory where you have extracted the zipped data
DATA_DIR = 'cifar-10-batches-py'

#hyper-parameters for the model

BATCH_SIZE = 128
CLASS_NUM = 10
EPOCHS = 20
DROPOUT = 0.5
LEARNING_RATE = 0.001
IMAGE_SIZE = (32, 32)
SEED = 2

class data:

    def __init__(self, dataDir, fileName, batchSize, seed, classNum = 10):

        self.dataDir = dataDir
        self.fileName = fileName
        self.classNum = classNum
        self.batchSize = batchSize
        self.seed = seed

        self.labelsDicti =
{0:'airplane',1:'automobile',2:'bird',3:'cat',4:'deer',5:'dog',6:'frog',7:'
```

```
horse',8:'ship',9:'truck'}
    self.inverseLabelsDicti = {v:k for k,v in self.labelsDicti.items()}

  def load_data_batch(self):

    with open(os.path.join(self.dataDir, self.fileName), 'rb') as f:

      dataBatch = pickle.load(f, encoding = 'latin1')
      #print(dataBatch['data'].shape)
      # latin1 encoding has been used to dump the data.

      # we don't need filename and other details,
      # we will keep only labels and images

    self.images = dataBatch['data']
    self.labels = dataBatch['labels']
```

Here, `dataBatch` will be a dictionary containing the following keys:

- `batch_label`: Representing which batch out of the 5 batches the file is in
- `labels`: Numeric labels for images from 0 to 9
- `data`: numpy array of shape (10,000 x 3,072), representing the data
- `filenames`: Contains names for the corresponding images

We will only keep the `data` and `labels` in two separate named attributes and ignore everything else. Next, we need to reshape the images into their original form. For this, we first need to separate out the three channels of each of the 10,000 images. Along with splitting them into three channels, we will reshape the images into the width and height dimensions; that is, 32 x 32. An important thing to note here is that we need to first split the image into a channel and then into width and height. Hence, we will need to swap the axes once we reshape the images into (10, 000, 3, 32, 32). The swapping can be done by the `transpose` function on `numpy` arrays:

```
def reshape_data(self):

    # function to reshape and transpose
    self.images = self.images.reshape(len(self.images), 3, 32,
32).transpose(0, 2, 3, 1)
```

Now, we can visualize some of our images and check out their corresponding labels. We will add a `visualise_data` function to the `data` class, which will take a list of 4 indices and plot the images at those indices in a subplot and display the classes of the images as titles:

 The plotted images will be quite blurred due to the small size of the images in the dataset.

```
def visualise_data(self, indices):

 plt.figure(figsize = (5, 5))

    for i in range(len(indices)):
        # take out the ith image in indices
        img = self.images[indices[i]]

        # it's corresponding label
        label =self.labels[indices[i]]

        plt.subplot(2,2,i+1)
        plt.imshow(img)
        plt.title(self.labelsDicti[label])

 plt.show()
```

You can make an object of the `data` class and call the functions we have built on the object to visualize it in the following manner:

```
dataObj = data(DATA_DIR, 'data_batch_1')
dataObj.load_data_batch()
dataObj.reshape_data()
dataObj.visualise_data([100, 4000, 2, 8000])
# here we have chosen indices 100, 4000, 2, 8000
```

The output from running the preceding code is shown in the following screenshot:

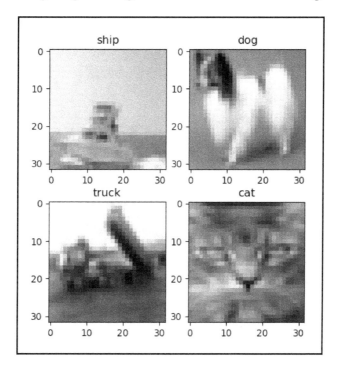

Next, we will convert the labels into one-hot encoding form. We have already discussed one-hot encoding in the Chapter 2, *Deep Feedforward Networks*. If you cannot remember it, you can go back and refer to one-hot encoding under Chapter 2, *Deep Feedforward Networks*. The number of classes for CIFAR-10 is 10 and the class attribute, classNum, has a default value of 10. The following function converts the labels into one-hot encoding:

```
def one_hot_encoder(self):

    # this function will convert the labels into one-hot vectors
    # initially the label vector is a list, we will convert it to numpy
array,

    self.labels = np.array(self.labels, dtype = np.int32)

    #converting to one-hot
    self.labels = np.eye(self.classNum)[self.labels]

    #print(self.labels.shape)
```

We normalize the images. Here, by normalizing, we mean we are bringing the pixel values between 0 to 1. This is helpful as the activation functions are sensitive when they are between 0 and 1. The pixel values range from 0 to 255 in each channel. Therefore, we will divide the image array by 255 (which is the highest possible value) to bring everything between 0 and 1:

```
def normalize_images(self):

    # just simply dividing by 255
    self.images = self.images / 255
```

To facilitate proper training, we need to bring up random samples. Therefore, we will shuffle the data using sklearn's `shuffle` function:

```
def shuffle_data(self):

    # shuffle the data so that training is better
    self.images, self.labels = shuffle(self.images, self.labels, random_state
=          self.seed)
```

The next function will be an important function for the `data` class. The function will generate batches of data and labels from the loaded file. We know that we train our model in batches and that we have declared a hyper-parameter, `BATCH_SIZE`, which decides the number of images in one batch. Hence, the function will keep on looping through the data loaded from file and yield a batch of size `BATCH_SIZE` each time. Here, `yield` is used instead of `return` because `yield` holds the function control, and we create generator objects instead of lists that get destroyed once they are used, thus saving us memory:

```
def generate_batches(self):

    # function to yield out batches of batchSize from the loaded file
    for i in range(0, len(self.images), self.batchSize):

        last = min(i + self.batchSize, len(self.images))

        yield (self.images[i: last], self.labels[i: last])
```

Now, we will focus on building our CNN model. Let's define another class, `model`, which will contain our model graph. We will also define the hyper-parameters as attributes of the class:

```
class model:

    def __init__(self, batchSize, classNum, dropOut, learningRate, epochs,
imageSize, savePath):
```

```
        self.batchSize = batchSize
        self.classNum = classNum
        self.dropOut = dropOut
        self.imageSize = imageSize

        self.learningRate = learningRate
        self.epochs = epochs
        self.savePath = savePath
```

First, we will make placeholders to hold the data and labels. Here, note that the dimensions of the placeholder will be 4. The first dimension will represent the batch size and, as we have discussed earlier, the input layer holds the data in 3D volume. The remaining three dimensions will be width, height, and the channel of the images.

One more thing to do here is to make another placeholder for the dropOut value. Since TensorFlow takes everything as tensors, the value of dropOut must also be a tensor. Hence, through the keepProb, we will add the dropOut placeholder value:

```
with tf.name_scope('placeholders') as scope:

        self.x = tf.placeholder(shape = [None, self.imageSize[0],
self.imageSize[1], 3], dtype = tf.float32, name = 'inp_x')

        self.y = tf.placeholder(shape = [None, self.classNum], dtype =
tf.float32, name = 'true_y')

        self.keepProb = tf.placeholder(tf.float32)
```

You can play around with the network architecture by using different filter numbers, kernel sizes, and a varying number of layers in the network. Let's define the first layer of our model. We will use 64 filters in the first layer with a kernel size of 3 x 3:

```
#first conv layer with 64 filters
    with tf.name_scope('conv_1') as scope:

        #tensorflow takes the kernel as a 4D tensor. We can initialize the
values    with tf.zeros

        filter1 = tf.Variable(tf.zeros([3, 3, 3, 64], dtype=tf.float32),
name='filter_1')

        conv1 = tf.nn.relu(tf.nn.conv2d(self.x, filter1, [1, 1, 1, 1],
padding='SAME', name = 'convo_1'))
```

In TensorFlow, we need to define the filters as a variable 4D tensor. The first three dimensions represent the width, height, and depth of the filter, and the fourth dimension is the output number of filters we want. Here, the third dimension has to be the current depth and the fourth dimension has to be the number of filters we want (here, 64).

Next, we will add a maxpooling layer to the network:

```
with tf.name_scope('pool_1') as scope:

    pool1 = tf.nn.max_pool(conv1, ksize = [1, 2, 2, 1], strides = [1, 2,
2, 1],padding='SAME', name = 'maxPool_1')
```

Here, the second and third dimensions represent the width and height of the pooling kernel. Similarly, we will define the further layers of the network. We will gradually increase the depth and reduce the width and height:

```
with tf.name_scope('conv_2') as scope:

    filter2 = tf.Variable(tf.zeros([2, 2, 64, 128], dtype=tf.float32),
name='filter_2')

    conv2 = tf.nn.relu(tf.nn.conv2d(pool1, filter2, [1, 1, 1, 1],
padding='SAME', name = 'convo_2'))


    with tf.name_scope('conv_3') as scope:

    filter3 = tf.Variable(tf.zeros([2, 2, 128, 128], dtype=tf.float32),
name='filter_3')

    conv3 = tf.nn.relu(tf.nn.conv2d(conv2, filter3, [1, 1, 1, 1],
padding='SAME', name = 'convo_3'))


    with tf.name_scope('pool_2') as scope:

    pool2 = tf.nn.max_pool(conv3, ksize = [1, 2, 2, 1], strides = [1, 2,
2, 1],
                padding='SAME', name = 'maxPool_2')


    with tf.name_scope('conv_4') as scope:

    filter4 = tf.Variable(tf.zeros([1, 1, 128, 256], dtype=tf.float32),
name='filter_4')

    conv4 = tf.nn.relu(tf.nn.conv2d(pool2, filter4, [1, 1, 1, 1],
```

```
padding='SAME', name = 'convo_4'))


    with tf.name_scope('pool_3') as scope:

        pool3 = tf.nn.max_pool(conv4, ksize = [1, 2, 2, 1], strides = [1, 2,
2, 1],
                    padding='SAME', name = 'maxPool_3')


    with tf.name_scope('conv_5') as scope:

        filter5 = tf.Variable(tf.zeros([1, 1, 256, 512], dtype=tf.float32),
name='filter_5')

        conv5 = tf.nn.relu(tf.nn.conv2d(pool3, filter5, [1, 1, 1, 1],
padding='SAME', name = 'convo_5'))
```

Now, it's time to add the fully connected layers. To add the fully connected layers, we will first need to flatten the output coming from previous layer. You can use either the Flatten() function in TensorFlow or you can reshape the output from the previous layer:

```
    with tf.name_scope('flatten') as scope:

        flatt = tf.layers.Flatten()(conv5)

        #shape = conv5.get_shape().as_list()
        #flatt = tf.reshape(conv5, [-1, shape[1]*shape[2]*shape[3]])
```

We will add three fully connected layers with units of 1,024, 512, and 256. The layers will use dropOut, as defined earlier, and the rely activation function. The fully connected layers are also called **dense layers** as they create a dense structure with global connections:

```
    with tf.name_scope('dense_1') as scope:

        dense1 = tf.layers.dense(flatt, units = 1024, activation =
'relu',name='fc_1')

        dropOut1 = tf.nn.dropout(dense1, self.keepProb)


    with tf.name_scope('dense_2') as scope:

        dense2 = tf.layers.dense(dropOut1, units = 512, activation =
'relu',name='fc_2')

        dropOut2 = tf.nn.dropout(dense2, self.keepProb)
```

```
    with tf.name_scope('dense_3') as scope:

        dense3 = tf.layers.dense(dropOut2, units = 256, activation =
'relu',name='fc_3')

        dropOut3 = tf.nn.dropout(dense3, self.keepProb)
```

The output layer will also be a fully connected layer, the difference being that we won't use any activation function in this layer:

```
with tf.name_scope('out') as scope:
        outLayer = tf.layers.dense(dropOut3, units = self.classNum,
activation = None, name='out_layer')
```

As we defined the loss function and optimizer for the deep feedforward networks, we will define them similarly here:

```
    with tf.name_scope('loss') as scope:

        self.loss =
tf.reduce_mean(tf.nn.softmax_cross_entropy_with_logits(logits = outLayer,
labels = self.y))

    with tf.name_scope('optimizer') as scope:

        optimizer = tf.train.AdamOptimizer(learning_rate = self.learningRate)

        self.train = optimizer.minimize(self.loss)


    with tf.name_scope('accuracy') as scope:

        correctPredictions = tf.equal(tf.argmax(outLayer, axis=1),
tf.argmax(self.y, axis = 1))

        # calculating average accuracy
        self.avgAccuracy = tf.reduce_mean(tf.cast(correctPredictions,
tf.float32))
```

Now, let's create an object of the `model` class to initiate our model graph:

```
modelGraph = model(batchSize = BATCH_SIZE, classNum = CLASS_NUM, dropOut =
DROPOUT,
        learningRate = LEARNING_RATE, epochs = EPOCHS, imageSize =
IMAGE_SIZE,        savePath = 'model')
```

Next, we will create a TensorFlow session and loop around the batch file. For each batch file from 1 to 5, we will create an object of the data class and call the functions we created to load and pre-process the data. Furthermore, the `generate_batches` function keeps generating the batches for training. You can save the model, say, after every 10th epoch:

```
with tf.Session() as sess:

    sess.run(tf.global_variables_initializer())
    saver = tf.train.Saver()

    for epoch in range(modelGraph.epochs):

        for iBatch in range(1, 6):

            dataObj = data(DATA_DIR, 'data_batch_' + str(iBatch), BATCH_SIZE,
SEED)
            dataObj.load_data_batch()
            dataObj.reshape_data()
            #dataObj.visualise_data([100, 4000, 2, 8000])
            dataObj.one_hot_encoder()
            dataObj.normalize_images()
            dataObj.shuffle_data()
            #print(dataObj.generate_batches()[0])

            for batchX, batchY in dataObj.generate_batches():

                #print(batchX[0])
                #print(batchY[0])

                _, lossT, accT = sess.run([modelGraph.train, modelGraph.loss,
modelGraph.avgAccuracy],
                        feed_dict = {modelGraph.x: batchX, modelGraph.y: batchY,
modelGraph.keepProb: modelGraph.dropOut})

                print('Epoch: '+str(epoch)+' Minibatch_Loss:
'+"{:.6f}".format(lossT)+' Train_acc: '+"{:.5f}".format(accT)+"\n")

            if epoch % 10 == 0:

                saver.save(sess, modelGraph.savePath)
```

The next section will deal with the task of object detection with CNNs. We will learn about some successful object detection architectures, and also implement object detection with TensorFlow.

Object detection with CNN

Most of the natural images that we come across in everyday life don't consist of a single object covering the whole image. Often, it's a mixture of different objects located at different positions. In such cases, simple object recognition is not going to work. Hence, detecting various objects that are present in an image along with their position becomes challenging. This is where deep learning shines!

So, object detection can be broken down into two parts:

- **Object localization**: Determining the x, y co-ordinates of an object in the image
- **Object recognition**: Determining whether the location has an object or not and, if so, what object it is

Thus, object detection networks have two separate sub-networks to perform these two tasks. The first network generates different regions of interest in the image while the second network classifies them.

R-CNN

This is one of the early phases of the deep learning approach for object detection. It utilizes the selective search algorithm to generate region proposals. A region proposal is a bounded box of any aspect ratio in an image that has a large probability of containing an object. Selective search is a graph-based algorithm, which first uses pixel intensity to divide regions and then groups them hierarchically based on color, texture, and size to generate regions. The problem with this algorithm is that it produces too many region proposals even for low resolution images. Hence, R-CNN limits the region proposals to 2,000.

These proposals are resized to the same shape and fed into a CNN network, which extracts features from the regions and outputs a feature vector. Each class of object has a SVM classifier, which is fed with this feature vector to predict the probability of the region containing that object. Also, the same feature vector is fed into a linear regressor to predict the offsets in bounding box of object. It may happen that though the region proposal contains the object, it doesn't cover the whole of the object. Hence, predicting offsets helps to rectify the co-ordinates of the bounding box. The following diagram shows the steps involved in the R-CNN architecture:

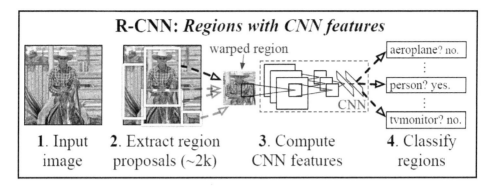

R-CNN: *Regions with CNN features*

warped region

aeroplane? no.

person? yes.

CNN

tvmonitor? no.

1. Input image **2**. Extract region proposals (~2k) **3**. Compute CNN features **4**. Classify regions

The link to the paper, *Rich feature hierarchies for accurate object detection and semantic segmentation,* can be found at `https://arxiv.org/abs/1311.2524`.

Next, we will look at an architecture that improved R-CNN by replacing selective search with a separate region proposal network.

Faster R-CNN

R-CNN turned out to be quite slow, due to the 2,000 region proposals being generated for each image. The selective search algorithm, doesn't always produce good candidate region proposals either. Faster R-CNN introduced a Region Proposal Network to generate region proposals, replacing the selective search algorithm. It has the following features:

- A CNN to initially extract feature maps from the input image
- Nine anchors (three ratios and three scales) to cover objects of different sizes and scale in feature maps
- A **region proposal network (RPN)** to generate regions of interests and rank them
- **Region of Interest (ROI)** pooling to reshape the different shaped proposals to a fixed size

First, the input image is fed into a CNN to produce feature maps. The feature maps go into the RPN, which uses a 3 x 3 convolution kernel to resize the feature maps to a fixed size. For each point on the feature map, nine anchor boxes are predicted, along with their objectless (object present or not) and bounding box coordinates (center-x, center-y, width, and height). A lot of generated proposals from the RPN overlap each other. The overlapping bounding boxes are eliminated by non-maximum suppression, which calculates the **Intersection Over Union (Iou)** of bounding boxes and eliminates boxes that have more than a set threshold score. The RPN gives us the proposed regions but of different sizes. In order to classify them through R-CNN, we need to get the proposals in the same size. The ROI pooling performs the job by splitting the proposed region into an equal number of parts and then applying maxpooling. This way, the output will always be of a fixed size, irrespective of the initial size. These ROI pooled outputs are then fed into the R-CNN module for classification. In the following diagram, you can observe the complete pipeline for the architectures:

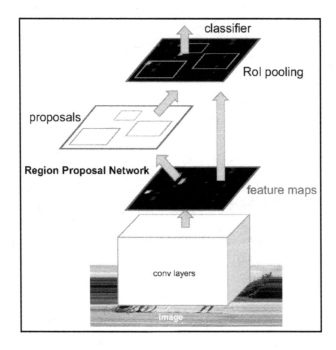

Image sourced from paper, Faster R-CNN: Towards Real-Time Object Detection with Region Proposal Networks

The link to the original paper of Faster-RCNN can be found at https://arxiv.org/pdf/1506.01497.pdf.

Next, we will look at another class of object detectors, regression-based object detectors, which have significantly simplified the task of object detection.

You Only Look Once (YOLO)

The object detection architectures we've discussed so far rely on region proposals (either through selective search or the separate region proposal network). The problem with these types of architectures is that they are quite complex to implement due to the ensemble of multiple networks present inside them. These architectures involve a huge number of parameters, which makes them computationally too expensive. Also, the networks begin with proposing a lot of regions of interests, which makes it impossible to perform detection in real time.

To counter these challenges, a new prediction-based (regression-based) architecture was developed by Joseph Redmon, Santosh Divvala, Ross Girshick, and Ali Farhadi in 2015-16, which was capable of performing detection in real time. The architecture was called **YOLO**, which is short for **You Only Look Once**. YOLO is an end-to-end trainable architecture that uses just a single CNN for detecting objects.

YOLO divides the image into S x S grids. Two bounding boxes are predicted for each grid along with the probability of the object belonging to a particular class. The bounding box sizes are not restricted to be inside the grid. Each bounding box has five values predicted—(x, y, w, h). x and y represent the center of the bounding box relative to the grid, while w and h represent the width and height of the bounding box relative to the image size. Hence, the network makes $S \times S \times (B \times 5 + C)$ predictions, where B is the number of bounding boxes predicted for each cell (say, two) and C is the class probabilities for C classes. You will now notice that the network relies on predicting values and thus is a regression based object detection network. In the following diagram, you can observe how the image is divided into grids to predict bounding boxes and class scores:

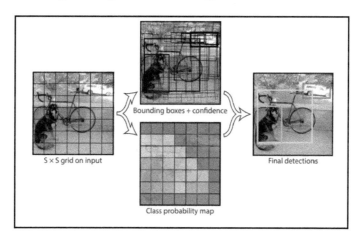

Image sourced from the paper, You Only Look Once: Unified, Real-Time Object Detection

The link to the paper, *You Only Look Once: Unified, Real-Time Object Detection*, can be found at https://arxiv.org/pdf/1506.02640.pdf.

YOLO uses 24 convolution layers. The layers follow a simple structure, repeatedly using 1 x 1 and 3 x 3 convolutions, one after the other. In the end, two fully connected layers are present to output the tensor of predictions. The architecture can be observed in the following diagram:

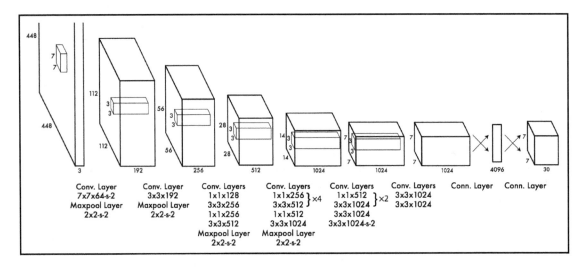

Image sourced from the paper, You Only Look Once: *Unified, Real-Time Object Detection*

The loss function used in YOLO can be divided into four parts:

- Squared-sum loss for prediction on positions x and y of bounding boxes
- Square-root loss for prediction in the width and height of bounding boxes
- Loss for the confidence score of bounding boxes
- Classification loss

The following equation contains the combined loss function for YOLO:

$$\lambda_{\text{coord}} \sum_{i=0}^{S^2} \sum_{j=0}^{B} \mathbb{1}_{ij}^{\text{obj}} \left[(x_i - \hat{x}_i)^2 + (y_i - \hat{y}_i)^2 \right]$$

$$+ \lambda_{\text{coord}} \sum_{i=0}^{S^2} \sum_{j=0}^{B} \mathbb{1}_{ij}^{\text{obj}} \left[\left(\sqrt{w_i} - \sqrt{\hat{w}_i} \right)^2 + \left(\sqrt{h_i} - \sqrt{\hat{h}_i} \right)^2 \right]$$

$$+ \sum_{i=0}^{S^2} \sum_{j=0}^{B} \mathbb{1}_{ij}^{\text{obj}} \left(C_i - \hat{C}_i \right)^2$$

$$+ \lambda_{\text{noobj}} \sum_{i=0}^{S^2} \sum_{j=0}^{B} \mathbb{1}_{ij}^{\text{noobj}} \left(C_i - \hat{C}_i \right)^2$$

$$+ \sum_{i=0}^{S^2} \mathbb{1}_{i}^{\text{obj}} \sum_{c \in \text{classes}} (p_i(c) - \hat{p}_i(c))^2$$

Image sourced from the original paper, You Only Look Once: Unified, Real-Time Object Detection

The first term in the loss function takes the squared sum of difference in positions of the bounding boxes for all the *B* bounding box predictors. The second term does the same thing but with the width and height. You will notice extra square roots. According to the authors, small deviations in large bounding boxes should matter less than in smaller bounding boxes. Square-rooting the terms helps us achieve less sensitivity toward larger values. We also predict the confidence scores, C_i, along with the bounding boxes (how confident our model while predicting a bounding box). The third term in the loss function is related to the confidence score. The final term in the loss function is about the classification of objects into different classes.

Although YOLO hugely simplifies object detection architectures and is capable of making predictions in real time, there are certain drawbacks as well. The model doesn't extract features at different scales and hence is not robust for objects of different sizes and scales. The model also struggles in detecting objects of smaller sizes that are grouped together. Next, we will look at another regression- based object detection architecture, the **Single Shot Multibox Detector** (**SSD**), which improvises on the drawbacks of YOLO.

Single Shot Multibox Detector

The SSD is also a regression-based object detector, like YOLO, but the creators of SSD claim faster and more accurate performance of SSD over YOLO. We can break the SSD into four major parts:

- The base network—VGG16
- Multiple scaled feature maps
- Convolution for bounding box prediction
- Default bounding boxes for prediction

The first job of any convolution network is to reduce the dimensions of the input and increase the depth of feature maps so that features can be extracted. The extracted features in the feature maps can then be used differently for different tasks, be it classification or detection. SSD also does the same! SSD uses the famous VGG16 architecture as the initial layers (base network) of the model for feature extraction (remember that this is different from YOLO, as the image itself is first divided into grids and then the convolution is applied for prediction). The fully connected layers at the end of the VGG16 architecture have been removed, as the purpose of using VGG16 is just to provide rich feature learning and not classification. At the end of the modified VGG16 network, SSD introduces six more layers of convolution. The sizes of these extra six layers are progressively reduced. The purpose of adding the extra layers is to make the network capable of extracting features from objects of different sizes and at different scales. That's why the feature maps in these layers keep decreasing in size (multiple scaled feature maps). The following diagram represents the overall architecture for SSD:

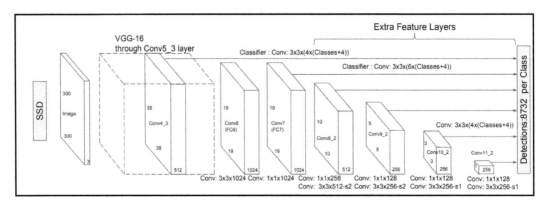

Image sourced from the paper, SSD: Single Shot MultiBox Detector

The link to the original paper, *SSD: Single Shot MultiBox Detector*, can be found at: https://www.cs.unc.edu/~wliu/papers/ssd.pdf.

The first feature map set is extracted from the 23rd layer of the VGG 16 architecture and has size 38 x 38 x 512 (here 512 is the depth or number of filters). The second set of feature maps has size 19 x 19 x 1,024 and is suitable for capturing slightly larger objects. Further sets of feature maps keep reducing the size to 10 x 10 x 512, 5 x 5 x 256, 3 x 3 x 256, and finally, to 1 x 1 x 256.

For predictions, SSD uses a 3 x 3 x d (d represents the depth of filters) convolution kernel over the extracted feature maps. For each point on the feature map, the 3 x 3 kernel outputs bounding box offsets and the class scores. SSD has default boxes assigned for each point in the feature map. The job of the 3 x 3 convolution is then to predict the four offset values from the default bounding box that will cover the object. Along with the offsets, it also predicts c class scores for the classes. If we have an m x n size feature map and k default bounding boxes at each position, the total number of predictions made out of this layer would be $(c + 4)$ x k x m x n. The number of default boxes at each location typically ranges from four to six. The scale and size of these default bounding boxes are decided by the scale of the lowest and highest feature map in the network. Suppose we have m feature maps; then the scale of default bounding boxes (s_k) is given by the following equation:

$$s_k = s_{min} + \frac{s_{max} - s_{(min)}}{m - 1}(k - 1), k \in [1, m]$$

Here, s_{min} is the scale of lowest feature map and s_{max} is the scale of highest feature map. The height and width of the default boxes is then defined by the following relations:

$$w_k = s_k \sqrt{a_r}, \quad h_k = s_k / \sqrt{a_r}, \quad where \ a_r \in \{1, 2, 3, 1/2, 1/3\}$$

The following screenshot illustrates SSD making predictions with the 8 x 8 feature map and 4 x 4 feature map. The bounding box offsets, $\triangle(cx, cy, w, h)$ and class scores for p classes (c_1, c_2, ... , c_p) are predicted:

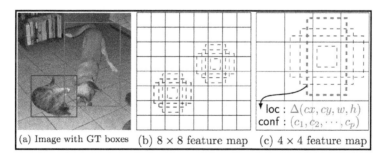

(a) Image with GT boxes (b) 8 × 8 feature map (c) 4 × 4 feature map

Image sourced from the paper, SSD: Single Shot MultiBox Detector

The loss function used in SSD is a combination of localization loss and classification loss. The localization loss is smooth L1 loss defined in the following manner:

$$smooth_{L1}(x) = \begin{cases} 0.5x^2 \ if \ |x| < 0.5 \\ |x| - 0.5 \ otherwise \end{cases}$$

$$L_{loc}(x, l, g) = \sum_{N} \sum_{m \in \{cx, cyw, h\}} x_{ij} smooth_{L1}(l_i^m - g_j^m)$$

Here, smooth loss is calculated for all the N default bounding boxes between the parameters of the predicted bounding box (l) and ground truth bounding box (g). The classification loss is simple cross-entropy loss over softmax calculated class scores for the classes. Classification loss is given by the following equation:

$$L_{conf}(x, c) = -\sum_{N} x_{ij} log(\hat{c}_i^p) - -\sum_{N} log(\hat{c}_i^0)$$

Here, the first term is if a bounding box contains the object and the second term is when there is no object. $\hat{c}$ represents the softmax score of the class.

So far, we have learned how SSD works. Now, let's use SSD to detect objects using TensorFlow!

TensorFlow object detection zoo

Object detection models are quite tricky to train. This is due to their complex architectures and the requirement to make a lot of predictions. To train an object detection model, such as Faster RCNN, YOLO, or SSD, a great deal of parallel processing power is required, which is not accessible to everyone. Even if you have such computation at your disposal, it would take you hours and hours of time and careful monitoring to train an end-to-end object detection model. This could restrict the easy use of these models, despite being highly accurate.

To overcome this commonly faced problem, researchers came up with the idea of pre-trained networks. The model is trained using the state-of-art resources available over publicly available large datasets, such as the COCO dataset, PASCAL VOC dataset, Kitti dataset, and so on. Links to these datasets can be found at `http://cocodataset.org/#home`, `PASCAL VOC :http://host.robots.ox.ac.uk/pascal/VOC/`.

The weights and graph of the models are then made public. Anyone who is interested in object detection deep learning models can download these weights and graph to implement them for object detection.

TensorFlow has taken a step forward with their TensorFlow object detection API and TensorFlow model zoo to open source various pre-trained model weights and TensorFlow frozen graphs to help out the deep learning developers. You can check out the following link for the TensorFlow model zoo and compare the running time and **mean average precision** (**MAP**) for different object detections models: `https://github.com/tensorflow/models/blob/master/research/object_detection/g3doc/detection_model_zoo.md`.

Next, we will look at how we can use the TensorFlow model zoo for object detection. Let's build our model based on the SSD we discussed earlier. Our first step would be to download the pre-trained weights for the model we wish to implement. Here, we will consider the model `ssd_mobilenet_v2_coco`. The idea behind MobileNet will be discussed in the up coming chapter. For now, consider this as an SSD object detection network trained on the COCO dataset. You can download the directory containing all related files in zipped form by clicking the model name, as shown in the following screenshot:

ssd_mobilenet_v1_0.75_depth_coco ☆	26	18	Boxes
ssd_mobilenet_v1_quantized_coco ☆	29	18	Boxes
ssd_mobilenet_v1_0.75_depth_quantized_coco ☆	29	16	Boxes
ssd_mobilenet_v1_ppn_coco ☆	26	20	Boxes
ssd_mobilenet_v1_fpn_coco ☆	56	32	Boxes
ssd_resnet_50_fpn_coco ☆	76	35	Boxes
ssd_mobilenet_v2_coco	31	22	Boxes
ssd_mobilenet_v2_quantized_coco	29	22	Boxes
ssdlite_mobilenet_v2_coco	27	22	Boxes
ssd_inception_v2_coco	42	24	Boxes

Once you have downloaded the `.zip` file, you can extract it to the `deep_learning` folder. Next, we will look at a script that will load the model and weights from frozen graph and detect objects in the input image. Let's begin by importing our required dependencies:

> Remember to activate the environment in which you have installed the Python libraries and TensorFlow for deep learning. We created an environment named `test_env` in Chapter 1, *Getting started with Deep Learning*. You can use that! In case you are missing out any of the dependencies, you can simply execute the `conda install <dependency_name>` command in your terminal (under the activated environment).

```
import tensorflow as tf
import numpy as np
import matplotlib.pyplot as plt
import cv2
import os
import argparse
```

We will be using the `argparse` module to pass the path of the images on which detection needs to be performed. With `argparse`, you can give the path of the directory in which you have stored images to be detected at the time of running the script:

```
parser.add_argument('--im_path', type=str, help='path to input image')
#parser.add_argument('--save_path', type=str, help='save path to output
image')
args = parser.parse_args()
IM_PATH = args.im_path
```

Next, we will define a simple function using `opencv` to read the image:

```
def read_image(imPath):
    img = cv2.imread(imPath)
    return img
```

The extracted folder must contain the frozen graph of the model in `protobuf` format (with the `.pb` extension). We need to read this file in order to load the frozen graph:

```
FROZEN_GRAPH_FILE = 'frozen_inference_graph.pb'  #path to frozen graph
```

We are using TensorFlow in Python, but the actual library of TensorFlow is written in C++. TensorFlow uses a module called `protobuf` to make transfers of graphs into different language. Hence, while reading a graph stored by `protobuf` (generally with the `.pb` extension), we need to define a serial graph first with `tf.GraphDef` and then put it inside an empty graph that we will create. The following code does the same:

```
# making an empty graph

graph = tf.Graph()
with graph.as_default():

  # making a serial graph
  serialGraph = tf.GraphDef()

  # reading from saved frozen graph

  with tf.gfile.GFile(FROZEN_GRAPH_FILE, 'rb') as f:

      serialRead = f.read()
      serialGraph.ParseFromString(serialRead)
      tf.import_graph_def(serialGraph, name = '')
```

Next, we initialize the session with our loaded graph:

```
sess = tf.Session(graph = graph)
```

Now, we will read the images in the specified directory path. Here, we are considering only `.jpeg` images, but you can change it into an other format if you want:

```
for dirs in os.listdir(IM_PATH):
  if not dirs.startswith('.'):
    for im in os.listdir(os.path.join(IM_PATH, dirs)):
      if im.endswith('.jpeg'):

        image = read_image(os.path.join(IM_PATH, dirs, im))
        if image is None:
          print('image read as None')
        print('image name: ', im)
```

A TensorFlow graph consists of tensor variables and placeholders, which are used to flow and feed data during a session. To take output and feed input to the model, we need to take out the tensors that are responsible for the input and output. We can fetch the tensors by their names in the graph. We fetch the tensors for the output detected bounding boxes, the class, and the input placeholder for the image with the following code:

```
imageTensor = graph.get_tensor_by_name('image_tensor:0')

bboxs = graph.get_tensor_by_name('detection_boxes:0')

classes = graph.get_tensor_by_name('detection_classes:0')
```

Now, we are ready to perform object detection on our image. Here, we need to use `np.expand_dims()` to add an extra dimension in the image, as TensorFlow keeps the first dimension for the batch size:

```
(outBoxes, classes) = sess.run([bboxs, classes],feed_dict =
{imageTensor:np.expand_dims(image, axis=0)})
```

We can extract our result to be visual using simple `np.squeeze()` operations to remove the extra dimension by using the following code:

```
cnt = 0
imageHeight, imageWidth = image.shape[:2]
boxes = np.squeeze(outBoxes)
classes = np.squeeze(classes)
boxes = np.stack((boxes[:,1] * imageWidth, boxes[:,0] * imageHeight,
                  boxes[:,3] * imageWidth, boxes[:,2] *
imageHeight),axis=1).astype(np.int)
```

Once we have the predicted bounding boxes, we will draw a rectangular box around them with `opencv`. Optionally, you can print the class value as well. A numeric class value will be printed; you can refer to the COCO dataset and convert the numeric label into an actual label. We'll leave that to you as an exercise:

```
for i, bb in enumerate(boxes):
    print(classes[i])
    cv2.rectangle(image, (bb[0], bb[1]), (bb[2], bb[3]), (100,100,255),
thickness = 1)
```

After this, we just need to plot the final image in order to see our bounding boxes on the image:

```
plt.figure(figsize = (10, 10))
plt.imshow(image)
plt.show()
```

So, that's it! If you got caught up in the indent or flow of the preceding snippets, the following is the code in its entirety for your reference:

```
import tensorflow as tf
import numpy as np
import matplotlib.pyplot as plt
import cv2
import os
import argparse

parser = argparse.ArgumentParser()

parser.add_argument('--im_path', type=str, help='path to input image')

args = parser.parse_args()
IM_PATH = args.im_path

def read_image(imPath):
  img = cv2.imread(imPath)
  return img

FROZEN_GRAPH_FILE = 'frozen_inference_graph.pb' #path to frozen graph

# making an empty graph
graph = tf.Graph()
with graph.as_default():

  serialGraph = tf.GraphDef()

  with tf.gfile.GFile(FROZEN_GRAPH_FILE, 'rb') as f:
    serialRead = f.read()
    serialGraph.ParseFromString(serialRead)
    tf.import_graph_def(serialGraph, name = '')

sess = tf.Session(graph = graph)

for dirs in os.listdir(IM_PATH):
  if not dirs.startswith('.'):
    for im in os.listdir(os.path.join(IM_PATH, dirs)):
      if im.endswith('.jpeg'):
```

```
image = read_image(os.path.join(IM_PATH, dirs, im))
if image is None:
  print('image read as None')
print('image name: ', im)

# here we will bring in the tensors from the frozen graph we
loaded,
# which will take the input through feed_dict and output the
bounding boxes

imageTensor = graph.get_tensor_by_name('image_tensor:0')

bboxs = graph.get_tensor_by_name('detection_boxes:0')


classes = graph.get_tensor_by_name('detection_classes:0')

(outBoxes, classes) = sess.run([bboxs,
classes],feed_dict={imageTensor: np.expand_dims(image, axis=0)})


# visualize
cnt = 0
imageHeight, imageWidth = image.shape[:2]
boxes = np.squeeze(outBoxes)
classes = np.squeeze(classes)
boxes = np.stack((boxes[:,1] * imageWidth, boxes[:,0] *
imageHeight,
          boxes[:,3] * imageWidth, boxes[:,2] *
imageHeight),axis=1).astype(np.int)

for i, bb in enumerate(boxes):

  print(classes[i])
  cv2.rectangle(image, (bb[0], bb[1]), (bb[2], bb[3]), (255,255,0),
thickness = 1)
plt.figure(figsize = (10, 10))
plt.imshow(image)
plt.show()
```

Let's pick up an image to show you what it looks like. We picked up the following image of two humans standing (image sourced from Wikipedia):

And here's the detected result:

Summary

We begun this chapter by discussing the drawbacks of deep feedforward networks and how CNNs had evolved to overcome their drawbacks. Next, we dived deep into the architecture of CNNs, understanding the different layers of CNN—the input layer, convolution layer, maxpooling layer, and fully connected layer. We looked at the architectures of some famous image classification CNNs and then built our first CNN image classifier on the CIFAR-10 dataset. Then, we moved on to object detection with CNNs. We discussed various object detectors, such as RCNN, Faster-RCNN, YOLO, and SSD. Lastly, we used the TensorFlow detection model zoo to implement our first object detector using SSD.

In the next chapter, we will look at CNN architectures that require less computational power and are lightweight to run on a mobile device. They are called **MobileNets**!

5
Mobile Neural Networks and CNNs

The computation costs required by deep learning networks have always been a concern for expansion. Millions of multiplication operations are required to run an inference. This has limited the practical use of developed **convolutional neural network** (**CNN**) models. The mobile neural network provides a breakthrough to this problem. They are super small and computationally light deep learning networks, and achieve performance that's equivalent to their original counterparts. Mobile neural networks are just CNNs that have been modified to have far fewer parameters, which means they are consuming less memory. This way, they are capable of working on mobile devices with limited memory and processing power. Hence, mobile neural networks are playing a crucial role in making CNNs work for real-time applications. In this chapter, we will cover two benchmark mobile CNN architectures that were introduced by Google—MobileNet and MobileNetV2. After completion of this chapter, you will have learned about the following topics:

- How MobileNet evolved
- The architecture and structure of MobileNet
- Implementing MobileNet with Keras
- MobileNetV2
- Motivation behind MobileNetV2
- The architecture and structure of MobileNetV2
- Comparing the two mobile nets
- SSD-MobileNet

Evolution path to MobileNets

CNNs present a promising future for computer vision. CNNs have laid out a benchmark for complex computer vision tasks such as detection and recognition with their remarkable performance in the ILSVRC competition over consecutive years. But the computation power required by these CNN models has always been quite high. This could lead to a major setback for the commercial use of CNNs. Almost all object detection-related tasks in the real world are performed through portable devices, such as mobile phones, surveillance cameras, or any other embedded device. These devices have limited computational abilities and memory. To make any deep learning network running on a portable device, the network weights and the number of calculations occurring in the network (that is, the number of parameters in the network) have to very small. CNNs have millions of parameters and weights, and it thus seems impossible to pack and run a CNN on any mobile device!

It early 2017, a group of researchers at Google made a breakthrough and introduced a new class of CNN called MobileNets for mobile and embedded vision. MobileNet featured the concept of depth-wise separable convolution, significantly reducing the number of parameters of a convolution network while maintaining the same depth of model. MobileNets were a huge success! A lot of companies began using MobileNets for real-time detection on mobile devices.

In 2018, Google launched the second version of MobileNets, referred to as MobileNetV2. The newer MobileNetV2 features inverted residual blocks. Various successful object detection architectures, such as SSD, were also combined with MobileNetV2 to create efficient mobile architectures for object detection. So, let's understand the architecture of MobileNets in the next section.

Architecture of MobileNets

At the heart of the MobileNets architecture lies the concept of depth-wise separable convolution. The standard convolution operations of CNNs are substituted by depth-wise convolution and point-wise convolution. So, let's first see what depth-wise separable convolution is in the next sub-section.

Depth-wise separable convolution

As the name suggests, depth-wise separable convolution must have something to do with the depths of feature maps rather than their width and height. Remember that when we used a filter over the input image in a CNN, the filter covered all the channels of the image (say the three RGB channels of the colored image). No matter how many channels were present in the input, the convolution kernel always covered all the channels and produced output in a single channel feature map.

In any layer, if we wanted n number of feature maps, we ran n number of kernels over the previous layer as each kernel output a single channel. The following diagram shows the output response of a standard convolution:

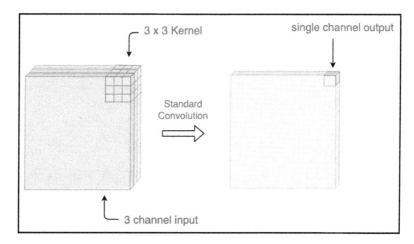

But unlike the standard convolution, the depth-wise convolution doesn't consider all the channels in the input together to output a single channel. Rather, it performs a convolution on each channel separately. So, performing depth-wise convolution on an n channel image would produce n channels in the output. Depth-wise separable convolution has two parts—depth-wise convolution (which we just discussed) and point-wise convolution. Depth-wise convolution is followed by point-wise convolution, which is just a regular convolution operation with a 1 x 1 kernel. Point-wise convolution is required to combine the results of depthwise convolution.

The following diagram shows the output response of a depth-wise separable convolution:

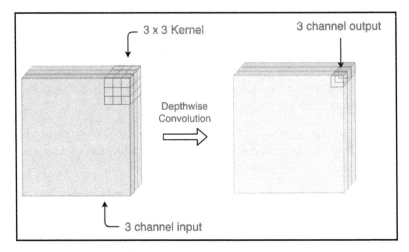

So, what's the problem in using n convolution filters for generating a feature map of depth n? Why do we need to substitute standard convolution with depth-wise separable convolution? We will look at the reasons why in the next sub-section.

The need for depth-wise separable convolution

The purpose of introducing depth-wise separable convolution in MobileNets is to reduce the computation expense that's required. So, let's compare the computation cost of depth-wise separable convolution with standard convolution. The major computation cost is incurred due to multiplication operations (operations such as addition are computationally simple). The greater the number of multiplications, the higher the computation that's required. Let's consider a case of an $M \times M \times N$ image. This is a typical dimension for an RGB image. Suppose we are using $K \times K \times N$ sized standard convolution kernels and we want the feature map of dimensions to be $G \times G \times D$. For this, we have to use D number of filters:

- Hence the number of multiplication operations required for one convolution filter at a location is $K.K.N = K^2N$.
- This filter slides $G \times G$ times for generating complete output for one filter. This makes the number of multiplications G^2K^2N.
- We have D such kernels. Hence, this makes our total cost of the required convolution G^2K^2ND.

Now, let's calculate the number of multiplication operations required for generating the same results using depth-wise separable convolution. We know that there are two parts in depth-wise separable convolution—depth-wise convolution and point-wise convolution. The major difference between standard convolution and depth-wise convolution is that depth-wise convolution uses a depth of 1 in convolution kernels. Let's consider the same scenario we mentioned previously. We have an M x M x N image:

- The kernel size here would be K x K x 1. We would require N number of kernels to fit through the complete image, which would then give us an output dimension of G x G x N. So, here, the number of multiplications required is $G^2 K^2 N$.

- Now, it's time for point-wise convolution. This involves combining the outputs from depth-wise convolution. The kernel for point-wise convolution is 1 x 1 x N. If this kernel slides all over the output of depth-wise convolution, the number of multiplication operations required for one kernel would be $G^2 N$.

- If we want depth D in the final output feature map, then D number of point-wise kernels are used to give the final output as G x G x D. Hence, the number of multiplications becomes G^2ND.

- The total number of multiplications required in depth-wise separable convolution is the sum of multiplications required for depth-wise convolution and point-wise convolution, which would be as follows:

$$G^2 K^2 N + G^2 ND = G^2 N(K^2 + D)$$

We can compare the number of multiplications required for standard convolution and depth-wise separable convolution in the following manner:

$$\frac{Depthwise\ Separable\ Conv.}{Standard\ Conv.} = \frac{G^2 N(K^2 + D)}{G^2 K^2 ND} = \frac{1}{D} + \frac{1}{K^2}$$

In general, if we put $D = 256$ and $K = 3$, then the ratio is 0.115. This means that depth-wise separable convolution has nine times more parameters than standard convolution.

Hopefully, you now have an idea of how MobileNet is able to reduce the number of parameters with depth-wise separable convolution. Now, let's look at the structure of MobileNet in our next sub-section.

Structure of MobileNet

The structure of MobileNet consists of 30 layers. It starts with a standard convolution of 3 x 3 as the first layer. Thereafter, the pair of depth-wise convolution and pointwise convolution continues. The depthwise separable convolution block is the consecutive combination of depth-wise separable and point-wise convolution, as shown in the following diagram:

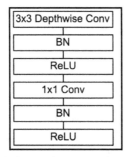

Image sourced from the paper, *MobileNets: Efficient Convolutional Neural Networks for Mobile Vision Applications*. BN represents batch normalization.

The preceding block is repeated 13 times in the structure. In order to reduce the width and height of the feature maps, MobileNet uses stride two in depth-wise convolution. Yes, it doesn't use maxpooling! And to increase the depth of feature maps, the point-wise convolution doubles the number of channels. The doubling of channels occurs in the corresponding point-wise layer where stride two is used in depth-wise convolution.

The link to the research paper of MobileNets can be found at `https://arxiv.org/pdf/1704.04861.pdf`.

MobileNet was trained on data from ImageNet, where the input dimensions of an image is 224 x 224 x 3. According to the input size of ImageNet images, the final output coming out from the convolution layers is of size 7 x 7 x 1,024. After the convolutions are over, a **global average pooling** (**GAP**) layer is applied to make the dimension 1 x 1 x 1,024. Assuming a feature map of size H x W x D, the GAP layer calculates the average of $H.W$ values and replaces the H x W values with a single average value, resulting in an output dimension of 1 x 1 x D always.

Since MobileNet was primarily used for classification, the ending layer is a fully connected layer. The activation functions that are used in MobileNets are ReLU6. We have learned about ReLU, but what is ReLU6? ReLU6 is the same ReLU function, but the upper bound is limited to six. The authors claim that ReLU6 helps the model learn sparse features earlier. The following equation defines the ReLU6 activation function:

$$y = min(max(0, x), 6)$$

Let's look at the complete architecture of MobileNet in the following table:

Type / Stride	Filter Shape	Input Size
Conv / s2	$3 \times 3 \times 3 \times 32$	$224 \times 224 \times 3$
Conv dw / s1	$3 \times 3 \times 32$ dw	$112 \times 112 \times 32$
Conv / s1	$1 \times 1 \times 32 \times 64$	$112 \times 112 \times 32$
Conv dw / s2	$3 \times 3 \times 64$ dw	$112 \times 112 \times 64$
Conv / s1	$1 \times 1 \times 64 \times 128$	$56 \times 56 \times 64$
Conv dw / s1	$3 \times 3 \times 128$ dw	$56 \times 56 \times 128$
Conv / s1	$1 \times 1 \times 128 \times 128$	$56 \times 56 \times 128$
Conv dw / s2	$3 \times 3 \times 128$ dw	$56 \times 56 \times 128$
Conv / s1	$1 \times 1 \times 128 \times 256$	$28 \times 28 \times 128$
Conv dw / s1	$3 \times 3 \times 256$ dw	$28 \times 28 \times 256$
Conv / s1	$1 \times 1 \times 256 \times 256$	$28 \times 28 \times 256$
Conv dw / s2	$3 \times 3 \times 256$ dw	$28 \times 28 \times 256$
Conv / s1	$1 \times 1 \times 256 \times 512$	$14 \times 14 \times 256$
$5\times$ Conv dw / s1	$3 \times 3 \times 512$ dw	$14 \times 14 \times 512$
Conv / s1	$1 \times 1 \times 512 \times 512$	$14 \times 14 \times 512$
Conv dw / s2	$3 \times 3 \times 512$ dw	$14 \times 14 \times 512$
Conv / s1	$1 \times 1 \times 512 \times 1024$	$7 \times 7 \times 512$
Conv dw / s2	$3 \times 3 \times 1024$ dw	$7 \times 7 \times 1024$
Conv / s1	$1 \times 1 \times 1024 \times 1024$	$7 \times 7 \times 1024$
Avg Pool / s1	Pool 7×7	$7 \times 7 \times 1024$
FC / s1	1024×1000	$1 \times 1 \times 1024$
Softmax / s1	Classifier	$1 \times 1 \times 1000$

Image sourced from the paper, *MobileNets: Efficient Convolutional Neural Networks for Mobile Vision Applications*

Now that we know about the architecture of MobileNet and how the number of parameters are reduced through depth-wise separable convolution, let's look at the implementation of MobileNet.

MobileNet with Keras

MobileNet was trained on ImageNet data. We can implement MobileNet using the pre-trained weights for the model by using the Keras application class. Inside the Keras application, you can find a lot of pre-trained models for use. You can go through the documentation of the Keras application at `https://keras.io/applications/`.

So, let's get started! First, obviously, we will import the required dependencies:

```
import keras
from keras.preprocessing import image
from keras.applications import imagenet_utils
from keras.models import Model
from keras.applications.mobilenet import preprocess_input

import numpy as np
import argparse
import matplotlib.pyplot as plt
```

The Keras `preprocessing` provides a class such as the `ImageDataGenerator` class which helps to draw batches of images from the dataset. Our next job is to fetch the model weights and graph. The download will happen only once on your system as we add the following step to our script:

```
model = keras.applications.mobilenet.MobileNet(weights = 'imagenet')
```

The download may take some time depending on your internet connectivity. Keras will keep updating the status, which would look like the following image on completion:

```
Downloading data from https://github.com/fchollet/deep-learning-model
s/releases/download/v0.6/mobilenet_1_0_224_tf.h5
17227776/17225924 [==============================] - 288s 17us/step
>>>
```

We will use the `argparse` module to aid passing the image path to our script for the image we want MobileNet to classify:

```
parser = argparse.ArgumentParser()
parser.add_argument('--im_path', type = str, help = 'path to the image')
args = parser.parse_args()

# adding the path to image
IM_PATH = args.im_path
```

We will use the `load_img` function provided by Keras to load this image and convert it into an array with `img_to_array`:

```
img = image.load_img(IM_PATH, target_size = (224, 224))
img = image.img_to_array(img)
```

Images in ImageNet have a width and height of 224. Hence, the target size is set to (224, 224) by default. As we saw earlier, the first dimension is always kept for the batch size. We will expand the dimensions of our image to accommodate the batch size as the first dimension (as we are using a single image, we can assume it to be batch size 1):

```
img = np.expand_dims(img, axis = 0)
```

Finally, we will pass `img` through the `preprocess_input()` function from `mobilenet`, which performs basic pre-processing operations, such as reshaping and normalizing the pixel values of the image:

```
img = preprocess_input(img)
```

Now, it's time for MobileNet to make a prediction on the image we gave:

```
prediction = model.predict(img)
```

As the model predicts classes according to the ImageNet dataset, we will use the `decode_predictions` function to bring back the top five predictions in human-readable form:

```
output = imagenet_utils.decode_predictions(prediction)
print(output)
```

Let's use the following image of a Pelican bird and checkout whether MobileNet is able to classify it or not:

Image sourced from Wikipedia

You need to run the script from a Terminal under the environment you are working on, along with the path to the image in the following manner:

```
$python mobilenet_keras.py --im_path=pelican.jpg
```

The following is the output from our script. You can see that MobileNet predicted the image as a Pelican with a probability of 0.99! In the top five predicted classes are some other birds that look similar to a Pelican, but their probabilities are suppressed due to softmax activations:

```
[[('n02051845', 'pelican', 0.99999094), ('n02006656', 'spoonbill', 5.054373e-06), ('n0205822
1', 'albatross', 2.0289876e-06), ('n02009912', 'American_egret', 7.567513e-07), ('n02002724'
, 'black_stork', 4.1900924e-07)]]
```

You can explore the performance of MobileNet with different images relating to the ImageNet data classes. After the success of MobileNet, the Google research team launched an updated version of MobileNet in April, 2018. We will learn about the second version of MobileNet in the next section.

MobileNetV2

The second version of MobileNet, referred to as MobileNetV2, is even faster than MobileNet. The second version has fewer parameters as well. Since its launch, MobileNetV2 has been widely used in state-of-the-art object detection and segmentation architectures to make object detection or segmentation possible on devices with limited resources. Let's look at the motivation behind the creation of MobileNetV2.

Motivation behind MobileNetV2

The researchers at Google wanted MobileNet to be even lighter. How can we make MobileNet have fewer parameters? All the CNN-based models increase the number of feature maps (depth channel) while reducing the width and height. One easy way to reduce the network size would be to reduce the depth of the feature maps. The fewer the number of channels, the fewer the parameters. But this would weaken the CNN! The convolution filters won't be able to extract features from shallow feature maps. So, what do we do now?

The Google researchers found an answer to this problem and introduced two major changes in the existing MobileNet architecture: the **expansion-linear bottleneck layer** and the **inverted residual block.** We will look at the detailed structure of MobileNetV2 in the next sub-section.

Structure of MobileNetV2

The core architecture of MobileNetV2 still relies on depth-wise separable convolution layers. Remember the building block of MobileNet? It had the 3 x 3 depth-wise convolution layer, followed by 1 x 1 point-wise convolution and batch normalization, with ReLU6 in-between. MobileNetV2 follows the same block, except with an additional expansion layer at the top and a linear bottleneck layer in place of 1 x 1 point-wise convolution. Let's first see what the linear bottleneck layer does.

Linear bottleneck layer

In MobileNet, the 1 x 1 pointwise convolution was responsible for increasing the depth of feature maps through the network. The linear bottleneck layer in MobileNetV2 does the opposite job. It actually reduces the depth of feature maps. The ReLU activation function, in order to preserve the non-linearity in layers, drops the negative values. This leads to information loss in channels. To counter this, a lot of channels are used in feature maps, so there's a high chance that information loss in one channel is preserved in any other channel.

However, the authors of MobileNetV2 proved that if input channels are projected into much lower-dimensional space rather than higher-dimensional space, then ReLU activation is capable of preserving all the information coming from the input channels. This is a major breakthrough! The authors also provide supplementary material in the original paper to prove this.

 The link to the research paper of MobileNetV2 can be found at `https://arxiv.org/pdf/1801.04381.pdf`.

Thus, the authors introduced the so-called linear bottleneck layer after the convolution, which reduces dimensionality. For example, if an intermediate layer has 384 channels, it will be reduced to 128 channels. But the reduction in dimensions is not all that we need! For performing depth-wise convolution, we need the dimensionality to be higher. Hence, an expansion layer is used before the depth-wise convolution to increase the number of channels. Let's look at the functionality of the expansion layer.

Expansion layer

The **expansion layer** is a 1 x 1 convolution layer which always has a higher output channel dimension than the input dimension. The amount of expansion to be done is controlled by a hyperparameter called the **expansion factor**. The expansion factor throughout MobileNetV2 is set to 6. For example, if the input has 64 channels, it will be expanded into *64*6 = 384* channels. Depth-wise convolution is performed over it, and then the bottleneck layer brings it back to 128 channels.

The architecture of MobileNetV2 first expands the channel, performs convolution, and then reduces it. This keeps the end-to-end dimensionality of the architecture low and thus reduces the number of required parameters.

The overall building block of MobileNetV2 is shown in the following diagram:

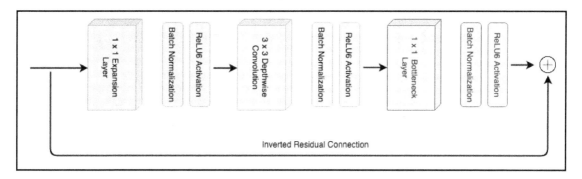

Now, there's one more thing left in the architecture: the residual layer. Although it is similar to the skip connections from the ResNet model, we will look at some details about it.

Inverted residual block

As a deep learning model becomes too deep by stacking a lot layers together, training the network becomes very difficult. This is not only due to the enormous computation power that's required, but also because of the vanishing flow of gradients through the layer. We know that all the learning in deep learning models depend on the flow of gradients through backpropagation. In large networks, the gradient becomes smaller with each step and vanishes before passing through all layers. This phenomenon restricts us from making a network too deep. The residual connections, or skip connections, introduced in the ResNet architecture help us overcome this problem. A connection from a previous layer is added to a layer so that the gradients get an easy path to flow through. These skip connections have allowed the ResNet model to be deeper than usual.

Inspired by skip connections, the authors of MobileNetV2 claim that the useful information lies only in the bottleneck layers and, therefore, to allow the easy flow of gradients through the multiple bottleneck blocks, they have added residual connections from one bottleneck layer to another. The authors chose to call this an inverted residual due to the design difference between the original residual connections in ResNet and the residual connections in MobileNetV2.

The difference can be observed in the following diagram:

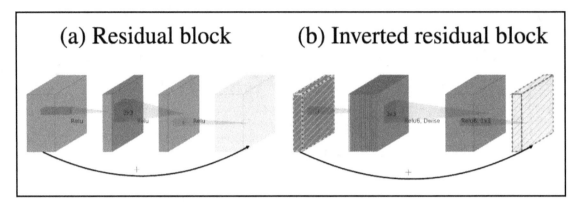

Image sourced from research paper, *MobileNetV2: Inverted Residuals and Linear Bottlenecks*

Now that we have covered all the elements of MobileNetV2, we will look at the overall structure of MobileNetV2.

Overall architecture

MobileNetV2 began by performing a standard convolution over an image to create a 32 filters feature map. Thereafter, there are 19 blocks of residual bottleneck layers (the block that we saw in the expansion layer sub-section). All the convolution kernels are of size 3 x 3. A constant expansion factor of six has been used throughout the network. The overall architecture of MobileNetV2 can be observed in the following table:

Input	Operator	t	c	n	s
$224^2 \times 3$	conv2d	-	32	1	2
$112^2 \times 32$	bottleneck	1	16	1	1
$112^2 \times 16$	bottleneck	6	24	2	2
$56^2 \times 24$	bottleneck	6	32	3	2
$28^2 \times 32$	bottleneck	6	64	4	2
$14^2 \times 64$	bottleneck	6	96	3	1
$14^2 \times 96$	bottleneck	6	160	3	2
$7^2 \times 160$	bottleneck	6	320	1	1
$7^2 \times 320$	conv2d 1x1	-	1280	1	1
$7^2 \times 1280$	avgpool 7x7	-	-	1	-
$1 \times 1 \times 1280$	conv2d 1x1	-	k	-	

Image sourced from research paper, *MobileNetV2: Inverted Residuals and Linear Bottlenecks*

In the preceding table, the column *n* represents the number of times that particular layer is repeated. The column *s* represents the stride that was used for that layer. Columns *c* and *t* represent the number of channels and expansion factors that are used in the layers, respectively.

Similar to MobileNet, we can use Keras to implement MobileNetV2 as well.

Implementing MobileNetV2

We will follow a process that's similar to the one we followed for MobileNet. You can find MobileNetV2 in the Keras applications. We will use the same codes as we did for MobileNet, except we will use MobileNetV2 this time. For your reference, the code is as follows:

```
import keras
from keras.preprocessing import image
from keras.applications import imagenet_utils
from keras.applications.mobilenet import preprocess_input
from keras.models import Model


import numpy as np
import argparse
import matplotlib.pyplot as plt


model = keras.applications.mobilenet_v2.MobileNetV2(weights = 'imagenet')

parser = argparse.ArgumentParser()
parser.add_argument('--im_path', type = str, help = 'path to the image')
args = parser.parse_args()

# adding the path to image
IM_PATH = args.im_path

img = image.load_img(IM_PATH, target_size = (224, 224))
img = image.img_to_array(img)

img = np.expand_dims(img, axis = 0)
img = preprocess_input(img)
prediction = model.predict(img)

output = imagenet_utils.decode_predictions(prediction)

print(output)
```

The script will first download the weights for MobileNetV2, which may take time depending on your internet connection. It will look something like this:

```
Downloading data from https://github.com/JonathanCMitchell/mobilenet_v2_keras/
releases/download/v1.1/mobilenet_v2_weights_tf_dim_ordering_tf_kernels_1.0_224
.h5
14540800/14536120 [==============================] - 67s 5us/step
```

Let's use the following Flamingo image to checkout the output:

Here's what the output will look like. We can see that the network is around 86% sure that the image is of a Flamingo. You can observe that the probabilities of other classes are suppressed due to softmax:

```
[[('n02007558', 'flamingo', 0.864596), ('n02006656', 'spoonbill', 0.004185393), ('n0201284
9', 'crane', 0.0026652862), ('n02009912', 'American_egret', 0.0019446992), ('n01860187', '
black_swan', 0.0018243799)]]
```

The two versions of MobileNet were introduced within a year. The second version includes significant changes, which we have already discussed. Now, let's compare the two networks on some standard parameters.

Comparing the two MobileNets

MobileNetV2 has introduced significant changes in the architecture of MobileNet. Were the changes worth making? How much better is MobileNetV2 than MobileNet in regards to performance? We can compare the models in terms of the number of multiplication operations required for one inference, which is commonly known as **MACs** (number of multiply-accumulates). The higher the MAC value, the heavier the network is. We can also compare the models in terms of the number of parameters in the model. The following table shows the MACs and the number of parameters for both MobileNet and MobileNetV2:

Network	Number of Parameters	MACs/ MAdds
MobileNet V1	4.2M	575M
MobileNet V2	3.4M	300M

We can also compare the models in terms of memory that's required for the different number of channels and resolution. The following table provides the comparison data. The memory is measured is **kilobytes (Kb)**:

Size	MobileNetV1	MobileNetV2
112x112	64/1600	16/400
56x56	128/800	32/200
28x28	256/400	64/100
14x14	512/200	160/62
7x7	1024/199	320/32
1x1	1024/2	1280/2
max	1600K	**400K**

TensorFlow also offers an **Accuracy vs Latency** comparison between the two MobileNets running on a pixel 1 mobile phone. The latency basically represents how much time is required to run the model. The following diagram shows the comparison:

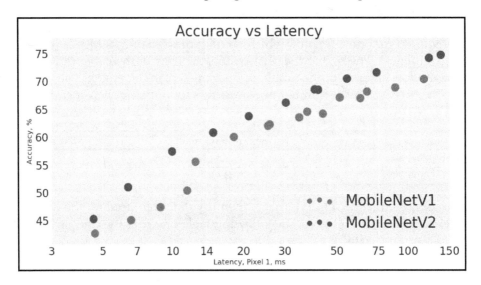

You can find more details about the comparison at `https://github.com/tensorflow/models/tree/master/research/slim/nets/mobilenet`.

There's more to MobileNetV2 than just classification. The authors of the architecture have come up with the idea of combining object detection and segmentation architectures. We will look at a very successful combination of MobileNetV2 and SSD for object detection in the next section.

SSD MobileNetV2

The makers of MobileNetV2 also made real-time object detection possible for mobile devices. They introduced a combination of the SSD Object Detector and MobileNetV2, which is called **SSDLite.** Remember that in `Chapter 4`, *CNN Architecture*, we used `ssd_mobilenetv2` for object detection. It is the same as SSDLite. The reason for choosing SSD is quite simple. SSD is built independent of the base network and hence the convolutions are replaced by depth-wise separable convolution. The first layer of SSDLite is attached to the expansion of layer 15 of MobileNetV2. Replacing standard convolutions with depth-wise separable convolution significantly reduces the number of parameters that are required by the network for object detection.

The following table shows a comparison of the number of parameters and multiplication operations required by the original SSD network and SSDLite:

	Params	MAdds
SSD[ ]	14.8M	1.25B
SSDLite	**2.1M**	**0.35B**

Image sourced from the research paper, MobileNetV2: *Inverted Residuals and Linear Bottlenecks*

Summary

We began this chapter by discussing the need for mobile neural networks to make CNNs work in real-time applications. We discussed the two benchmark MobileNet architectures that were introduced by Google—MobileNet and MobileNetV2. We looked at how modifications such as depth-wise separable convolution work and replaced the standard convolutions, enabling the network to achieve the same results with significantly fewer parameters. With MobileNetV2, we looked at the possibility of reducing the network even further with expansion layers and bottleneck layers. We also looked at the implementation of both the networks in Keras and compared both the networks in terms of the number of parameters, MACs, and memory required. Finally, we discussed the successful combination of MobileNets with object detection networks, such as SSD, to achieve object detection on mobile devices.

In the next chapter, we will look at yet another successful type of deep learning architecture, called **recurrent neural networks** (**RNNs**). These networks are designed to capture temporal information in sequences, such as sentences or any other text.

Section 3: Sequence Modeling 3

In this section, we will learn about two important DL models, along with the evolution paths of those models. We will explore their architectures and various engineering best practices through some examples.

The following chapters will be covered in this section:–

- Chapter 6, *Recurrent Neural Networks*

6
Recurrent Neural Networks

In this chapter, we will explain one of the most important deep learning models, **recurrent neural networks** (**RNNs**). We will start by reviewing what RNNs are and why they are well-suited for processing sequential data. After briefing the evolution paths of RNN models, we will illustrate a variety of RNN architectures that have been categorized by the different forms of input and output data, along with industrial examples. We will figure out the answers to questions such as, *how can we generate only one output?*, *Can output be a sequence?*, and *does it work with only one input element?*

We will follow this by discussing several architectures categorized by the recurrent layer. First, we will apply the basic RNN architecture to write our own *War and Peace*. The RNNs with vanilla architecture are not good at preserving long-term dependent information. To get around this, we will learn about *memory-boosted* architectures, including long short-term memory and the gated recurrent unit. We will also employ gated architectures in stock price prediction. Finally, not satisfied with capturing past information, we will introduce a bidirectional architecture that allows the model to preserve information from both past and future contexts of the sequence. A bidirectional model with LSTM will be used to classify the sentiment of movie reviews.

In this chapter, we will cover the following topics:

- What are RNNs?
- The evolution path of RNNs
- RNN architectures by input and output (one-to-many, many-to-one, synced, and unsynced many-to-many)
- Vanilla RNN architecture
- Vanilla RNNs for text generation
- Long short-term memory
- LSTM RNNs for text generation
- Gated recurrent unit

- GRU RNNs for stock price prediction
- Bidirectional RNNs
- BRNNs for sentiment classification

What are RNNs?

Recall that in deep feedforward networks, autoencoder neural networks, and CNNs, which we discussed in the previous chapters, data flows one-way from the input layer to the output layer. However, deep learning models allow data to proceed in any direction—even circle back to the input layer—and are not limited to feedforward architectures. Data looping back from the previous output becomes a part of the next input data. RNNs are great examples of this. The general form of RNNs is depicted in the following diagram, and we will be working on several variants of RNNs throughout this chapter:

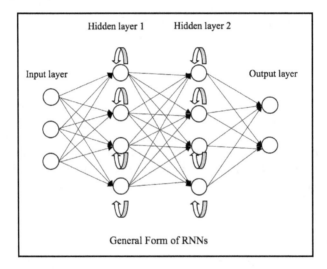

General Form of RNNs

As we can see in the preceding diagram, data from previous time points goes into the training of the current time point. The recurrent architecture makes the models work well with time series (such as product sales, stock price) or sequential inputs (words in articles—DNA sequences, for example).

Suppose we have some inputs, x_t (where t represents a time step or a sequential order), in a traditional neural network, as shown in the following diagram. Let's assume that the inputs at different t are independent of each other. The output of the network at any t can be written as $h_t = f(x_t)$, as shown here:

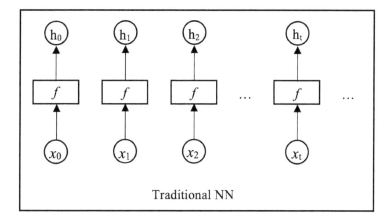

Traditional NN

In RNNs, the feedback loop passes information of the current state to the next, as shown in the unrolled version of the network in the following diagram. The output of the RNN network at any t can be written as $h_t = f(h_{t-1}, x_t)$. The same task f is performed on each element of the sequence, and an output h_t is dependent on the output h_{t-1} of the previous computations. Thanks to this chain-like architecture, or the additional *memory* capturing of what has been calculated so far, there has been great success in applying RNNs to time series and sequence data. Before we apply variants of RNNs to a variety of problems, first, we will take a look at the history of RNNs and their evolution path:

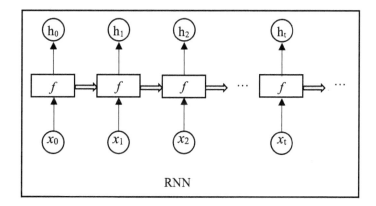

RNN

The evolution path of RNNs

RNNs actually have a long history and were first developed in the 1980s. The Hopfield network, as the first neural network with recurrent links, was invented by John Hopfield in *Neurons with graded response have collective computational properties like those of two-state neurons* (PNAS. 1984 May; 81(10): 3088-3092).

Inspired by the Hopfield network, the fully connected neural network—the Elman network—was introduced in *Finding structure in time* (Cognitive Science, 1990 March; 14(2): 179-211). The Elman network has one hidden layer and a set of context units connected to the hidden layer. At each time step, the context units keep track of the previous values of the hidden units.

In 1992, Schmidhuber discovered the vanishing gradient problem due to memorizing long-term dependencies. Five years later, the **long short-term memory** (**LSTM**) was proposed by Schmidhuber and Hochreiter in *LSTM* (neural computation. 9 (8): 1735-1780). LSTM was augmented by forget gate units, which drop old and irrelevant memory and hence avoid vanishing gradients.

In 1997, an RNN was extended to a bidirectional version (published in *Bidirectional recurrent neural networks*, Journal IEEE Transactions on Signal Processing, 1997 November; 45(11): 2673-2681), where the model was trained on both positive (from beginning to end) and negative (from end to beginning) time direction.

A hierarchical RNN that was introduced in *How Hierarchical Control Self-organizes in Artificial Adaptive Systems* (Adaptive Behavior, 2005 September; 13 (3): 211-225) had both horizontal and vertical recurrent connections, which decomposes complex and adaptive information.

LSTMs have started to prevail since 2007: they outperformed traditional models in certain speech recognition tasks, as reported in *An Application of Recurrent Neural Networks to Discriminative Keyword Spotting* (International Conference on Artificial Neural Networks: 220-229); in 2009, an LSTM model trained by **connectionist temporal classification** (**CTC**) was used for tasks like connected handwriting recognition and phoneme recognition in speech audio. LSTM models also become state-of-the-art solutions for machine translation and language modeling. LSTM is even incorporated with CNNs to automate image captioning, as presented in *Show and Tell: A Neural Image Caption Generator*.

Back in 2014, the GRU RNN was introduced as another improvement over regular RNNs, similar to LSTM. GRU RNNs perform in a similar way to LSTMs on many tasks. However, they demonstrate better performance on smaller datasets, partially because they have fewer parameters to tune, with one less gate in the architecture.

As promised, we will be studying the variants of RNNs in detail and then apply them to real-world problems.

RNN architectures and applications

RNNs can be categorized into *many-to-one*, *one-to-many*, *many-to-many* (synced), and *many-to-many* (unsynced) based on their input and output. From the perspective of hidden layers, the most commonly used RNN architectures include the basic, vanilla RNNs, and the bidirectional ones, LSTM and GRU. We will focus on these four architectures of RNNs, and will start by briefly mentioning those four categories by input and output.

Architectures by input and output

Many-to-one: The *many-to-one* architecture is probably the most intuitive one. We can input as many elements or time steps in the sequence, but the model produces only one output after going through the entire sequence. Its general structure is displayed in the following diagram, where *f* represents one or more recurrent layers:

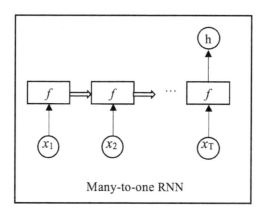

Many-to-one RNN

The **many-to-one** architecture can be used for sentiment analysis, where the model reads the entire customer review (for example) and outputs a sentiment score. Similarly, it can be used to identify the genre of a song after going through the entire audio stream.

One to many: Quite the opposite of a **many-to-one RNN**, the **one-to-many** architecture only takes in one input and produces a sequence of outputs. The **one-to-many** architecture can be presented as follows:

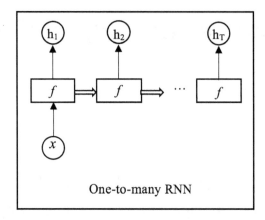

One-to-many RNN

RNNs like these are frequently used to generate sequences. For example, we can use the model to generate music with a starting note or a genre as the sole input. In a similar manner, we can even write a poem in Shakespeare's style with a starting word that we specify.

Many-to-many (synced): The third architecture, **many-to-many (synced)**, facilitates the need for one output per input. As we can see in the following network flow, each output is dependent on all the previous outputs and the current input:

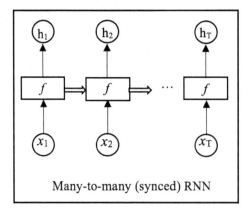

Many-to-many (synced) RNN

One of the common use cases for many-to-many (synced) architectures is time series forecasting, where we want to perform rolling prediction at each time step, given the current and all previous inputs. This architecture is also widely used in **natural language processing** (**NLP**) problems, such as **named-entity recognition** (**NER**), **part-of-speech** (**PoS**) tagging, and speech recognition.

Many-to-many (unsynced): As for the unsynced version of the many-to-many architecture, the model will not generate outputs until it finishes reading the entire input sequence. As a result, the number of outputs can be different from that of the inputs. As we can see in the following diagram, the length of output sequence Ty is not necessarily equal to that of input sequence Tx:

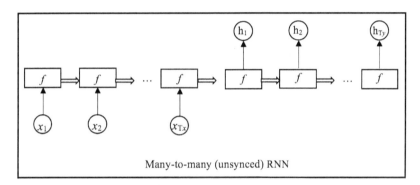

Many-to-many (unsynced) RNN

The unsynced many-to-many architecture is most commonly seen in machine translation. For example, the model reads a whole sentence in English, then starts producing the translated sentence in French. Another popular use case is multi-step ahead forecasting, where we are asked to predict several time steps ahead, given all previous inputs.

So far, we have learned about four RNN architectures by model input and output, and we will be incorporating some of them in the practical examples in rest of this chapter, where we will be mainly discussing architectures in the hidden layer—more specifically, the recurrent layer.

Let's start with the vanilla RNNs, which are the most basic form of recurrent architecture.

Vanilla RNNs

A basic RNN model with its weights annotated and its unfolded version looks as follows:

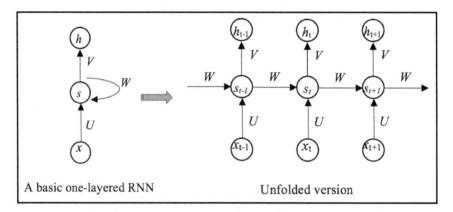

| A basic one-layered RNN | Unfolded version |

Here, **U** is the weights connecting the input layer and the hidden layer, **V** is the weights between the hidden layer and the output layer, and **W** is the weights of the recurrent layer, that is, the feedback layer; s_t is the hidden state at time step **t**, and x_t and h_t are the inputs and outputs at time step **t**, respectively.

Note that we are using only one recurrent layer from now on for simplicity, but we can stack up multiple recurrent layers together, which we will see soon.

The relationship between the layers can be described as follows:

- Hidden state at time step t, s_t is computed based on the current input x_t and the previous hidden state s_{t-1} via $s_t = a(Ux_t + Ws_{t-1})$, where a is the activation function. Typical choices of the activation function for hidden layers in RNNs include tanh and ReLU.
- Similarly, s_{t-1} depends on s_{t-2} : $s_{t-1} = a(Ux_{t-1} + Ws_{t-2})$ and so on. s_1 also depends on s_0, which is set to all zeros by convention.
- With such a dependency over time steps, the hidden states can be viewed as the memory of the network, capturing information from previous time steps.
- The output at time step t is calculated as $h_t = g(Vs_t)$, where g is the activation function. Depending on what task is being performed, it can be a sigmoid function for binary classification, a softmax function for multi-class classification, and a simple linear function for regression.

All the weights *U*, *V*, and *W* are trained using a backpropagation algorithm, similar to traditional neural networks. But the difference is that at current time *t*, we need to compute the loss over all previous *t*-1 time steps besides the current one. This is because weights are shared by all time steps, and outputs at a time step are indirectly dependent on all previous time steps, like the gradients of weights. For instance, if we want to compute the gradients at time step *t* = 5, we need to backpropagate the previous four time steps and sum up gradients over five time steps. This special backpropagation algorithm is called **backpropagation through time (BPTT)**.

In theory, RNNs can capture information from the beginning of the input sequence, which boosts the predictive capability of time series or sequence modeling. However, this is not the case for vanilla RNNs due to the vanishing gradient problem. We will explain this in detail later and will learn about other architectures such as LSTM and GRU that are specifically designed to get around this issue. But for now, let's assume that vanilla RNNs work fine for many cases and gain some hands-on experience with them, as they are the fundamental building blocks of any RNN.

Vanilla RNNs for text generation

As we mentioned previously, RNNs are usually used as language models in the NLP domain, which assign a probability distribution over sequences of words, such as machine translation, PoS tagging, and speech recognition. We are going to work on a rather interesting language for modeling problem-text generation, where RNN models are used to learn the text sequences of a specified domain and then generate entirely new and reasonable text sequences in the desired domain.

The RNN-based text generator can take any input text, such as novels like Harry Potter, poems from Shakespeare, and the movie scripts of Star Wars, and produce its own Harry Potter, Shakespeare poems, and Star Wars movie scripts. The artificial text should be plausible and read similar to the originals if the model has been trained well. In this section, we will use *War and Peace*, a novel by the Russian author Leo Tolstoy, as an example. Feel free to use any of your favorite books for training input. We recommend downloading text data from books that are free of copyright protection. Project Gutenberg (`www.gutenberg.org`) is a great resource for this, with over 57,000 free great books whose copyright has expired.

First, we need to download the `.txt` file of *War and Peace* directly from `https://cs.stanford.edu/people/karpathy/char-rnn/warpeace_input.txt`. Alternatively, we could download it from Project Gutenberg at `http://www.gutenberg.org/ebooks/2600`, but we will have to do some clean-ups, for example, removing the beginning section, *The Project Gutenberg EBook,* and the end section, *End of the Project,* from the file, as well as the table of contents.

We then read the file, convert the text into lower case, and take a quick look at it by printing out the first 100 characters:

```
>>> training_file = 'warpeace_input.txt'
>>> raw_text = open(training_file, 'r').read()
>>> raw_text = raw_text.lower()
>>> raw_text[:100]
'ufeff"well, prince, so genoa and lucca are now just family estates of
thenbuonapartes. but i warn you, i'
```

Now, we need to count how many characters there are in total:

```
>>> n_chars = len(raw_text)
>>> print('Total characters: {}'.format(n_chars))
Total characters: 3196213
```

Then, we can obtain the unique characters and the vocabulary size:

```
>>> chars = sorted(list(set(raw_text)))
>>> n_vocab = len(chars)
>>> print('Total vocabulary (unique characters): {}'.format(n_vocab))
Total vocabulary (unique characters): 57
>>> print(chars)
['n', ' ', '!', '"', "'", '(', ')', '*', ',', '-', '.', '/', '0', '1', '2',
'3', '4', '5', '6', '7', '8', '9', ':', ';', '=', '?', 'a', 'b', 'c', 'd',
'e', 'f', 'g', 'h', 'i', 'j', 'k', 'l', 'm', 'n', 'o', 'p', 'q', 'r', 's',
't', 'u', 'v', 'w', 'x', 'y', 'z', '!!CDP!E.agrave!!', '!!CDP!E.auml!!',
'!!CDP!E.eacute!!', '!!CDP!E.ecirc!!', 'ufeff']
```

Now, we have a raw training dataset composed of more than 3 million characters and 57 unique characters. But how can we feed it to the RNN model?

Recall that in the synced many-to-many architecture, the model takes in sequences and produces sequences at the same time. In our case, we can feed the model with fixed-length sequences of characters. The output sequences are the same length as the input ones, and one character is shifted from their input sequences. Let's say that we set the sequence length to 5, from the word *learning*. Now, we can construct a training sample with the input *learn* and the output *earni*. We can visualize this in the network, like so:

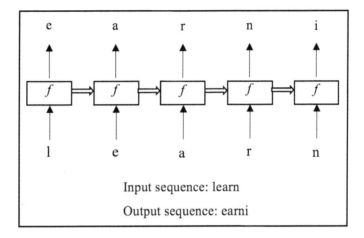

Input sequence: learn

Output sequence: earni

We just constructed a single training sample. As for the whole training set, we can split the raw text data into sequences of equal length, say 100. Each sequence of characters is the input of a training sample.

Next, we split the raw text data into sequences in the same manner, but starting from the second character this time. Each of the resulting sequences is the output of a training sample. For example, given the raw text *deep learning architectures* and 5 as the sequence length, we can create five training samples, as follows:

Input	Output
deep_	eep_l
learn	earni
ing_a	ng_ar
rchit	chite
ectur	cture

Here, _ denotes space.

Note that the last subsequence, *es*, is not long enough, so we can simply ignore it.

Since neural network models only take in numerical data, the input and output sequences of characters are represented by one-hot encoded vectors. We create a dictionary by mapping 57 characters to indices from 0 to 56 and another one the other way around:

```
>>> index_to_char = dict((i, c) for i, c in enumerate(chars))
>>> char_to_index = dict((c, i) for i, c in enumerate(chars))
>>> print(char_to_index)
{'n': 0, ' ': 1, '!': 2, '"': 3, "'": 4, '(': 5, ')': 6, '*': 7, ',': 8, '-
': 9, '.': 10, '/': 11, '0': 12, '1': 13, '2': 14, '3': 15, '4': 16, '5':
17, '6': 18, '7': 19, '8': 20, '9': 21, ':': 22, ';': 23, '=': 24, '?': 25,
'a': 26, 'b': 27, 'c': 28, 'd': 29, 'e': 30, 'f': 31, 'g': 32, 'h': 33,
'i': 34, 'j': 35, 'k': 36, 'l': 37, 'm': 38, 'n': 39, 'o': 40, 'p': 41,
'q': 42, 'r': 43, 's': 44, 't': 45, 'u': 46, 'v': 47, 'w': 48, 'x': 49,
'y': 50, 'z': 51, '!!CDP!E.agrave!!': 52, '!!CDP!E.auml!!': 53,
'!!CDP!E.eacute!!': 54, '!!CDP!E.ecirc!!': 55, 'ufeff': 56}
```

For instance, character e becomes a vector of length 57, with 1 in index 30 and 0s in all other indices. With the character lookup table ready, we can construct the training dataset as follows:

```
>>> import numpy as np
>>> seq_length = 100
>>> n_seq = int(n_chars / seq_length)
```

With the sequence length set to 100, we will have n_seq training samples. Next, we initialize training input and output:

 Note that the sequence length are of shape (number of samples, sequence length, feature dimensionality). Such form is required as we are going to use Keras for RNN model training.

```
>>> X = np.zeros((n_seq, seq_length, n_vocab))
>>> Y = np.zeros((n_seq, seq_length, n_vocab))
```

Assemble each of the n_seq samples:

```
>>> for i in range(n_seq):
...     x_sequence = raw_text[i * seq_length : (i + 1) * seq_length]
...     x_sequence_ohe = np.zeros((seq_length, n_vocab))
...     for j in range(seq_length):
...         char = x_sequence[j]
...         index = char_to_index[char]
...         x_sequence_ohe[j][index] = 1.
...     X[i] = x_sequence_ohe
...     y_sequence =
...             raw_text[i * seq_length + 1 : (i + 1) * seq_length + 1]
```

```
...        y_sequence_ohe = np.zeros((seq_length, n_vocab))
...        for j in range(seq_length):
...            char = y_sequence[j]
...            index = char_to_index[char]
...            y_sequence_ohe[j][index] = 1.
...        Y[i] = y_sequence_ohe
>>> X.shape
(31962, 100, 57)
>>> Y.shape
(31962, 100, 57)
```

Again, each sample is composed of 100 elements of one-hot encoded characters. We finally have the training dataset ready, and now it is the time to build our vanilla RNN model. Let's train a model with two recurrent layers stacked up, as follows:

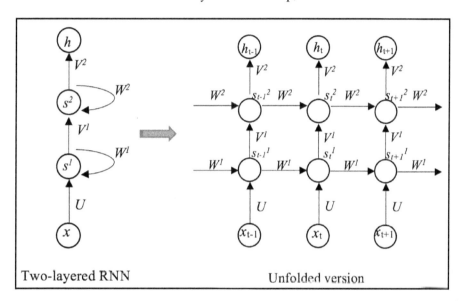

Each layer contains 800 units, with a dropout ratio of 0.3 and ReLU as the activation function. First, import all the necessary modules:

```
>>> from keras.models import Sequential
>>> from keras.layers.core import Dense, Activation, Dropout
>>> from keras.layers.recurrent import SimpleRNN
>>> from keras.layers.wrappers import TimeDistributed
>>> from keras import optimizers
```

Now, specify other hyperparameters, including batch size and number of epochs, besides the number of hidden layers and units and the dropout ratio:

```
>>> batch_size = 100
>>> n_layer = 2
>>> hidden_units = 800
>>> n_epoch= 300
>>> dropout = 0.3
```

Now, create and compile the network:

```
>>> model = Sequential()
>>> model.add(SimpleRNN(hidden_units, input_shape=
          (None, n_vocab),return_sequences=True, activation='relu'))
>>> model.add(Dropout(dropout))
>>> for i in range(n_layer - 1):
...      model.add(SimpleRNN(hidden_units, return_sequences=True,
                    activation='relu'))
...      model.add(Dropout(dropout))
>>> model.add(TimeDistributed(Dense(n_vocab)))
>>> model.add(Activation('softmax'))
```

There are a few things to note regarding the model we just put together:

- `return_sequences=True`: The output of the recurrent layers becomes a sequence, enabling a many-to-many architecture, like we wanted. Otherwise, it would become many-to-one, with the last element as output.
- `TimeDistributed`: Since the output of the recurrent layers is a sequence, while the next layer—the dense layer—doesn't take sequential input, a `TimeDistributed` wrap is used as an adaptor to get around this.
- `Softmax`: Such an activation is used since the model generates a one-hot encoded character vector.

As for the optimizer, we will choose RMSprop, with a learning rate of `0.001`:

```
>>> optimizer = optimizers.RMSprop(lr=0.001, rho=0.9,
                            epsilon=1e-08, decay=0.0)
>>> model.compile(loss="categorical_crossentropy",optimizer=optimizer)
```

With the loss metric of multi-class cross entropy added, we have finished building our model. We can take a look at the summary of the model by using the following code:

```
>>> print(model.summary())
```

```
Layer (type) Output Shape Param #
=================================================================
simple_rnn_1 (SimpleRNN) (None, None, 800) 686400

dropout_1 (Dropout) (None, None, 800) 0

simple_rnn_2 (SimpleRNN) (None, None, 800) 1280800

dropout_2 (Dropout) (None, None, 800) 0

time_distributed_1 (TimeDist (None, None, 57) 45657

activation_1 (Activation) (None, None, 57) 0
=================================================================
Total params: 2,012,857
Trainable params: 2,012,857
Non-trainable params: 0
```

We have more than 2 million parameters to train. But before we start the long training procedure, it is good practice to set up some callbacks in order to keep track of statistics and internal states of the model during training. The callback functions we will employ include the following:

- Model checkpoint, which saves the model after each epoch so that we can load the latest saved model and resume training from there if it stops unexpectedly.
- Early stopping, which stops training when performance in loss does not improve anymore.
- Checking text generation results on a regular base. We want to see how reasonable the generated text is, and the training loss is not tangible enough.

These functions are defined or initialized as follows:

```
>>> from keras.callbacks import Callback, ModelCheckpoint, EarlyStopping
>>> file_path =file_path =
                "weights/weights_epoch_{epoch:03d}_loss_{loss:.4f}.hdf5"
>>> checkpoint = ModelCheckpoint(file_path, monitor='loss',
                        verbose=1, save_best_only=True, mode='min')
```

The model checkpoints will be saved with the epoch number and the training loss in the filename. We also monitor the validation loss at the same time and see if it stops decreasing for 50 successive epochs:

```
>>> early_stop = EarlyStopping(monitor='loss', min_delta=0,
                               patience=50, verbose=1, mode='min')
```

Next, we have the callback for quality monitoring. First, we write a helper function that generates text of any length given our RNN model:

```
>>> def generate_text(model, gen_length, n_vocab, index_to_char):
...     """
...     Generating text using the RNN model
...     @param model: current RNN model
...     @param gen_length: number of characters we want to generate
...     @param n_vocab: number of unique characters
...     @param index_to_char: index to character mapping
...     @return: string of text generated
...     """
...     # Start with a randomly picked character
...     index = np.random.randint(n_vocab)
...     y_char = [index_to_char[index]]
...     X = np.zeros((1, gen_length, n_vocab))
...     for i in range(gen_length):
...         X[0, i, index] = 1.
...         indices = np.argmax(model.predict(
...                 X[:, max(0, i - seq_length -1):i + 1, :])[0], 1)
...         index = indices[-1]
...         y_char.append(index_to_char[index])
...     return ('').join(y_char)
```

It starts with a randomly picked character. The input model then predicts each of the remaining `gen_length-1` characters based on past generated characters that are of a length up to 100 (sequence length).

We can now define the `callback` class that generates text for every *N* epochs:

```
>>> class ResultChecker(Callback):
...     def __init__(self, model, N, gen_length):
...         self.model = model
...         self.N = N
...         self.gen_length = gen_length
...
...     def on_epoch_end(self, epoch, logs={}):
...         if epoch % self.N == 0:
...             result = generate_text(self.model, self.gen_length,
...                                     n_vocab, index_to_char)
...             print('nMy War and Peace:n' + result)
```

Now that all the components are ready, let's start training the model:

```
>>> model.fit(X, Y, batch_size=batch_size, verbose=1, epochs=n_epoch,
    callbacks=[ResultChecker(model, 10, 200), checkpoint, early_stop])
```

The generator writes 200 characters for every 10 epochs. We can see the progress bar for each epoch with verbose set to 1 (while 0 is silent mode and 2 shows no progress bar).

The followings are the results for epochs 1, 11, 51, and 101:

Epoch 1:

```
Epoch 1/300
 8000/31962 [======>.....................] - ETA: 51s - loss: 2.8891
31962/31962 [==============================] - 67s 2ms/step - loss: 2.1955
My War and Peace:
 5 the count of the stord and the stord and the stord and the stord and the
stord and the stord and the stord and the stord and the stord and the stord
and the stord and the stord and the stord and the
Epoch 00001: loss improved from inf to 2.19552, saving model to
weights/weights_epoch_001_loss_2.19552.hdf5
```

Epoch 11:

```
Epoch 11/300
  100/31962 [..............................] - ETA: 1:26 - loss: 1.2321
31962/31962 [==============================] - 66s 2ms/step - loss: 1.2493
My War and Peace:
 ?" said the countess was a strange the same time the countess was already
been and said that he was so strange to the countess was already been and
the same time the countess was already been and said
Epoch 00011: loss improved from 1.26144 to 1.24933, saving model to
weights/weights_epoch_011_loss_1.2493.hdf5
```

Epoch 51:

```
Epoch 51/300
 31962/31962 [==============================] - 66s 2ms/step - loss: 1.1562
My War and Peace:
 !!CDP!E.agrave!! to see him and the same thing is the same thing to him
and the same thing the same thing is the same thing to him and the same
thing the same thing is the same thing to him and the same thing the sam
Epoch 00051: loss did not improve from 1.14279
```

Epoch 101:

```
Epoch 101/300
 31962/31962 [==============================] - 67s 2ms/step - loss: 1.1736
My War and Peace:
 = the same thing is to be a soldier in the same way to the soldiers and
the same thing is the same to me to see him and the same thing is the same
to me to see him and the same thing is the same to me
Epoch 00101: loss did not improve from 1.11891
```

The training stops early at epoch 203:

```
Epoch 00203: loss did not improve from 1.10864
Epoch 00203: early stopping
```

Each epoch takes around 1 minute on a Tesla K80 GPU. With around 3.5 hours of training, loss decreases from 2.19552 to 1.10864.

It generates the following text at epoch 151:

```
which was a strange and serious expression of his face and shouting and
said that the countess was standing beside him.
"what a battle is a strange and serious and strange and so that the
countess was
```

Our *War and Peace* reads fine, although a little nonsensical. Can we do better by tweaking the hyperparameters of this vanilla RNN model? Absolutely, but it isn't worth it. As we mentioned earlier, it is very difficult to train a vanilla RNN model to solve problems that require learning long-term dependencies—dependencies between steps that are far away are usually critical to the prediction. However, due to the vanishing gradient issue, the vanilla RNNs are only able to capture the temporal dependencies between a few early steps in the sequence. Architectures such as LSTM and GRU are specifically designed to get around this issue. We will explain how they maintain information in memory over time in the following two sections.

LSTM RNNs

The architecture of LSTM is where its magic comes from: on top of the plain recurrent cell, a memory unit and three information gates are added to handle long-term dependencies. The recurrent cell of an LSTM is depicted as follows (we have also brought up the vanilla one for comparison):

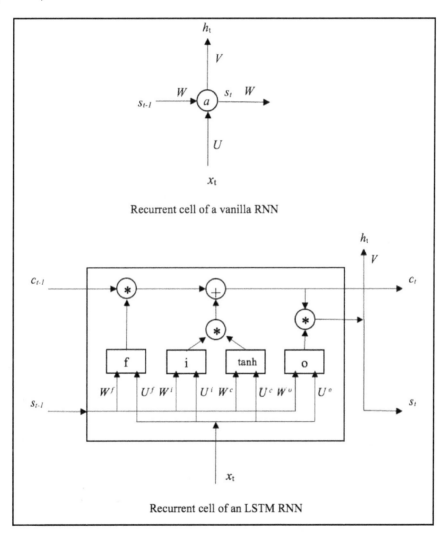

Recurrent cell of a vanilla RNN

Recurrent cell of an LSTM RNN

From left to right in the preceding diagram, the key components are explained as follows:

- c_t is the **memory unit**, which memorizes context from the very beginning of the input sequence.
- **f** represents the **forget gate**, which controls how much information from the previous memory state c_{t-1} can pass forward. Weights associated with the forget gate include W^f, which is connected with the previous hidden state S_{t-1}, and u^f, which is connected with the current input x_t.
- **i** stands for the **input gate**, which determines how much information from the current input can go through. Weights W^i and U^i connect it with the previous hidden state and current input, respectively.
- The **tanh** is just the activation function for the hidden state, and is computed based on the current input x_t and the previous hidden state s_{t-1} with their corresponding weights, W^c and U^c. It is exactly the same as the "a" in vanilla RNN.
- **o** serves as the **output gate**, which defines how much information from the internal memory is used as the output of the entire recurrent cell. Similarly, W^o and U^o are the associated weights.

Accordingly, the relationship between these components can be summarized as follows:

- Output of the forget gate *f* at time step t is computed as $f = sigmoid(U^f x_t + W^f s_{t-1})$.
- Output of the input gate *i* at time step t is computed as $i = sigmoid(U^i x_t + W^i s_{t-1})$.
- Output of the tanh activation *c'* at time step t is computed as $c' = tanh(U^c x_t + W^c s_{t-1})$.
- Output of the output gate *o* at time step t is computed as $o = sigmoid(U^o x_t + W^o s_{t-1})$.
- Memory unit c_t at time step *t* is updated by $c_t = f.\ast c_{t-1} + i.\ast c'$, where $.\ast$ denotes element-wise multiplication. It is worth noting that the sigmoid function in *f* and *i* transform their outputs to the range from *0* to *1*, governing the proportion of previous memory c_{t-1} and current memory input c' passing through, respectively.
- Finally, hidden state s_t at time step *t* is updated as $s_t = o.\ast c_t$. Again, *o* decides the proportion of the updated memory unit c_t that's used as the output of the entire cell.

All four sets of weights *U* and *W* are trained using backpropagation through time, which is identical to vanilla RNNs. By learning these weights for three information gates, the network explicitly models long-term dependencies. Next, we will take advantage of the LSTM architecture and invent a more powerful text generator.

LSTM RNNs for text generation

In the LSTM-based text generator, we will increase the sequence length to 160 characters, since it handles long sequences better. Remember to regenerate the training set *X* and *Y* with the new `seq_length` = 160.

In order to easily compare this model's performance with the previous vanilla model, we will keep a similar structure—two recurrent layers, with each of the two recurrent layers containing 800 units, a dropout ratio of 0.4, and *tanh* (by default) as the activation function:

```
>>> from keras.layers.recurrent import LSTM
>>> batch_size = 100
>>> n_layer = 2
>>> hidden_units = 800
>>> n_epoch= 300
>>> dropout = 0.4
```

Now, create and compile the network:

```
>>> model = Sequential()
>>> model.add(LSTM(hidden_units, input_shape=(None, n_vocab),
                                     return_sequences=True))
>>> model.add(Dropout(dropout))
>>> for i in range(n_layer - 1):
...     model.add(LSTM(hidden_units, return_sequences=True))
...     model.add(Dropout(dropout))
>>> model.add(TimeDistributed(Dense(n_vocab)))
>>> model.add(Activation('softmax'))
```

The optimizer, RMSprop, comes with a learning rate of 0.001:

```
>>> optimizer = optimizers.RMSprop(lr=0.001, rho=0.9,
                                     epsilon=1e-08, decay=0.0)
>>> model.compile(loss="categorical_crossentropy", optimizer=optimizer)
```

Let's summarize the LSTM model we just assembled:

```
>>> print(model.summary())
```

Layer (type)	Output Shape	Param #
lstm_1 (LSTM)	(None, None, 800)	2745600
dropout_1 (Dropout)	(None, None, 800)	0
lstm_2 (LSTM)	(None, None, 800)	5123200
dropout_2 (Dropout)	(None, None, 800)	0
time_distributed_1 (TimeDist	(None, None, 57)	45657
activation_1 (Activation)	(None, None, 57)	0

```
Total params: 7,914,457
Trainable params: 7,914,457
Non-trainable params: 0
```

There are 8 million parameters to train—almost four times as many as there were in the vanilla model. Let's start training them:

```
>>> model.fit(X, Y, batch_size=batch_size, verbose=1, epochs=n_epoch,
        callbacks=[ResultChecker(model, 10, 500), checkpoint, early_stop])
```

The generator writes 500 characters long text for every 10 epochs.

The followings are the results for epochs 151, 201, and 251:

Epoch 151:

```
Epoch 151/300
 19976/19976 [==============================] - 250s 12ms/step - loss:
0.7300
My War and Peace:
 ing to the countess. "i have nothing to do with him and i have nothing to
do with the general," said prince andrew.

"i am so sorry for the princess, i am so since he will not be able to say
anything. i saw him long ago. i am so sincerely that i am not to
 blame for it. i am sure that something is so much talk about the emperor
alexander's personal attention."

"why do you say that?" and she recognized in his son's presence.
```

"well, and how is she?" asked pierre.

"the prince is very good to make

Epoch 00151: loss improved from 0.73175 to 0.73003, saving model to
weights/weights_epoch_151_loss_0.7300.hdf5

Epoch 201:

Epoch 201/300
 19976/19976 [==============================] - 248s 12ms/step - loss:
0.6794
My War and Peace:
 was all the same to him. he received a story proved that the count had not
yet seen the countess and the other and asked to be able to start a tender
man than the world. she was not a family affair and was at the same time as
in the same way. a few minutes later the count had been at home with his
smile and said:

"i am so glad! well, what does that mean? you will see that you are always
the same."

"you know i have not come to the conclusion that i should like to
 send my private result. the prin

Epoch 00201: loss improved from 0.68000 to 0.67937, saving model to
weights/weights_epoch_151_loss_0.6793.hdf5

Epoch 251:

Epoch 251/300
 19976/19976 [==============================] - 249s 12ms/step - loss:
0.6369
My War and Peace:
 nd the countess was sitting in a single look on
 her face.

"why should you be ashamed?"

"why do you say that?" said princess mary. "why didn't you say a word of
this?" said prince andrew with a smile.

"you would not like that for my sake, prince vasili's son, have you seen
the rest of the two?"

"well, i am suffering," replied the princess with a sigh. "well, what a
delightful norse?" he shouted.

```
the convoy and driving away the flames of the battalions of the first
  day of the orthodox russian

Epoch 00251: loss improved from 0.63715 to 0.63689, saving model to
weights/weights_epoch_251_loss_0.6368.hdf5
```

Finally, at epoch 300, the training stops with a loss of 0.6001.

Each epoch takes around four to five minutes to complete on a Tesla K80 GPU. With around 22 hours of training, the text generator is able to write a more realistic and interesting *War and Peace* script thanks to the LSTM architecture.

Moreover, LSTM RNNs for character generation are not limited to text. They can learn from any character data, such as source codes, HTML, LaTex, and hopefully write software programs, web pages, and scientific papers automatically.

GRU RNNs

GRU, the alternative architecture with a gating mechanism, was invented more than a decade after LSTM. GRU and LSTM perform comparably, with one outperforming the other in some cases. However, GRU has only two information gates, which is slightly less complex than LSTM. The recurrent cell of a GRU is depicted as follows:

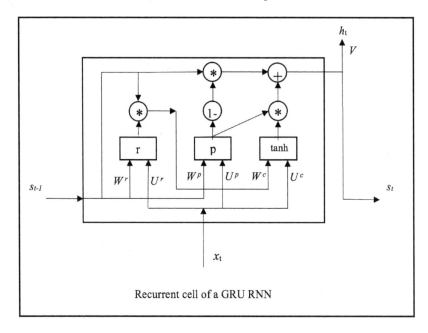

Recurrent cell of a GRU RNN

The key components, from left to right in the preceding diagram, are explained as follows:

- **r** represents the **reset gate**, which controls how much information from the previous memory s_{t-1} to forget. Given the weights W^r connected to the previous hidden state s_{t-1} and U^r connected to the current input x_t, the output of the reset gate r at time step t is computed as $r = sigmoid(U^r x_t + W^r s_{t-1})$.

- **p** stands for the **update gate**, which determines how much information from the previous memory can pass through. With weights W^p and U^p connected to the previous memory state and current input, respectively, the output of the update gate p at time step t is computed as $p = sigmoid(U^p x_t + W^p s_{t-1})$.

- The **tanh** is the activation function for the hidden state, and is computed based on the current input x_t and the reset of the previous memory state. Given their corresponding weights, W^c and U^c, the output of the current memory c' at time step t is computed as $c' = tanh[U^c x_t + W^c(r.*s_{t-1})]$.

- Finally, hidden state s_t at time step t is updated as $s_t = (1-p).*c' + p.*s_{t-1}$. Again, p decides the proportion of previous memory that's used to update the current one—the closer to 1, the more previous memory to keep; the closer to 0, the more current memory take place.

- Interestingly, if p is an all-zero vector and r is an all-one vector—say we don't explicitly keep any previous memory—the network is simply a vanilla RNN.

Overall, GRU is very similar to LSTM. Both of them use a grating mechanism to model long-term, and the gate-related parameters are trained via BPTT. However, there are a few differences worth noting:

- There are three information gates in LSTM, while there are only two in GRU.
- The update gate in GRU takes the responsibility of the input gate and the forget gate in LSTM.
- The reset gate in GRU is directly applied to the previous hidden state.
- LSTM explicitly models memory unit C_t, while GRU doesn't.
- Additional nonlinearity is applied to the updated hidden state in LSTM.
- LSTM was introduced in 1997 and has been studied and widely used for recent years; GRU was invented in 2014 and has not been fully explored yet. That is why LSTM is more popular than GRU, even though one outperforming the other is not guaranteed.
- It is commonly believed that training GRU RNNs is relatively faster and requires less data than LSTM since GRU RNNs have fewer parameters. Hence, some argue that GRU works better with small training sets.

Despite the remaining mystery, we are going to apply GRU RNNs to a billion (or trillion) dollar problem: stock price prediction.

GRU RNNs for stock price prediction

Predicting stocks interests many people. For years, a large number of methods have been developed to predict stock prices using machine learning techniques. For example, in *Chapter 7* of *Python Machine Learning by Example* by Yuxi Hayden Liu (Packt Publishing), linear regression, random forest, and support vector machines were used to predict stock prices. In traditional machine learning solutions like this, feature engineering is probably the stage taking the most effort. It is the process of manually creating domain-specific features or signals that are more significant for targeting prediction than the raw inputs. Typical invented features include x-day moving average, volatility over periods of time, and x-day return. On the contrary, RNN-based deep learning solutions do not involve manual featuring crafting, but figure out timely or sequential relationships themselves. We will demonstrate the power of the recurrent architecture by forecasting the **Dow Jones Industrial Average** (**DJIA**) with GRU RNNs.

Although we are emphasizing the advantages of deep learning, we do not assert that deep learning methods are superior to traditional machine learning methods. There is no *one size fits all* in machine learning.

Consisting of 30 large and significant stocks (such as Apple, IBM, GE, and Goldman Sachs) in the United States, DJIA is one of the most commonly watched market indexes by investors worldwide. It represents a quarter of the value of the entire US market, which makes the project more exciting.

We can view its historical daily data at `https://finance.yahoo.com/quote/%5EDJI/history?p=%5EDJI`. A screenshot of some of this data is as follows:

Dow Jones Industrial Average (^DJI)						

DJI - DJI Real Time Price. Currency in USD

24,361.45 -391.64 (-1.58%)

At close: 4:53PM EDT

Summary Chart Conversations Options Components **Historical Data**

Time Period: May 29, 2017 - May 29, 2018 ∨   Show: Historical Prices ∨   Frequency: Daily ∨   **Apply**

Currency in USD   ⬇ Download Data

Date	Open	High	Low	Close*	Adj Close**	Volume
May 29, 2018	24,606.59	24,635.18	24,247.84	24,361.45	24,361.45	395,810,000
May 25, 2018	24,781.29	24,824.22	24,687.81	24,753.09	24,753.09	257,210,000
May 24, 2018	24,877.36	24,877.36	24,605.90	24,811.76	24,811.76	347,050,000
May 23, 2018	24,757.71	24,889.46	24,667.12	24,886.81	24,886.81	399,610,000
May 22, 2018	25,047.55	25,064.99	24,812.06	24,834.41	24,834.41	288,200,000
May 21, 2018	24,883.06	25,086.49	24,883.06	25,013.29	25,013.29	308,920,000
May 18, 2018	24,707.72	24,774.97	24,664.87	24,715.09	24,715.09	269,700,000
May 17, 2018	24,752.40	24,839.49	24,639.40	24,713.98	24,713.98	314,650,000
May 16, 2018	24,722.32	24,801.19	24,672.79	24,768.93	24,768.93	280,810,000

Five values illustrate the stock movements on trading days over time: open and close, that is, the starting and final price on a trading day, low and high, that is, the range of prices stock traded at, and volume, that is, the total number of shares traded on a trading day. As an example, we will be focusing on using historical close prices to forecast future close prices. But it is also feasible to incorporate four other indicators.

Let's start with data acquisition and exploration. First, we will download the data from 2001-01-01 to 2017-12-31: in the same web page, change the time period to **Jan 01, 2001 - Dec 31, 2017**. Click the **Apply** button, and finally click **Download Data**. We can then load and take a peek at the data:

```
>>> import numpy as np
>>> import matplotlib.pyplot as plt
>>> import pandas as pd
>>> raw_data = pd.read_csv('^DJI.csv')
>>> raw_data.head()
       Date        Open        High        Low        Close
```

```
0  2001-01-02  10790.919922  10797.019531  10585.360352  10646.150391
1  2001-01-03  10637.419922  11019.049805  10581.089844  10945.750000
2  2001-01-04  10944.940430  11028.000000  10888.419922  10912.410156
3  2001-01-05  10912.809570  10919.419922  10627.750000  10662.009766
4  2001-01-08  10658.730469  10700.849609  10516.019531  10621.349609

     Adj Close     Volume
0  10646.150391  253300000
1  10945.750000  420720000
2  10912.410156  382800000
3  10662.009766  272650000
4  10621.349609  225780000
```

Plot the close price data using the following lines of codes:

```
>>> data = raw_data.Close.values
>>> len(data)
4276
>>> plt.plot(data)
>>> plt.xlabel('Time period')
>>> plt.ylabel('Price')
>>> plt.show()
```

The previous code will create the following graph:

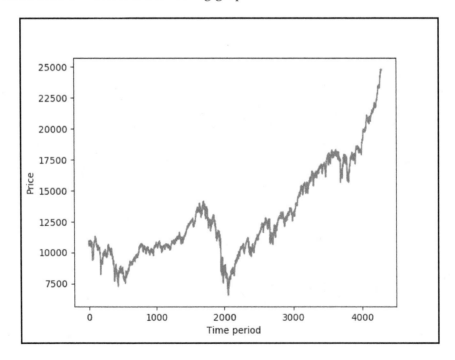

There are, on average, 252 trading days in a year. That is why there are only 4,276 data points over the 17 years that have been selected.

Next, we need to construct sequential inputs from the raw time series in order to feed the RNN model, similar to what we did in text generation. Recall that in the "many-to-one" architecture, the model takes in a sequence and produces one output after going through all the time steps in the sequence. In our case, we can feed the RNN model with sequences of prices in the past T days and output the price of the next day.

Denote the price time series as $x_1, x_2, \ldots, x_n$ (N=4276), and take $T=5$ as an example. By doing this, we can create training samples, as follows:

Input	Output
$\{x_1, x_2, x_3, x_4, x_5\}$	x_6
$\{x_2, x_3, x_4, x_5, x_6\}$	x_7
$\{x_3, x_4, x_5, x_6, x_7\}$	x_8
......	...
$\{x_{n-1}, x_{N-4}, x_{N-3}, x_{N-2}, x_{N-1}\}$	x_n

Here, we forecast the price of the next day by looking back at the previous 5 trading days (a week). We also depict it in the network:

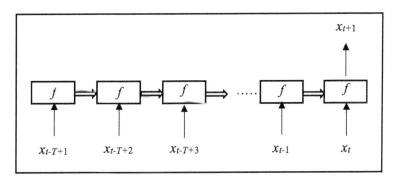

Accordingly, we implement the sequence generation function:

```
>>> def generate_seq(data, window_size):
...     """
...     Transform input series into input sequences and outputs based
        on a specified window size
...     @param data: input series
...     @param window_size: int
...     @return: numpy array of input sequences, numpy array of outputs
...     """
...     X, Y = [], []
...     for i in range(window_size, len(data)):
...         X.append(data[i - window_size:i])
...         Y.append(data[i])
...     return np.array(X), np.array(Y)
```

Then, we construct the input and output dataset with *T=10* (2 week look back):

```
>>> window_size = 10
>>> X, Y = generate_seq(data, window_size)
>>> X.shape
(4266, 10)
>>> Y.shape
(4266,)
```

Next, we split the data into 70% training and 30% testing:

```
>>> train_ratio = 0.7
>>> train_n = int(len(Y) * train_ratio)
>>> X_train = X[:train_n]
>>> Y_train = Y[:train_n]
>>> X_test = X[train_n:]
>>> Y_test = Y[train_n:]
```

Can we now start modelling on the training data? Of course not—data scaling or preprocessing is needed. As we can see from the preceding plot, the testing data is out of scale with the training data, not to mention future data. The regression model is unable to predict values that are out of scale. To solve this issue, we usually scale the data to a given range, such as 0 to 1, using min-max scaling $(x_{scaled} = (x - x_{min})/(x_{max} - x_{min}))$. However, there is no reliable way to predict x_{max} (or x_{min}) for stocks. This is unlike cases where min and max value are known, for instance, 0 and 255 in image prediction. To get around this, we normalize the prices within each window. We simply divide each price in a time window by the last known price. Using the previous *T=5* example again, we can preprocess the training samples as follows:

Input	Output
$\left\{ \dfrac{x_1}{x_1}, \dfrac{x_2}{x_2}, \dfrac{x_3}{x_3}, \dfrac{x_4}{x_4}, \dfrac{x_5}{x_5} \right\}$	$\dfrac{x_6}{x_5}$
$\left\{ \dfrac{x_2}{x_6}, \dfrac{x_3}{x_6}, \dfrac{x_4}{x_6}, \dfrac{x_5}{x_6}, \dfrac{x_6}{x_6} \right\}$	$\dfrac{x_7}{x_6} \dfrac{x_7}{x_6}$
$\left\{ \dfrac{x_1}{x_5}, \dfrac{x_2}{x_5}, \dfrac{x_3}{x_5}, \dfrac{x_4}{x_5}, \dfrac{x_5}{x_5} \right\}$	$\dfrac{x_8}{x_7} \dfrac{x_8}{x_7}$
......	...
$\left\{ \dfrac{x_{n-5}}{x_{n-1}}, \dfrac{x_{n-4}}{x_{n-1}}, \dfrac{x_{n-3}}{x_{n-1}}, \dfrac{x_{n-2}}{x_{n-1}}, \dfrac{x_{n-1}}{x_{n-1}} \right\}$	$\dfrac{x_N}{x_{N-1}}$

We basically convert the absolute values into relative values. The preprocessing function is implemented as follows:

```
>>> def scale(X, Y):
...        """
...        Scaling the prices within each window
...        @param X: input series
...        @param Y: outputs
...        @return: scaled input series and outputs
...        """
...        X_processed, Y_processed = np.copy(X), np.copy(Y)
...        for i in range(len(X)):
...            x = X[i, -1]
...            X_processed[i] /= x
...            Y_processed[i] /= x
...        return X_processed, Y_processed
```

Scale both the training and testing data:

```
>>> X_train_scaled, Y_train_scaled = scale(X_train, Y_train)
>>> X_test_scaled, Y_test_scaled = scale(X_test, Y_test)
```

It is finally time to build the GRU RNN model:

```
>>> from keras.models import Sequential
>>> from keras.layers import Dense, GRU
>>> from keras import optimizers
>>> model = Sequential()
>>> model.add(GRU(256, input_shape=(window_size, 1)))
>>> model.add(Dense(1))
```

Here, we are designing a relatively simple model, with one recurrent layer of 256 units since we only have 2,986 training samples. For the optimizer, RMSprop is used, with a learning rate of 0.006 to minimize the mean squared error:

```
>>> optimizer = optimizers.RMSprop(lr=0.0006, rho=0.9,
                                   epsilon=1e-08, decay=0.0)
>>> model.compile(loss='mean_squared_error', optimizer=optimizer)
```

We also use TensorBoard as the callback function, besides early stopping and model checkpoint. TensorBoard is a performance visualization tool from TensorFlow that provides dynamic graphs for training and validation metrics:

```
>>> from keras.callbacks import TensorBoard, EarlyStopping, ModelCheckpoint
>>> tensorboard = TensorBoard(log_dir='./logs/run1/',
                             write_graph=True, write_images=False)
```

Validation loss is the metric that's used in both early stopping and model checkpoint:

```
>>> early_stop = EarlyStopping(monitor='val_loss', min_delta=0,
                              patience=100, verbose=1, mode='min')
>>> model_file = "weights/best_model.hdf5"
>>> checkpoint = ModelCheckpoint(model_file, monitor='val_loss',
                                verbose=1, save_best_only=True, mode='min')
```

As always, reshape the input data in order to feed the Keras RNN model:

```
>>> X_train_reshaped = X_train_scaled.reshape(
                          (X_train_scaled.shape[0], X_train_scaled.shape[1],
1))
>>> X_test_reshaped = X_test_scaled.reshape(
                          (X_test_scaled.shape[0], X_test_scaled.shape[1], 1))
```

The model is fit against the training set and validated by the testing set, with a maximum epoch of `300` and a batch size of `100`:

```
>>> model.fit(X_train_reshaped, Y_train_scaled, validation_data=
            (X_test_reshaped, Y_test_scaled), epochs=300, batch_size=100,
            verbose=1, callbacks=[tensorboard, early_stop, checkpoint])
```

Here are results from epochs 1, 11, 52, and 99:

Epoch 1:

```
Epoch 1/300
2986/2986 [==============================] - 1s 386us/step - loss: 0.0641 -
val_loss: 0.0038
Epoch 00001: val_loss improved from inf to 0.00383, saving model to
weights/best_model.hdf5
```

Epoch 11:

```
Epoch 11/300
2986/2986 [==============================] - 1s 353us/step - loss: 0.0014 -
val_loss: 9.0839e-04
Epoch 00011: val_loss improved from 0.00128 to 0.00091, saving model to
weights/best_model.hdf5
```

Epoch 52:

```
Epoch 52/300
2986/2986 [==============================] - 1s 415us/step - loss:
4.2122e-04 - val_loss: 6.0911e-05
Epoch 00052: val_loss improved from 0.00010 to 0.00006, saving model to
weights/best_model.hdf5
```

Epoch 99:

```
Epoch 99/300
2986/2986 [==============================] - 1s 391us/step - loss:
2.1644e-04 - val_loss: 5.2291e-05
Epoch 00099: val_loss improved from 0.00005 to 0.00005, saving model to
weights/best_model.hdf5
```

Each epoch takes about 1 second to complete on a CPU (Core i7). Training stops at epoch 242 as validation loss does not decrease anymore:

```
Epoch 241/300
2986/2986 [==============================] - 1s 370us/step - loss:
1.9895e-04 - val_loss: 7.5277e-05
Epoch 00241: val_loss did not improve

Epoch 242/300
2986/2986 [==============================] - 1s 368us/step - loss:
1.9372e-04 - val_loss: 9.1636e-05
Epoch 00242: val_loss did not improve
Epoch 00242: early stopping
```

Meanwhile, we can check out TensorBoard by typing the following command line in the Terminal:

```
tensorboard --logdir=logs
```

It returns the following output:

```
Starting TensorBoard b'41' on port 6006
(You can navigate to http://192.168.0.12:6006)
```

If you go to http://192.168.0.12:6006, you will be able to see the training losses and validation losses over time.

Training losses with smoothing = 0 (no exponential smoothing):

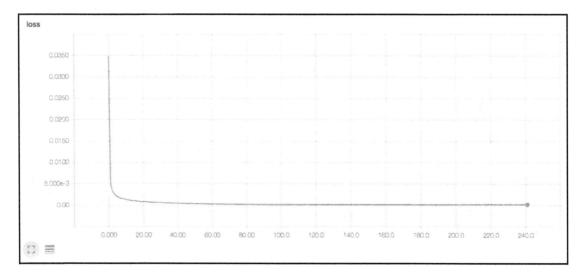

Validation losses with smoothing = 0 (no exponential smoothing):

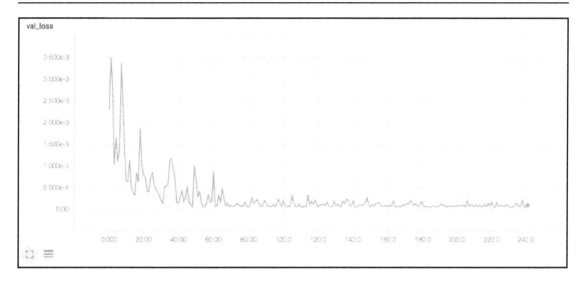

Learning goes well, with both losses decreasing over time. We can further visualize the prediction by comparing it with the ground truth. First, load the best model we just obtained and compute the prediction for both of the training data and the testing data:

```
>>> from keras.models import load_model
>>> model = load_model(model_file)
>>> pred_train_scaled = model.predict(X_train_reshaped)
>>> pred_test_scaled = model.predict(X_test_reshaped)
```

We also need to convert the scaled predictions back into their original scale. We can write a function to facilitate this:

```
>>> def reverse_scale(X, Y_scaled):
...     """
...     Convert the scaled outputs to the original scale
...     @param X: original input series
...     @param Y_scaled: scaled outputs
...     @return: outputs in original scale
...     """
...     Y_original = np.copy(Y_scaled)
...     for i in range(len(X)):
...         x = X[i, -1]
...         Y_original[i] *= x
...     return Y_original
```

Apply reverse scaling to the scaled predictions:

```
>>> pred_train = reverse_scale(X_train, pred_train_scaled)
>>> pred_test = reverse_scale(X_test, pred_test_scaled)
```

Finally, plot the prediction, along with the ground truth:

```
>>> plt.plot(Y)
>>> plt.plot(np.concatenate([pred_train, pred_test]))
>>> plt.xlabel('Time period')
>>> plt.ylabel('Price')
>>> plt.legend(['original series','prediction'],loc='center left')
>>> plt.show()
```

The previous code will create the following graph:

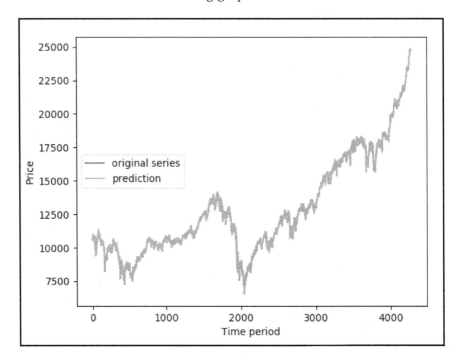

The resulting plot shows that the prediction is quite accurate. For comparison purposes, we also included an under performing result by using a model that was trained with only 10 epochs:

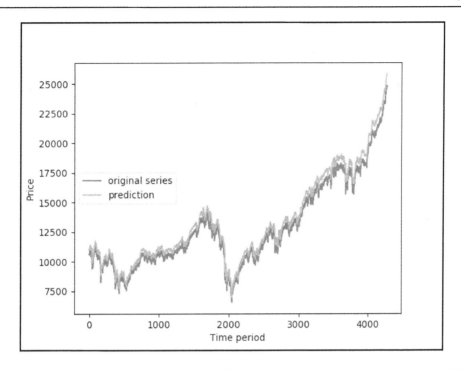

It should be noted that this project is mainly for demonstrating the application of GRU RNNs and not for actual stock trading. In reality, it is a lot more complicated and many external and internal factors should be considered, such as fundamentals, technical patterns, interest rates, volatility, cycles, news, and sentiment.

Bidirectional RNNs

In the RNN architectures we've discussed so far, information of the input sequence is learned in one direction—from the past to the current state, to the future. It restricts the current state from leveraging future input information. Let's look at a simple example of missing word generation:

```
He said, "Machine __ combines computer science and statistics."
```

It is difficult for an RNN model learning only the first three words to generate the next word that fits in the entire sentence. However, if the remaining words are given, the model will capture the context better and have a higher chance of predicting the next word, that is, `learning`. **Bidirectional RNNs (BRNNs)** were introduced to overcome the limitations of one-directional RNNs.

In BRNNs, a hidden layer is composed of two independent recurrent layers. These two layers are of opposite directions: one for positive time direction, also called **forward direction**, where input information flows from the past to the current state; and another one for negative time direction, also called **backward direction**, where input information is processed from the future to the current state. The general structure of BRNNs is depicted in the following diagram:

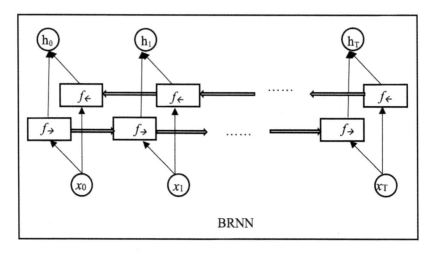

BRNN

Here, $f \rightarrow$ and $f \leftarrow$ represent the forward and backward recurrent layers, respectively. Concatenated together, they form the hidden layer f and preserve information from both past and future states.

BRNNs are especially useful when the complete context, including past and future information, is needed and available. For example, in part-of-speech tagging, entity recognition, or handwritten recognition, the performance can be enhanced by knowing the words or letters after the current one. Other excellent use cases include speech recognition, machine translation, and image captioning.

Next, we are going to apply BRNN, combined with LSTM, to sentiment classification. We will see whether capturing full contextual information of a move review helps augment its sentiment polarity.

Bidirectional RNNs for sentiment classification

Keras contains a dataset of 50,000 movie reviews from IMDb (www.imdb.com), labeled by sentiment polarity (1 as positive, 0 as negative). The reviews have been preprocessed, and each word is represented by the corresponding index in the dictionary. Words in the dictionary are sorted based on their frequencies in the entire dataset. For example, a word encoded as 4 is the 4th most frequent word among the data. You can guess that 1 represents the, 2 represents and, and the top indexes are for stop words.

The word-to-index dictionary can be obtained via the following code:

```
>>> from keras.datasets import imdb
>>> word_to_id = imdb.get_word_index()
```

We can use the load_data function to load the data, which returns two tuples, that is, the training dataset and the testing dataset:

```
>>> max_words = 5000
>>> (x_train, y_train), (x_test, y_test) =
                 imdb.load_data(num_words=max_words, skip_top=10, seed=42)
```

Here, we are only considering the top 5,000 most common words, but eliminate the top 10 most common words. The seed is for reproduction purposes:

```
>>> print(len(y_train), 'training samples')
25000 training samples
>>> print(len(y_test), 'testing samples')
25000 testing samples
```

You will find many 2s in some of the input samples. This is because 2 is used to represent words that were cut out because of the frequency filters we applied, including the top 10 most frequent words and those after the 5,000th most frequent. Actual words start from index 3.

You may notice that the input samples are of different lengths; for example, there are 467 words in the first training sample, and 138 words in the second one. However, training an RNN model requires input samples of the same length. We need to pad sequences to the same length: short samples are padded with 0s at the end, while long samples are truncated. We do so with the `pad_sequences` function, and specify the sequence length to be 200:

```
>>> from keras.preprocessing import sequence
>>> maxlen = 200
>>> x_train = sequence.pad_sequences(x_train, maxlen=maxlen)
>>> x_test = sequence.pad_sequences(x_test, maxlen=maxlen)
>>> print('x_train shape:', x_train.shape)
x_train shape: (25000, 200)
>>> print('x_test shape:', x_test.shape)
x_test shape: (25000, 200)
```

Now, we have input sequences of 200 words, with each word represented by an integer from 0 to 4999. We can conduct traditional one-hot encoding, but the resulting sparse 3,000-dimension outputs will make it excessively slow to train the corresponding RNN model. Instead, we perform word embedding to convert the word indexes into dense vectors of lower dimensions. In Keras, we employ the embedding layer as the first layer in the model:

```
>>> from keras.models import Sequential
>>> from keras.layers import Embedding
>>> model = Sequential()
>>> model.add(Embedding(max_words, 128, input_length=maxlen))
```

The embedding layer converts the index inputs of 5000 (`max_words`) values into 128-dimension vectors. Next, we add the bidirectional RNN, combined with LSTM:

```
>>> from keras.layers import Dense, Embedding, LSTM, Bidirectional
>>> model.add(Bidirectional(LSTM(128, dropout=0.2, recurrent_dropout=0.2)))
```

We simply apply a `Bidirectional` wrapper on an LSTM layer. The LSTM layer comes with 128 hidden units, with 20% dropout for input units and 20% dropout for recurrent connections.

The last layer generates logistic output:

```
>>> model.add(Dense(1, activation='sigmoid'))
```

For the optimizer, RMSprop is used with a learning rate of 0.001 to minimize cross entropy for binary classification:

```
>>> optimizer = optimizers.RMSprop(0.001)
>>> model.compile(optimizer=optimizer, loss='binary_crossentropy',
                   metrics=['accuracy'])
```

Finally, we train the model with the testing set as validation data and an early stop based on validation loss:

```
>>> from keras.callbacks import EarlyStopping
>>> early_stop = EarlyStopping(monitor='val_loss', min_delta=0,
                               patience=10, verbose=1, mode='min')
>>> model.fit(x_train, y_train, batch_size=32, epochs=100,
              validation_data=[x_test, y_test], callbacks=[early_stop])
```

Let's look at the logs from epochs 1, 5, 8, and 15:

Epoch 1:

```
Train on 25000 samples, validate on 25000 samples
Epoch 1/100
 5504/25000 [=====>........................] - ETA: 15:04 - loss: 0.6111 -
acc: 0.6672
25000/25000 [==============================] - 1411s 56ms/step - loss:
0.4730 - acc: 0.7750 - val_loss: 0.3765 - val_acc: 0.8436
```

Epoch 5:

```
Epoch 5/100
 5088/25000 [=====>........................] - ETA: 15:22 - loss: 0.2395 -
acc: 0.9025
25000/25000 [==============================] - 1407s 56ms/step - loss:
0.2367 - acc: 0.9070 - val_loss: 0.2069 - val_acc: 0.8848
Epoch 00005: val_loss did not improve from 0.27994
```

Epoch 8:

```
Epoch 8/100
 5088/25000 [=====>........................] - ETA: 15:16 - loss: 0.1760 -
acc: 0.9347
25000/25000 [==============================] - 1404s 56ms/step - loss:
0.1815 - acc: 0.9314 - val_loss: 0.2703 - val_acc: 0.8960
```

Epoch 15:

```
Epoch 15/100
 5408/25000 [=====>......................] - ETA: 15:08 - loss: 0.0936 -
acc: 0.9680
25000/25000 [==============================] - 1413s 57ms/step - loss:
0.0975 - acc: 0.9656 - val_loss: 0.3588 - val_acc: 0.8816
Epoch 00015: val_loss did not improve from 0.27034
```

Training stops at epoch 18 as early stopping triggers:

```
Epoch 00018: val_loss did not improve from 0.27034
Epoch 00018: early stopping
```

A testing accuracy of 89.6% is achieved with BRNN and LSTM.

Summary

We just accomplished an important part of our learning journey regarding DL architectures—RNNs! In this chapter, we got more familiar with RNNs and their variants. We started with what RNNs are, the evolution paths of RNNs, and how they became the state-of-the-art solutions to sequential modeling. We also explored four RNN architectures categorized by the forms of input and output data, along with industrial examples.

We followed by discussing a variety of architectures categorized by the recurrent layer, including vanilla RNNs, LSTM, GRU, and bidirectional RNNs. First, we applied the vanilla architecture to write our own *War and Peace*, albeit a bit nonsensical. We produced a better version by using LSTM architecture RNNs. Another memory-boosted architecture, GRU, was employed in stock price prediction.

Finally, beyond past information, we introduced the bidirectional architecture, which allows the model to preserve information from both past and future contexts of the sequence. We also worked on movie reviews sentiment classification using bidirectional RNNs combined with LSTM. In the next chapter, we will explore another great invention of the DL model: generative adversarial networks.

4

Section 4: Generative Adversarial Networks (GANs)

In this chapter, you will learn about GANs, along with their benchmarks. Along with the evolution paths of the GAN models, the architectures and engineering best practices will be illustrated with industrial examples. We will also explore how we can generate only one output, whether an output can be a sequence, and whether it works with only one input element.

The following chapters will be covered in this section:

- Chapter 7, *Generative Adversarial Networks*

7

Generative Adversarial Networks

In this chapter, we will explain one of the most interesting deep learning models, **Generative Adversarial Networks (GANs)**. We will start by reviewing what GANs are and what they are used for. After briefly covering the evolution paths of GAN models, we will illustrate a variety of GAN architectures, along with image generation examples.

Imagine you are in a competition of mimicking an artwork (such as Vincent van Gogh's *The Starry Night*) that you don't know enough about initially. You are allowed to participate as many times as you wish. And every time you submit your entry, the judge gives you feedback on what the real artwork looks like and how close your replica is. In the first few trials, your work does not score high, owing to your very limited knowledge of the original piece. After a few trails, your submissions are getting closer to the real artwork thanks to the useful tips provided by the judge. You keep trying and improving, and incorporating the judge's feedback into your attempts, and in your last few attempts, your work looks very close to the original. Hopefully, you win the competition in the end.

GANs do pretty much the same thing to synthesize images, sound waves, videos, and any other signals, and we will be exploring this in depth in this chapter.

In this chapter, we will cover the following topics:

- What are GANs?
- Generative models
- Adversarial training
- The evolution path of GANs
- Vanilla GAN architecture
- Implementing vanilla GANs
- Generating images
- Deep convolutional GAN architecture
- Implementing deep convolutional GANs
- Conditional GAN architecture
- Implementing conditional GANs
- Information-maximizing GAN architecture
- Implementing information-maximizing GANs

What are GANs?

GANs are probably one of the most interesting types of deep neural networks. Ever since GANs were first introduced by Goodfellow et al. in 2014, there have been more and more research projects and applications built around them, some of which are really intriguing. The following are the interesting ones we picked up on:

- **Image generation**, such as cat pictures, fake celebrity faces, and even modern artwork
- **Audio or video synthesis**, for instance, DeepMind's WaveNets, which are able to generate human speech and 3D reconstruction for astronomical images
- **Time-series generation**, such as medical data and high-frequency data for stock-market prediction
- **Statistical inference**, such as Amazon's algorithm that designs clothing by analyzing a bunch of pictures

So, why are GANs so powerful? When it comes to GANs, it is better to first talk about the generative model, since a GAN is basically a generative model.

Generative models

There are two main types of models in machine learning, the **generative model** and the **discriminative model**. A discriminative model, as its name implies, tries to distinguish data between two (or more) classes. For example, the CNN models we talked about in Chapter 4, *CNN Architecture*, learn to tell us whether an image is of a cat or dog, given an image of one of them, and the RNN models in Chapter 6, *Recurrent Neural Networks*, are trained to output positive or negative sentiment given a paragraph. Discriminative models focus on predicting the classes of data given their features. The generative model, on the contrary, does not try to map the features to the classes, but it generates the features given a certain class. For instance, the **Gaussian Mixture Model** (**GMM**) is trained to generate new data that fits the distribution of the training set. Generative models model the distribution of features given individual classes. That said, generative models can be used to classify data, such as Naive Bayes and Boltzmann machines, which we talked about in Chapter 3, *Restricted Boltzmann Machines and Autoencoders*. However, their priority is figuring out how likely certain features are, rather than recognizing the label. The learned feature distribution is then utilized for classification. If you are still confused, here is an easy way to distinguish a generative model from a discriminative model:

- The discriminative model is interested in finding boundaries or rules to segregate data
- The generative model focuses on modeling the data distribution

A GAN model is composed of two networks. One network, called the generator, is responsible for generating new data samples, which makes GANs generative models. Another network, called the discriminator, conducts authenticity evaluation for the generated data. To be specific, it determines whether individually generated samples belong to the real training dataset. Again, GANs are still generative models since they focus on generating a data distribution of particular interest, and the discriminator is added to provide feedback for better data generation. Let's see how it works in detail.

Adversarial – training in an adversarial manner

If we remember our Van Gogh example, the GAN model is doing similar things. We mimic the artwork, while the generator in a GAN generates candidates, say, a particular data distribution of interest; the judge assesses our replica, while the discriminator in the GAN evaluates the generated candidates by distinguishing between generated candidates and instances from the real data distribution.

The generator and discriminator in a GAN are trained in an adversarial manner, that is, they are contesting with each other in a zero-sum framework in order to generate data mimicking the real data distribution. Just as in the artwork competition, we constantly improve the replica with the goal of achieving a high score from the judge, and the judge keeps evaluating our work and offering feedback. The generator in a GAN aims at producing synthesized instances that are deemed as coming from the real data distribution, even though they are *fake*, and the goal of the discriminator is to identify whether individual instances are fake (synthesized) or real. From optimization perspectives, the training objective of the generator is to increase the errors of the discriminator—the more mistakes that are made by the discriminator, the generator performs better. The objective of the discriminator is to reduce its error, which is obvious enough. In each iteration, both networks are working toward their objectives using gradient descent, which is nothing new. What's interesting is that each network is trying to beat another—the generator is trying to fool the discriminator, while the discriminator is trying not to be fooled. Eventually, the synthesized data (such as images, audio, video, time series) from the generator is (hopefully) able to fool the most sophisticated discriminator, similar to the artwork replica competition where we are able to achieve the highest score from the strictest but most helpful judge.

In practice, the generator takes in random samples from a predefined distribution with multivariate Gaussian distribution as the most popular input and produces data that looks as if it could come from the target distribution. This is quite similar to the replica competition where we have little knowledge about the artwork initially and work all the way toward a decent replica.

Using image generation as an example, a GAN model can be represented in the following diagram:

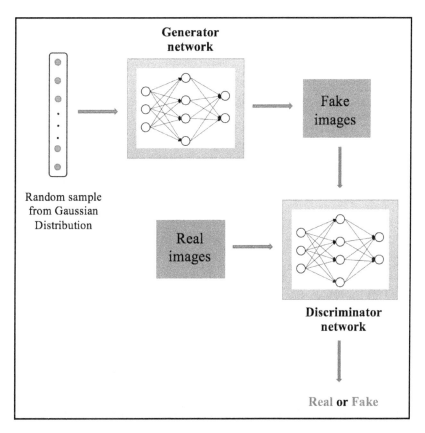

The following are the steps taken by the GAN:

1. The generator network takes in random samples from the Gaussian distribution and outputs the images.
2. These generated images are then fed into the discriminator network.
3. The discriminator network takes in both the generated images and the images that were taken from the actual dataset.
4. The discriminator outputs probabilities with upper bound 1, representing the input image being deemed authentic, and lower bound 0, indicating the input image being deemed fake.
5. The loss (cost function) of the generator is calculated based on the cross entropy of fake images being deemed authentic by the discriminator.

6. The loss (cost function) of the discriminator is calculated based on the cross entropy of fake images being deemed fake, plus the cross entropy of real images being deemed authentic.

7. For each epoch, both networks are optimized toward minimizing their individual losses, respectively.

8. At some point, the model is well-trained when the images generated by the converged generator are deemed authentic by the converged discriminator.

9. Finally the well-trained generator generates images as final outputs, which mimic the real images' input.

The evolution path of GANs

The idea of adversarial training can be dated back to early works in the 1990s, such as Schmidhuber's *Learning Factorial Codes by Predictability Minimization* (Neural Computation, 1992, 4(6): 863-879). In 2013, adversarial model inferring without any prior information was proposed in *A Coevolutionary Approach to Learn Animal Behavior Through Controlled Interaction* (Li, et al., Proceedings of the 15th Annual Conference on Genetic and Evolutionary Computation, 2013, 223-230). In 2014, GANs were first introduced by Goodfellow et al. in *Generative Adversarial Networks*.

Li, et al., the same authors who proposed animal behavior inferring, proposed the term **Turing learning** in 2016 in *Turing learning: a metric-free approach to inferring behavior and its application to swarms* (Swarm Intelligence, 10 (3): 211-243). Turing learning is related to the Turing test, and is a generalization of GANs, as concluded in *Generalizing GANs: A Turing Perspective* (by Gross, et al., Proceedings of the 31st Annual Conference on Neural Information Processing Systems, 2017, 1-11). In Turing learning, models are not limited to GANs or neural networks; the discriminator can influence the inputs of the generator, acting as the interrogator in the Turing test.

The first GANs that were proposed were composed of fully connected layers for both the generator and discriminator. Ever since the vanilla architecture, there have been many new innovative ones developed, for example, the deep convolutional GANs, conditional GANs, and the information-maximizing GANs. In the next section, we will be studying these architectures in detail and implementing each one from scratch.

GAN architectures and implementations

As promised, we will be taking a closer look at variants of the GANs we mentioned in detail in the previous sections and apply them on real-world problems. The most commonly used GANs include deep convolutional GANs, conditional GANs, and the information-maximizing GANs. Let's start with the most basic architecture.

Vanilla GANs

In a most basic GAN model, both the generator and discriminator are fully connected neural networks. The architecture of a vanilla GAN can be depicted as follows:

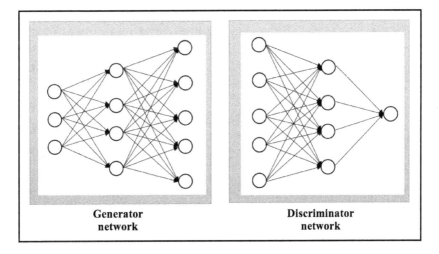

The input of the generator is the random samples from a particular distribution, which we usually call **noise** or **latent variables**. The second layer and several ones after are the hidden layers, which are fully connected layers in this case. A hidden layer usually has more units than its previous hidden layer. The output layer is the same size as the expected generation, which is the same as that of the real data. As for the discriminator, its input is the real or generated data, followed by one or more hidden layers, and an output layer with one unit. Each hidden layer usually has fewer units than its previous hidden layer. In general, the generator and discriminator have the same number of hidden layers. Moreover, two sets of hidden layers are often symmetrical. For example, the generator and discriminator of a vanilla GAN can look as follows:

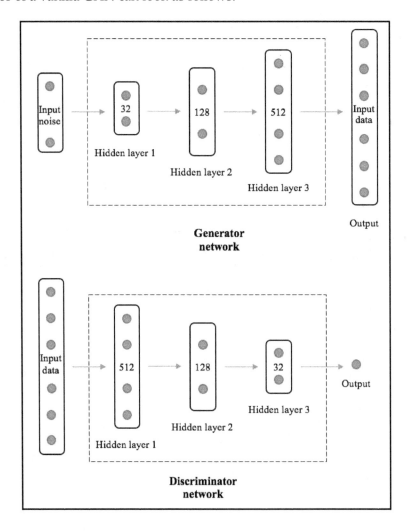

Now that we've understood what vanilla GANs are we can start to implement them from scratch in TensorFlow. From here onwards we will use the MNIST handwritten digits dataset as an example so that we can apply GANs to generate our own MNIST.

We will start by loading the MNIST dataset that's used for model training:

```
>>> import numpy as np
>>> import tensorflow as tf
>>> def load_dataset():
...        (x_train, y_train), (x_test, y_test) =
...                tf.keras.datasets.mnist.load_data('./mnist_data')
...        train_data = np.concatenate((x_train, x_test), axis=0)
...        train_data = train_data / 255.
...        train_data = train_data * 2. - 1
...        train_data = train_data.reshape([-1, 28 * 28])
...        return train_data
```

The function reads and combines the original training and testing set, excluding the labels, since they are not needed in the vanilla model. It also rescales the data from the range of [0, 255] to [-1, 1], which is a very important part of preprocessing for neural network models, and also reshapes individual samples into one-dimensional ones.

Call this function and check the size of the loaded data:

```
>>> data = load_dataset()
>>> print("Training dataset shape:", data.shape)
Training dataset shape: (70000, 784)
```

There are 70,000 training samples in total, and each is 784 dimensions (28 x 28). If you forget what the MNIST data look like, we will display some samples using the functions that are defined as follows:

```
>>> import matplotlib.pyplot as plt
>>> def display_images(data, image_size=28):
...        fig, axes = plt.subplots(4, 10, figsize=(10, 4))
...        for i, ax in enumerate(axes.flatten()):
...            img = data[i, :]
...            img = (img - img.min()) / (img.max() - img.min())
...            ax.imshow(img.reshape(image_size, image_size), cmap='gray')
...            ax.xaxis.set_visible(False)
...            ax.yaxis.set_visible(False)
...        plt.subplots_adjust(wspace=0, hspace=0)
...        plt.show()
```

This function exhibits 40 images in 4 rows and 10 columns. It will be reused to display the generated images later. Take a look at the first 40 real samples:

```
>>> display_images(data)
```

Refer to the following screenshot for the end result:

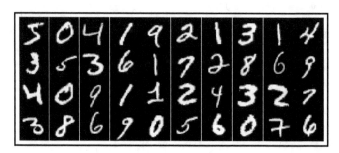

You will need to come back to these images later when evaluating how authentic our generated images are.

Now, let's get started with building the GAN model. First, we define a wrapper function for the fully connected layer since it is used the most frequently in vanilla GANs:

```
>>> def dense(x, n_outputs, activation=None):
...        return tf.layers.dense(x, n_outputs, activation=activation,
                    kernel_initializer=
                    tf.random_normal_initializer(mean=0.0,stddev=0.02))
```

By putting in a few dense layers, we build the generator:

```
>>> def generator(z, alpha=0.2):
...        """
...        Generator network
...        @param z: input of random samples
...        @param alpha: leaky relu factor
...        @return: output of the generator network
...        """
...        with tf.variable_scope('generator', reuse=tf.AUTO_REUSE):
...            fc1 = dense(z, 256)
...            fc1 = tf.nn.leaky_relu(fc1, alpha)
...            fc2 = dense(fc1, 512)
...            fc2 = tf.nn.leaky_relu(fc2, alpha)
...            fc3 = dense(fc2, 1024)
...            fc3 = tf.nn.leaky_relu(fc3, alpha)
...            out = dense(fc3, 28 * 28)
...            out = tf.tanh(out)
...            return out
```

The generator feeds the input random noise into three hidden layers in sequence, with 256, 512, and 1,024 hidden units, respectively. Note that the activation function for each hidden layer is **leaky ReLU**, which is a variant of ReLU. It was invented to fix the dying ReLU problem where the output becomes zero for any negative input to the function. It is defined as $f(x) = max(x, \alpha x)$ where α, is a slope factor ranging from 0 to 1 (but a small value is more often seen). A comparison between ReLU and the leaky version (*slope = 0.2*, as an example) can be seen in the following diagram:

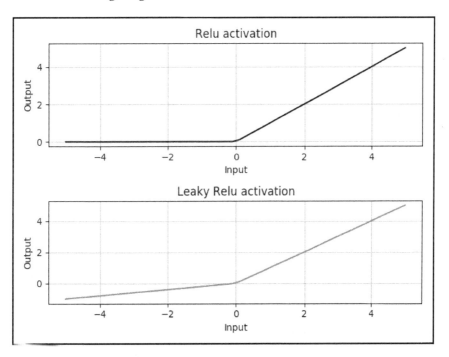

After three hidden layers, the output layer, followed by a tanh activation, maps the data to the same size and range of the expected image. Similarly, we build the discriminator with four dense layers, three of which are hidden layers with sizes in the opposite order of the hidden layers in the generator:

```
>>> def discriminator(x, alpha=0.2):
...         """
...         Discriminator network
...         @param x: input samples, can be real or generated samples
...         @param alpha: leaky relu factor
...         @return: output logits
...         """
...         with tf.variable_scope('discriminator', reuse=tf.AUTO_REUSE):
...             fc1 = dense(x, 1024)
```

```
...              fc1 = tf.nn.leaky_relu(fc1, alpha)
...              fc2 = dense(fc1, 512)
...              fc2 = tf.nn.leaky_relu(fc2, alpha)
...              fc3 = dense(fc2, 256)
...              fc3 = tf.nn.leaky_relu(fc3, alpha)
...              out = dense(fc3, 1)
...              return out
```

The output layer maps the data to a single unit logit. We can now define placeholders for the real input data of size 784 and the noise input data of size 100:

```
>>> noise_size = 100
>>> tf.reset_default_graph()
>>> X_real = tf.placeholder(tf.float32, (None, 28 * 28), name='input_real')
>>> z = tf.placeholder(tf.float32, (None, noise_size), name='input_noise')
```

Apply a generator to the input noise and a discriminator to the generated image, as well as the real image data:

```
>>> g_sample = generator(z)
>>> d_real_out = discriminator(X_real)
>>> d_fake_out = discriminator(g_sample)
```

With all these outputs from networks, we develop the `loss` computation for the generator, which is based on fake images being deemed authentic:

```
>>> g_loss = tf.reduce_mean(
...              tf.nn.sigmoid_cross_entropy_with_logits(logits=d_fake_out,
...              labels=tf.ones_like(d_fake_out)))
>>> tf.summary.scalar('generator_loss', g_loss)
```

We also log the loss for visualizing the learning progress using TensorBoard.

The `loss` computation for the discriminator comes next, which is based on two components: real images being deemed fake and fake images being deemed authentic:

```
>>> d_real_loss = tf.reduce_mean(
...              tf.nn.sigmoid_cross_entropy_with_logits(logits=d_real_out,
...              labels=tf.ones_like(d_real_out)))
>>> d_fake_loss = tf.reduce_mean(
...              tf.nn.sigmoid_cross_entropy_with_logits(logits=d_fake_out,
...              labels=tf.zeros_like(d_fake_out)))
>>> d_loss = d_real_loss + d_fake_loss
>>> tf.summary.scalar('discriminator_loss', d_loss)
```

Again, we log the discriminator loss. Then, we define optimizers for both networks, as follows:

```
>>> train_vars = tf.trainable_variables()
>>> d_vars = [var for var in train_vars
                    if var.name.startswith('discriminator')]
>>> g_vars = [var for var in train_vars
                    if var.name.startswith('generator')]
>>> learning_rate = 0.0002
>>> beta1 = 0.5
>>> with tf.control_dependencies(
                tf.get_collection(tf.GraphKeys.UPDATE_OPS)):
...     d_opt = tf.train.AdamOptimizer(learning_rate,
                beta1=beta1).minimize(d_loss, var_list=d_vars)
...     g_opt = tf.train.AdamOptimizer(learning_rate,
                beta1=beta1).minimize(g_loss, var_list=g_vars)
```

The optimizer implements the Adam algorithm, with a learning rate of 0.0002 and a first-moment decay rate of 0.5. Before model optimization, don't forget to define a function that returns batches of data for training:

```
>>> def gen_batches(data, batch_size, shuffle=True):
...     """
...     Generate batches for training
...     @param data: training data
...     @param batch_size: batch size
...     @param shuffle: shuffle the data or not
...     @return: batches generator
...     """
...     n_data = data.shape[0]
...     if shuffle:
...         idx = np.arange(n_data)
...         np.random.shuffle(idx)
...         data = data[idx]
...     for i in range(0, n_data, batch_size):
...         batch = data[i:i + batch_size]
...         yield batch
```

With all the components ready, we can start training our GAN model. For every 100 steps, we record generator loss and discriminator loss. And for performance inspection, we create a set of noise inputs and display the images that have been generated by the current generator for each epoch:

```
>>> epochs = 100
>>> steps = 0
>>> with tf.Session() as sess:
...     merged = tf.summary.merge_all()
```

```
...         train_writer = tf.summary.FileWriter(
                            './logdir/vanilla', sess.graph)
...         sess.run(tf.global_variables_initializer())
...         for epoch in range(epochs):
...             for batch_x in gen_batches(data, batch_size):
...             batch_z = np.random.uniform(
                            -1, 1, size=(batch_size,noise_size))
...             _, summary, d_loss_batch = sess.run(
                            [d_opt, merged, d_loss],
                            feed_dict={z: batch_z, X_real: batch_x})
...             sess.run(g_opt, feed_dict={z: batch_z})
...             _, g_loss_batch = sess.run(
                            [g_opt, g_loss], feed_dict={z: batch_z})
...             if steps % 100 == 0:
...                 train_writer.add_summary(summary, steps)
...                 print("Epoch {}/{} - discriminator loss:
                        {:.4f}, generator Loss: {:.4f}".format(
...                     epoch + 1, epochs, d_loss_batch,g_loss_batch))
...             steps += 1
...         gen_samples = sess.run(generator(z), feed_dict={z:sample_z})
...         display_images(gen_samples)
```

Note that in each epoch, the generator is updated twice while the discriminator is only updated once. This is because it is much easier to optimize the discriminator than the generator, which is intuitive; arbitrary images are just deemed fake effortlessly. If convergence of the discriminator occurs in early epochs, the incomplete generator will produce garbage. You can also specify different learning rates for two networks, for example, a slightly greater one, 0.001, for the generator and 0.0002 for the discriminator.

Refer to the following screenshot for the end result for epoch 25:

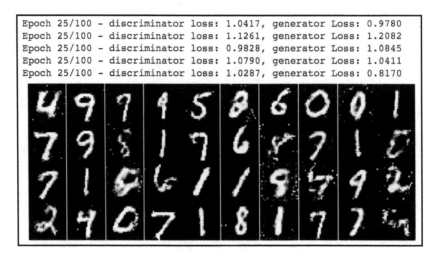

The following screenshot shows the output of epoch 50:

```
Epoch 50/100 - discriminator loss: 1.0954, generator Loss: 1.0482
Epoch 50/100 - discriminator loss: 0.8156, generator Loss: 1.3439
Epoch 50/100 - discriminator loss: 1.0247, generator Loss: 1.0905
Epoch 50/100 - discriminator loss: 1.0584, generator Loss: 1.0352
Epoch 50/100 - discriminator loss: 0.9823, generator Loss: 1.2046
```

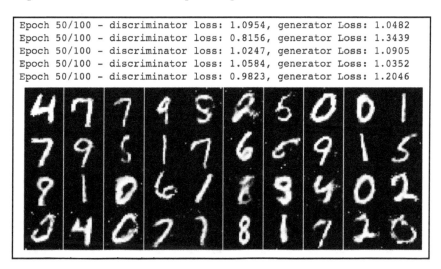

The following screenshot shows the output of epoch 75:

```
Epoch 75/100 - discriminator loss: 0.8683, generator Loss: 1.3016
Epoch 75/100 - discriminator loss: 0.9427, generator Loss: 1.0433
Epoch 75/100 - discriminator loss: 0.9479, generator Loss: 1.1799
Epoch 75/100 - discriminator loss: 0.9337, generator Loss: 1.3506
Epoch 75/100 - discriminator loss: 0.9523, generator Loss: 1.1126
Epoch 75/100 - discriminator loss: 0.9511, generator Loss: 1.6136
```

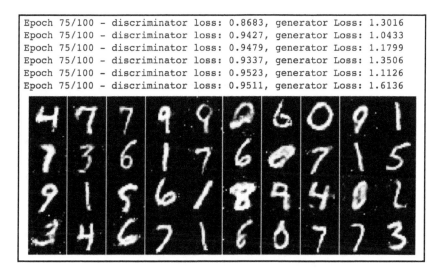

The following screenshot shows the output of epoch 100:

```
Epoch 100/100 - discriminator loss: 0.9049, generator Loss: 1.1243
Epoch 100/100 - discriminator loss: 0.7976, generator Loss: 1.6355
Epoch 100/100 - discriminator loss: 0.7642, generator Loss: 1.3923
Epoch 100/100 - discriminator loss: 1.0171, generator Loss: 2.0117
Epoch 100/100 - discriminator loss: 0.9927, generator Loss: 1.4057
```

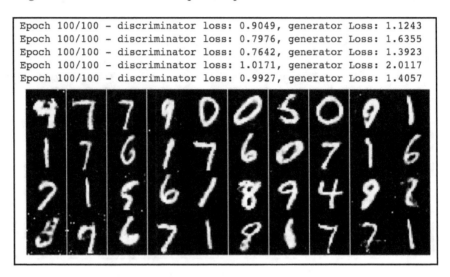

Our first GAN model is able to synthesize handwritten digits, and most of them look legit! Let's also take a look at the learning graph in TensorBoard. To run TensorBoard, enter the following command in the terminal:

```
tensorboard --logdir=logdir/
```

Then, go to `http://localhost:6006/` in a browser; we will see a diagram of the discriminator:

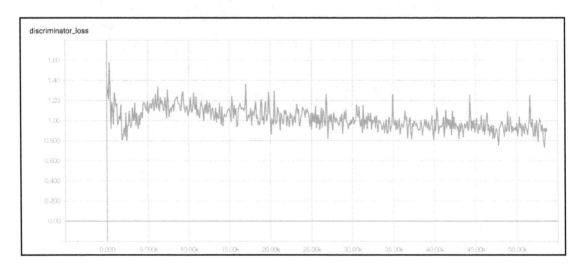

The following is a diagram of the generator:

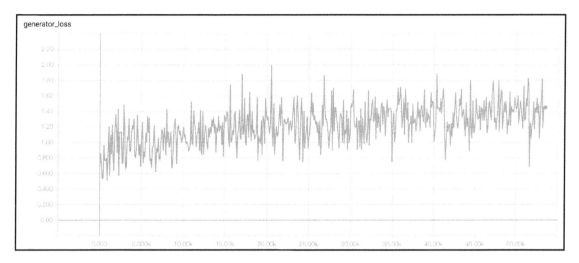

You may notice that there are several digits that look odd. What improvement can we make on top of the fully connected vanilla model? Using convolutional layers is probably the most intuitive approach when it comes to computer vision.

Deep convolutional GANs

Convolutional layers have become a must-have for image problems. Using GANs for image generation is no exception. Hence, **Deep Convolutional Generative Adversarial Networks (DCGANs)** were proposed by Radford, et al. in *Unsupervised Representation Learning with Deep Convolutional Generative Adversarial Networks* in 2016.

It is easy to understand the discriminator in DCGANs. It is also very similar to standard CNNs for classification, where one or more convolutional layers are employed and each is followed by a non-linear layer, and a fully connected layer at the end wraps things up. For example, we can have the following architecture:

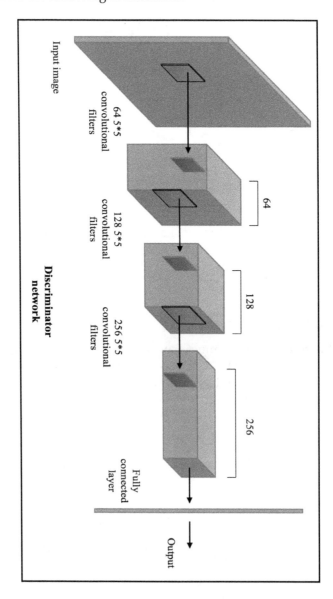

There are three convolutional layers, and they are composed of 64, 128, and 256 5 x 5 filters, respectively.

As we mentioned previously, the generator is usually symmetrical to the discriminator. The discriminator in DCGANs interprets an input image via convolutional layers and generates a numerical output. Hence, the generator needs to transform the numerical noise inputs into images using **transposed convolutional layers**, which are the exact opposite of convolutional layers. While convolutional layers perform downsampling, transposed convolutional layers perform upsampling. For example, we can have the following architecture for a generator:

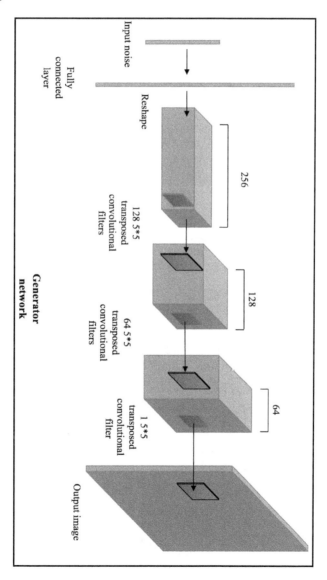

With all these concepts in mind, let's implement DCGANs. Similarly, we start by defining wrapper functions for the convolutional and transposed convolutional layers since they are used the most frequently in DCGANs:

```
>>> def conv2d(x, n_filters, kernel_size=5):
...     return tf.layers.conv2d(inputs=x, filters=n_filters,
                kernel_size=kernel_size, strides=2, padding="same",
                kernel_initializer=tf.random_normal_initializer(
                mean=0.0, stddev=0.02))

>>> def transpose_conv2d(x, n_filters, kernel_size=5):
...     return tf.layers.conv2d_transpose(inputs=x,
                filters=n_filters, kernel_size=kernel_size, strides=2,
                padding='same', kernel_initializer=
                tf.random_normal_initializer(mean=0.0, stddev=0.02))
```

The dense function that we defined is reused for the fully connected layer. Also, we apply batch normalization on the output of the convolutional layer. The idea behind batch normalization is similar to input data normalization, which speeds up learning. Batch normalization is performed by subtracting the batch mean from the output of an activation layer, and then dividing it by the batch standard deviation. We define a wrapper function for batch normalization as follows:

```
>>> def batch_norm(x, training, epsilon=1e-5, momentum=0.9):
...     return tf.layers.batch_normalization(x, training=training,
                            epsilon=epsilon, momentum=momentum)
```

We can now construct the discriminator using the components we just defined:

```
>>> def discriminator(x, alpha=0.2, training=True):
...     """
...     Discriminator network for DCGAN
...     @param x: input samples, can be real or generated samples
...     @param alpha: leaky relu factor
...     @param training: whether to return the output in training mode
...                     (normalized with statistics of the current batch)
...     @return: output logits
...     """
...     with tf.variable_scope('discriminator', reuse=tf.AUTO_REUSE):
...         conv1 = conv2d(x, 64)
...         conv1 = tf.nn.leaky_relu(conv1, alpha)
...         conv2 = conv2d(conv1, 128)
...         conv2 = batch_norm(conv2, training=training)
...         conv2 = tf.nn.leaky_relu(conv2, alpha)
...         conv3 = conv2d(conv2, 256)
...         conv3 = batch_norm(conv3, training=training)
...         conv3 = tf.nn.leaky_relu(conv3, alpha)
```

```
...             fc = tf.layers.flatten(conv3)
...             out = dense(fc, 1)
...             return out
```

This was nice and easy. The three convolutional layers involve 64, 128, and 256 5 x 5 filters, respectively.

It is a bit tricky to develop the generator. Recall that we need to first reshape the input one-dimensional noise to a three-dimensional image to enable transposed convolution. We know that the third dimension is 256 due to the symmetry of the two networks. So, what are the first two dimensions? They are *2 x 2*, becoming *4 x 4* after the first transposed convolutional layer, *8 x 8* after the second one, and *16 x 16* after the third one, which is far from our target of *28 x 28* if it is *3 x 3*. Similarly, it becomes 24 x 24 after the third transposed convolutional layer, which is again not big enough; if it is 4 x 4, then it becomes 32 x 32 after the third transposed convolutional layer. Hence, reshaping the linear input to a 4 x 4 image is sufficient. Note that the generated image output now has a size of 32 x 32, which is different than the size of our real image of 28 x 28. To ensure constant input to the discriminator, we just need to pad the real images with zeros. The zero padding for real images is implemented on top of the `load_dataset` function:

```
>>> def load_dataset_pad():
...     (x_train, y_train), (x_test, y_test)=
 tf.keras.datasets.mnist.load_data('./mnist_data')
...     train_data = np.concatenate((x_train, x_test), axis=0)
...     train_data = train_data / 255.
...     train_data = train_data * 2. - 1
...     train_data = train_data.reshape([-1, 28, 28, 1])
...     train_data = np.pad(train_data, ((0,0),(2,2),(2,2),(0,0)),
 'constant', constant_values=0.)
...     return train_data
```

The training data is also reshaped to (70000, 32, 32, 1), since the discriminator in DCGANs accepts three-dimensional image inputs:

```
>>> data = load_dataset_pad()
>>> print("Training dataset shape:", data.shape)
Training dataset shape: (70000, 32, 32, 1)
```

After the data has been loaded, we can continue defining the generator:

```
>>> def generator(z, n_channel, training=True):
...         """
...         Generator network for DCGAN
...         @param z: input of random samples
...         @param n_channel: number of output channels
...         @param training: whether to return the output in training
```

```
              mode (normalized with statistics of the current batch)
...       @return: output of the generator network
...       """
...       with tf.variable_scope('generator', reuse=tf.AUTO_REUSE):
...           fc = dense(z, 256 * 4 * 4, activation=tf.nn.relu)
...           fc = tf.reshape(fc, (-1, 4, 4, 256))
...           trans_conv1 = transpose_conv2d(fc, 128)
...           trans_conv1 = batch_norm(trans_conv1, training=training)
...           trans_conv1 = tf.nn.relu(trans_conv1)
...           trans_conv2 = transpose_conv2d(trans_conv1, 64)
...           trans_conv2 = batch_norm(trans_conv2, training=training)
...           trans_conv2 = tf.nn.relu(trans_conv2)
...           trans_conv3 = transpose_conv2d(trans_conv2, n_channel)
...           out = tf.tanh(trans_conv3)
...           return out
```

First, it maps the noise input to a fully connected layer with 4,096 units so that it can reshape the three-dimensional data of size 4 x 4 x 256 to be consumed by three transposed convolution layers afterwards.

We can now define placeholders for the real input data of size 28 x 28 x 1:

```
>>> image_size = data.shape[1:]
>>> tf.reset_default_graph()
>>> X_real = tf.placeholder(
            tf.float32, (None,) + image_size, name='input_real')
```

The noise input data and the rest of the parameters are identical to those in the last section, so we skip repeating the same code. Next, we apply the generator to the input noise:

```
>>> g_sample = generator(z, image_size[2])
```

The remainders, including discriminator on images, loss computation, and optimizers, reuse those in the last section.

With all the components ready, we can now start training our DCGAN model. Again, we record both losses for every 100 steps and display resulting synthesis images for each epoch (50 epochs in total at this time):

```
>>> epochs = 50
>>> steps = 0
>>> with tf.Session() as sess:
...     merged = tf.summary.merge_all()
...     train_writer = tf.summary.FileWriter(
                                './logdir/dcgan', sess.graph)
...     sess.run(tf.global_variables_initializer())
...     for epoch in range(epochs):
...         for batch_x in gen_batches(data, batch_size):
```

```
...                 batch_z = np.random.uniform(
                                -1, 1, size=(batch_size, noise_size))
...                 _, summary, d_loss_batch = sess.run(
                                [d_opt, merged,d_loss], feed_dict=
                                {z: batch_z, X_real: batch_x})
...                 sess.run(g_opt, feed_dict={z: batch_z, X_real:batch_x})
...                 _, g_loss_batch = sess.run([g_opt, g_loss], feed_dict=
                                {z: batch_z, X_real: batch_x})
...                 if steps % 100 == 0:
...                     train_writer.add_summary(summary, steps)
...                     print("Epoch {}/{} - discriminator loss: {:.4f},
                            generator Loss: {:.4f}".format(epoch + 1, epochs,
                            d_loss_batch, g_loss_batch))
...                 steps += 1
...             gen_samples = sess.run(generator(z, image_size[2],
                                training=False), feed_dict={z: sample_z})
...             display_images(gen_samples, 32)
```

Refer to the following screenshot for the end result for epoch 25:

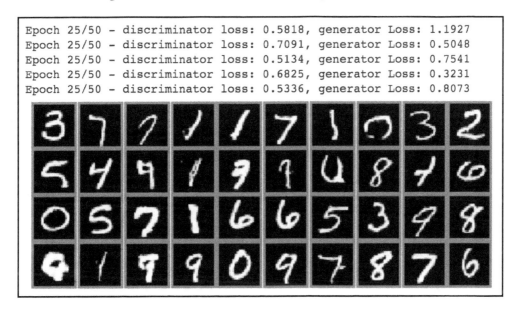

```
Epoch 25/50 - discriminator loss: 0.5818, generator Loss: 1.1927
Epoch 25/50 - discriminator loss: 0.7091, generator Loss: 0.5048
Epoch 25/50 - discriminator loss: 0.5134, generator Loss: 0.7541
Epoch 25/50 - discriminator loss: 0.6825, generator Loss: 0.3231
Epoch 25/50 - discriminator loss: 0.5336, generator Loss: 0.8073
```

And finally, refer to the following screenshot for the end result for epoch 50:

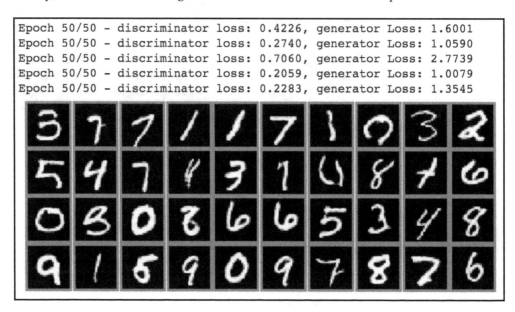

```
Epoch 50/50 - discriminator loss: 0.4226, generator Loss: 1.6001
Epoch 50/50 - discriminator loss: 0.2740, generator Loss: 1.0590
Epoch 50/50 - discriminator loss: 0.7060, generator Loss: 2.7739
Epoch 50/50 - discriminator loss: 0.2059, generator Loss: 1.0079
Epoch 50/50 - discriminator loss: 0.2283, generator Loss: 1.3545
```

The learning graph that's displayed in TensorBoard is as follows for the discriminator loss:

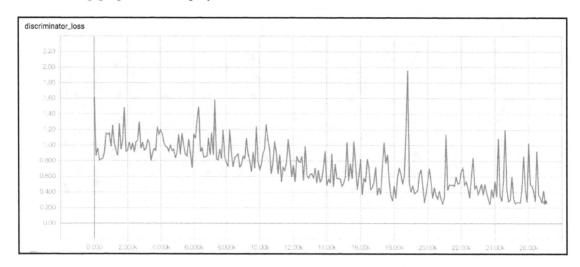

And the following graph shows the generator loss:

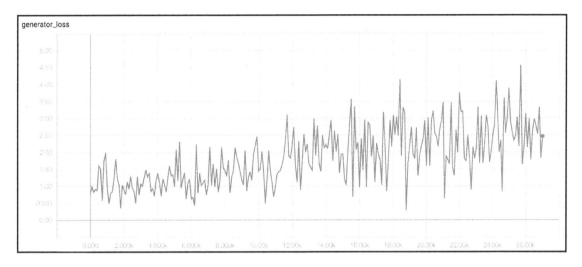

The generated images from our DCGAN model look a lot more authentic than those from the vanilla GAN. We also put them along with the real images; can you tell which set is real or fake without the hint?

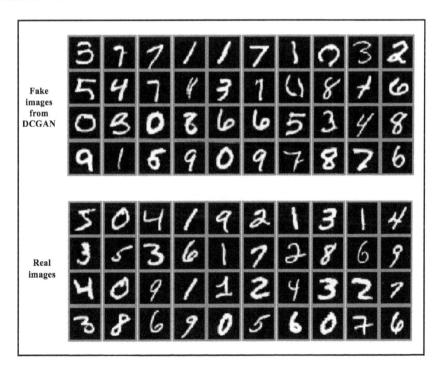

So far, the digits we have generated are quite random in the sense that we cannot control which one from 0 to 9 to produce. This is because the generator in vanilla GANs and DCGANs only take in random noise, with no more restrictions or conditions on what to generate, as long as the result appears real. We will see how conditional GANs and infoGANs enable this capability.

Conditional GANs

Conditional GANs (CGANs) grant us control over what to generate by feeding label information to both the generator and the discriminator with the hope that the data of particular labels will be generated. The architecture of a CGAN is presented in the following diagram:

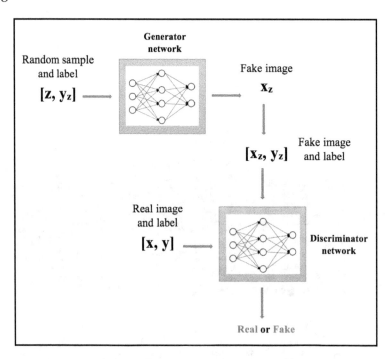

As we can see, the label data is an extension of the input space for both the generator and discriminator in CGANs. Note that the label data is represented as a one-hot vector. For example, digit 2 in the MNIST dataset becomes [0, 0, 1, 0, 0, 0, 0, 0, 0, 0]. The other parts of the CGANs, such as the cost function, are similar to regular GANs. So, it should be easy to implement CGANs. We can develop a fully connected CGAN, but the hidden layers in CGANs are not limited to fully connected layers. You can try implementing a convolutional version as an exercise.

First, we need to modify the `data load` function to include the label:

```
>>> def load_dataset_label():
...     from keras.utils import np_utils
...     (x_train, y_train), (x_test, y_test)
...                 =tf.keras.datasets.mnist.load_data('./mnist_data')
...     x_data = np.concatenate((x_train, x_test), axis=0)
...     y_train = np_utils.to_categorical(y_train)
...     y_test = np_utils.to_categorical(y_test)
...     y_data = np.concatenate((y_train, y_test), axis=0)
...     x_data = x_data / 255.
...     x_data = x_data * 2. - 1
...     x_data = x_data.reshape([-1, 28 * 28])
...     return x_data, y_data
```

The function also converts the label data from one-dimension into a one-hot encoded ten-dimension:

```
>>> x_data, y_data = load_dataset_label()
>>> print("Training dataset shape:", x_data.shape)
Training dataset shape: (70000, 784)
```

Accordingly, the `batch` generation function also needs updating so that it returns batches of images and labels:

```
>>> def gen_batches_label(x_data, y_data, batch_size, shuffle=True):
...     """
...     Generate batches including label for training
...     @param x_data: training data
...     @param y_data: training label
...     @param batch_size: batch size
...     @param shuffle: shuffle the data or not
...     @return: batches generator
...     """
...     n_data = x_data.shape[0]
...     if shuffle:
...         idx = np.arange(n_data)
...         np.random.shuffle(idx)
...         x_data = x_data[idx]
...         y_data = y_data[idx]
...     for i in range(0, n_data - batch_size, batch_size):
...         x_batch = x_data[i:i + batch_size]
...         y_batch = y_data[i:i + batch_size]
...         yield x_batch, y_batch
```

Later, we define a placeholder for the label data as a new input:

```
>>> n_classes = 10
>>> y = tf.placeholder(tf.float32, shape=[None,
n_classes],name='y_classes')
```

The, the generator takes label data and concatenates it with the input noise:

```
>>> def generator(z, y, alpha=0.2):
...         """
...         Generator network for CGAN
...         @param z: input of random samples
...         @param y: labels of the input samples
...         @param alpha: leaky relu factor
...         @return: output of the generator network
...         """
...         with tf.variable_scope('generator', reuse=tf.AUTO_REUSE):
...             z_y = tf.concat([z, y], axis=1)
...             fc1 = dense(z_y, 256)
...             fc1 = tf.nn.leaky_relu(fc1, alpha)
...             fc2 = dense(fc1, 512)
...             fc2 = tf.nn.leaky_relu(fc2, alpha)
...             fc3 = dense(fc2, 1024)
...             fc3 = tf.nn.leaky_relu(fc3, alpha)
...             out = dense(fc3, 28 * 28)
...             out = tf.tanh(out)
...             return out
```

The discriminator does the same thing:

```
>>> def discriminator(x, y, alpha=0.2):
...         """
...         Discriminator network for CGAN
...         @param x: input samples, can be real or generated samples
...         @param y: labels of the input samples
...         @param alpha: leaky relu factor
...         @return: output logits
...         """
...         with tf.variable_scope('discriminator', reuse=tf.AUTO_REUSE):
...             x_y = tf.concat([x, y], axis=1)
...             fc1 = dense(x_y, 1024)
...             fc1 = tf.nn.leaky_relu(fc1, alpha)
...             fc2 = dense(fc1, 512)
...             fc2 = tf.nn.leaky_relu(fc2, alpha)
...             fc3 = dense(fc2, 256)
...             fc3 = tf.nn.leaky_relu(fc3, alpha)
...             out = dense(fc3, 1)
...             return out
```

And now, we feed the y label to the `generator` and `discriminator`:

```
>>> g_sample = generator(z, y)
>>> d_real_out = discriminator(X_real, y)
>>> d_fake_out = discriminator(g_sample, y)
```

For quality inspection, we synthesize images for each epoch given noise inputs, along with the labels of sets of 10 classes. The sample labels are defined as follows:

```
>>> n_sample_display = 40
>>> sample_y = np.zeros(shape=(n_sample_display, n_classes))
>>> for i in range(n_sample_display):
...     j = i % 10
...     sample_y[i, j] = 1
```

The remainder of the codes before the training section is identical to those in the vanilla GAN model.

With all the components ready, we can start training our CGAN model:

```
>>> steps = 0
>>> with tf.Session() as sess:
...     merged = tf.summary.merge_all()
...     train_writer = tf.summary.FileWriter('./logdir/cgan', sess.graph)
...     sess.run(tf.global_variables_initializer())
...     for epoch in range(epochs):
...         for batch_x, batch_y in gen_batches_label(
...                                     x_data, y_data, batch_size):
...             batch_z = np.random.uniform(-1, 1,
...                                     size=(batch_size, noise_size))
...             _, summary, d_loss_batch = sess.run([d_opt, merged, d_loss],
...                                     feed_dict={z: batch_z,
...                                     X_real: batch_x, y: batch_y})
...             sess.run(g_opt, feed_dict={z: batch_z, y: batch_y})
...             _, g_loss_batch = sess.run([g_opt, g_loss], feed_dict=
...                                     {z: batch_z, y: batch_y})
...             if steps % 100 == 0:
...                 train_writer.add_summary(summary, steps)
...                 print("Epoch {}/{} - discriminator loss: {:.4f},
...                     generator Loss: {:.4f}".format(
...                     epoch + 1, epochs, d_loss_batch, g_loss_batch))
...             steps += 1
...         gen_samples = sess.run(generator(z, y),
...                                     feed_dict={z:sample_z, y: sample_y})
...         display_images(gen_samples)
```

Refer to the following screenshot for the end result for epoch 50:

```
Epoch 50/100 - discriminator loss: 1.3209, generator Loss: 0.8174
Epoch 50/100 - discriminator loss: 1.2812, generator Loss: 0.6854
Epoch 50/100 - discriminator loss: 1.2830, generator Loss: 0.8437
Epoch 50/100 - discriminator loss: 1.3071, generator Loss: 0.7735
Epoch 50/100 - discriminator loss: 1.2385, generator Loss: 0.8254
```

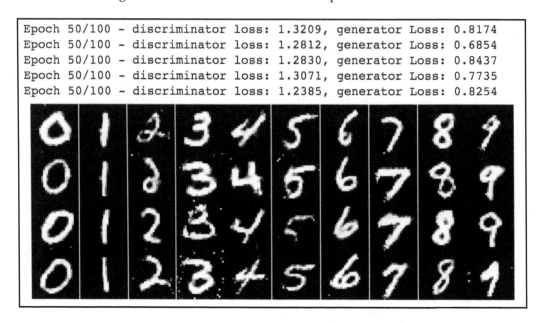

And refer to the following screenshot for the end result for epoch 100:

```
Epoch 100/100 - discriminator loss: 0.9967, generator Loss: 1.3391
Epoch 100/100 - discriminator loss: 1.0695, generator Loss: 0.9874
Epoch 100/100 - discriminator loss: 1.0823, generator Loss: 1.0086
Epoch 100/100 - discriminator loss: 1.1206, generator Loss: 0.9811
Epoch 100/100 - discriminator loss: 1.0257, generator Loss: 1.1568
```

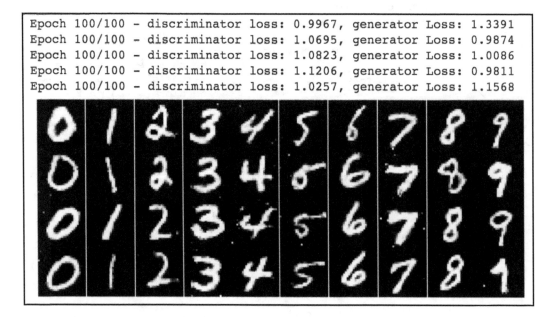

The learning graph that's displayed in TensorBoard is as follows for the discriminator loss:

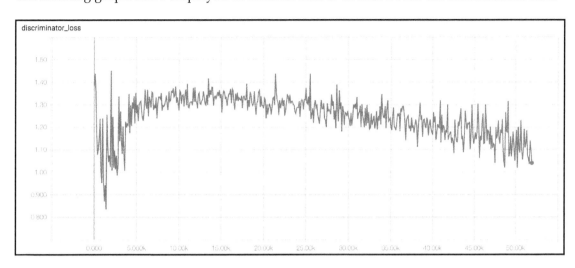

The following graph shows the generator loss:

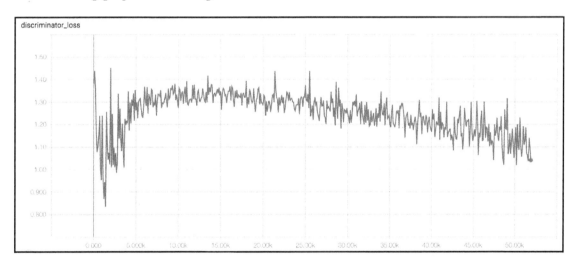

With CGANs, we have full control over what digits to generate, and we also have extensive control over other properties, such as the width or rotation, with InfoGANs.

InfoGANs

InfoGANs (short for **Information Maximizing Generative Adversarial Networks**) are somewhat similar to CGANs in the sense that both generator networks take in an additional parameter and the conditional variable, c, such as label information. They both try to learn the same conditional distribution, $P(X \mid z, c)$. InfoGANs differ from CGANs in the way they treat the conditional variable.

CGANs consider that the conditional variable is known. Hence, the conditional variable is explicitly fed into the discriminator during training. On the contrary, InfoGANs assume that the conditional variable is unknown and latent, which we need to infer based on the training data. The discriminator in an InfoGAN is responsible for deriving the posterior, $P(c \mid X)$. The architecture of an InfoGAN is presented in the following diagram:

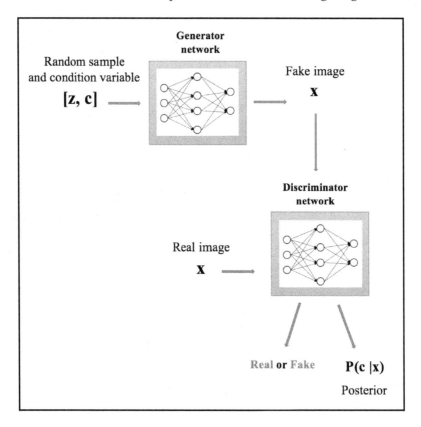

Since we do not need to supply the conditional variable to the discriminator where it will be inferred automatically, we can basically assign it to anything as long as it is related to the data. It is not limited to the label. It can be the width of the edges, the rotation angle, and a certain style. Moreover, it is not limited to just one variable or limited to a categorical value such as *label*. We can have multiple variables or a label variable, along with one or more continuous variables as the latent features.

So, how do InfoGANs learn the latent features? As the name implies, they do so by maximizing information, which refers to mutual information in information theory. We want to maximize the mutual information between c and the generated output from the generator. The `loss` function of InfoGANs can be summarized as follows:

$L_{InfoGAN}(D, G) = L(D,G) - I(c, G(z,c))$

Here, $L(D, G)$ is the `loss` function in regular GANs, $I(c, G(z, c))$ is the mutual information between c and the generated output. More accurately, $P(c \mid G(z, c))$ is predicted as the higher $I(c, G(z, c))$.

Mutual information $I(a, b)$ measures how much we know about a if we know b. The more accurately $P(a \mid b)$ (or $P(b \mid a)$) is predicted, the higher $I(a, b)$ becomes. $I(a, b) = 0$ means a and b are completely irrelevant.

Depending on what the latent variable is, $I(c, G(z, c))$ can be calculated differently. For a categorical variable, it is measured by the `cross` entropy. For the continuous variable, it can be computed as the variance between its distribution (such as a Gaussian distribution).

With all these concepts in mind, we can start developing our InfoGAN model. Recall that we do not need to supply label data in InfoGANs. Hence, we can reuse the `load_dataset_pad` and `gen_batches` functions as DCGANs. Let's load the data first, as always:

```
>>> data = load_dataset_pad()
>>> print("Training dataset shape:", data.shape)
>>> Training dataset shape: (70000, 32, 32, 1)
```

Now, we define a placeholder for the conditional variable as an extra input to the generator:

```
>>> n_classes = 10
>>> n_cont = 1
>>> c = tf.placeholder(tf.float32, shape=[None, n_classes + n_cont],
                       name='conditional_variable')
```

The latent features in this example include ten-dimension one-hot encoded features and a one-dimension continuous one. Now, we define the InfoGAN's generator, which takes in the conditional variable and concatenates it with the input noise:

```
>>> def generator(z, c, n_channel, training=True):
...         """
...         Generator network for InfoGAN
...         @param z: input of random samples
...         @param c: latent features for the input samples
...         @param n_channel: number of output channels
...         @param training: whether to return the output in training mode
...                          (normalized with statistics of the current batch)
...         @return: output of the generator network
...         """
...         with tf.variable_scope('generator', reuse=tf.AUTO_REUSE):
...             z_c = tf.concat([z, c], axis=1)
...             fc = dense(z_c, 256 * 4 * 4, activation=tf.nn.relu)
...             fc = tf.reshape(fc, (-1, 4, 4, 256))
...             trans_conv1 = transpose_conv2d(fc, 128)
...             trans_conv1 = batch_norm(trans_conv1, training=training)
...             trans_conv1 = tf.nn.relu(trans_conv1)
...             trans_conv2 = transpose_conv2d(trans_conv1, 64)
...             trans_conv2 = batch_norm(trans_conv2, training=training)
...             trans_conv2 = tf.nn.relu(trans_conv2)
...             trans_conv3 = transpose_conv2d(trans_conv2, n_channel)
...             out = tf.tanh(trans_conv3)
...             return out
```

As for the discriminator, its first half is the same as DCGAN's discriminator, which is composed of three sets of convolutional layers. Its second half is made up of two fully connected layers, followed by three sets of outputs, the discriminator logits (for determining whether an image is real or fake), the posterior for the continuous variable, and the posterior for the categorical variable:

```
>>> def discriminator(x, n_classes, n_cont=1, alpha=0.2, training=True):
...         """
...         Discriminator network for InfoGAN
...         @param x: input samples, can be real or generated samples
...         @param n_classes: number of categorical latent variables
...         @param n_cont: number of continuous latent variables
...         @param alpha: leaky relu factor
...         @param training: whether to return the output in training mode
...                          (normalized with statistics of the current batch)
...         @return: discriminator logits, posterior for the continuous
...                  variable, posterior for the categorical variable
...         """
...         with tf.variable_scope('discriminator', reuse=tf.AUTO_REUSE):
```

```
...             conv1 = conv2d(x, 64)
...             conv1 = tf.nn.leaky_relu(conv1, alpha)
...             conv2 = conv2d(conv1, 128)
...             conv2 = batch_norm(conv2, training=training)
...             conv2 = tf.nn.leaky_relu(conv2, alpha)
...             conv3 = conv2d(conv2, 256)
...             conv3 = batch_norm(conv3, training=training)
...             conv3 = tf.nn.leaky_relu(conv3, alpha)
...             fc1 = tf.layers.flatten(conv3)
...             fc1 = dense(fc1, 1024)
...             fc1 = batch_norm(fc1, training=training)
...             fc1 = tf.nn.leaky_relu(fc1, alpha)
...             fc2 = dense(fc1, 128)
...             d_logits = dense(fc2, 1)
...             cont = dense(fc2, n_cont)
...             classes = dense(fc2, n_classes)
...             return d_logits, cont, classes
```

Now, we apply the generator and discriminator on the input data, as well as the conditional variable:

```
>>> g_sample = generator(z, c, image_size[2])
>>> d_real_logits, d_real_cont, d_real_cat = discriminator(
                                    X_real, n_classes, n_cont)
>>> d_fake_logits, d_fake_cont, d_fake_cat = discriminator(
                                    g_sample, n_classes, n_cont)
```

Recall that the loss function in InfoGANs are composed of two parts. The first part is the same as that of standard GANs:

```
>>> g_loss = tf.reduce_mean(tf.nn.sigmoid_cross_entropy_with_logits(
                logits=d_fake_logits, labels=tf.ones_like(d_fake_logits)))
>>> d_real_loss = tf.reduce_mean(
...                 tf.nn.sigmoid_cross_entropy_with_logits(
                    logits=d_real_logits,
                    labels=tf.ones_like(d_real_logits)))
>>> d_fake_loss = tf.reduce_mean(tf.nn.sigmoid_cross_entropy_with_logits(
                    logits=d_fake_logits,
                    labels=tf.zeros_like(d_fake_logits)))
>>> d_loss = d_real_loss + d_fake_loss
```

The second part is mutual information. For the one-hot encoded categorical variable, it is measured by cross entropy:

```
>>> cat = c[:, n_cont:]
>>> d_cat_loss = tf.reduce_mean(
...                 tf.nn.softmax_cross_entropy_with_logits(
                    logits=d_fake_cat, labels=cat))
```

For the continuous variable, it can be computed as the variance between its distribution (such as Gaussian distribution):

```
>>> d_cont_loss = tf.reduce_sum(tf.square(d_fake_cont))
```

The information loss (which is the opposite of mutual information) is the weighted sum of these two types of loss:

```
>>> lambda_cont = 0.1
>>> lambda_cat = 1.0
>>> d_info_loss = lambda_cont * d_cont_loss + lambda_cat * cat_loss
```

The final loss for the generator and discriminator becomes the following:

```
>>> g_loss += d_info_loss
>>> tf.summary.scalar('generator_loss', g_loss)
>>> d_loss += d_info_loss
>>> tf.summary.scalar('discriminator_loss', d_loss)
```

We also need to develop a function to generate random conditional variables for training:

```
>>> def gen_condition_variable(n_size, n_classes, n_cont):
...     cont = np.random.randn(n_size, n_cont)
...     cat = np.zeros((n_size, n_classes))
...     cat[range(n_size), np.random.randint(0, n_classes, n_size)] = 1
...     return np.concatenate((cont, cat), axis=1)
```

For quality inspection, we synthesize images for each epoch given noise inputs, along with conditional variables of sets of 10 classes and sets of constant continuous variables. The sample conditional variable is defined as follows:

```
>>> n_sample_display = 40
>>> sample_c = np.zeros((n_sample_display, n_cont + n_classes))
>>> for i in range(n_sample_display):
...     j = i % 10
...     sample_c[i, j + 1] = 1
...     sample_c[i, 0] = -3 + int(i / 10) * 2
```

The 1st, 11th, 21st, and 31st samples are given label 0, the 2nd, 12th, 22nd, and 32nd samples are given label 1, and so forth. The first 10 samples are given the continuous value -3, the next 10 samples -1, then 1, and finally the last 10 samples are assigned 3. The training over 50 epochs is as follows:

```
>>> steps = 0
>>> with tf.Session() as sess:
...     merged = tf.summary.merge_all()
...     train_writer = tf.summary.FileWriter('./logdir/infogan',sess.graph)
```

```
...         sess.run(tf.global_variables_initializer())
...         for epoch in range(epochs):
...             for x in gen_batches(data, batch_size):
...                 batch_z = np.random.uniform(
                            -1, 1, size=(batch_size, noise_size))
...                 batch_c = gen_condition_variable(
                            batch_size, n_classes, n_cont)
...                 _, summary, d_loss_batch = sess.run([d_opt, merged,
                            d_loss], feed_dict=
                            {z: batch_z, X_real: x, c: batch_c})
...                 sess.run(g_opt, feed_dict=
                            {z: batch_z, X_real: x, c: batch_c})
...                 _, g_loss_batch = sess.run([g_opt, g_loss],
                            feed_dict={z: batch_z, X_real: x, c: batch_c})
...                 if steps % 100 == 0:
...                     train_writer.add_summary(summary, steps)
...                     print("Epoch {}/{} - discriminator loss: {:.4f},
                            generator Loss: {:.4f}".format(
...                         epoch + 1, epochs, d_loss_batch, g_loss_batch))
...                 steps += 1
...                 gen_samples = sess.run(generator(z, c,image_size[2],
                            training=False),
                            feed_dict={z: sample_z, c: sample_c})
...                 display_images(gen_samples, 32)
```

Refer to the following screenshot for the end result for epoch 20:

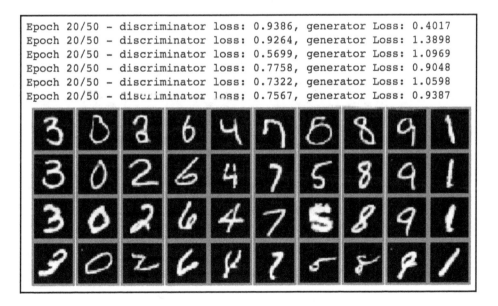

Refer to the following screenshot for the end result for epoch 40:

```
Epoch 40/50 - discriminator loss: 0.5233, generator Loss: 1.7111
Epoch 40/50 - discriminator loss: 0.3349, generator Loss: 1.1098
Epoch 40/50 - discriminator loss: 1.1865, generator Loss: 4.2708
Epoch 40/50 - discriminator loss: 0.3848, generator Loss: 1.8241
Epoch 40/50 - discriminator loss: 0.5007, generator Loss: 0.8337
```

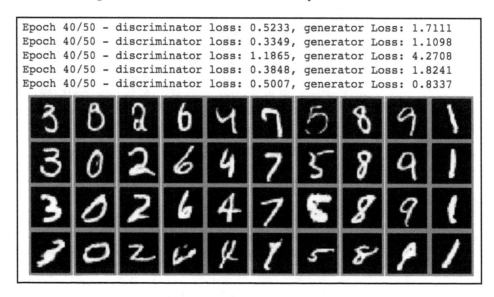

Refer to the following screenshot for the end result for the last epoch:

```
Epoch 50/50 - discriminator loss: 0.2468, generator Loss: 3.0000
Epoch 50/50 - discriminator loss: 0.2044, generator Loss: 1.5761
Epoch 50/50 - discriminator loss: 0.7732, generator Loss: 0.5251
Epoch 50/50 - discriminator loss: 0.2902, generator Loss: 0.9223
Epoch 50/50 - discriminator loss: 0.2233, generator Loss: 2.4616
```

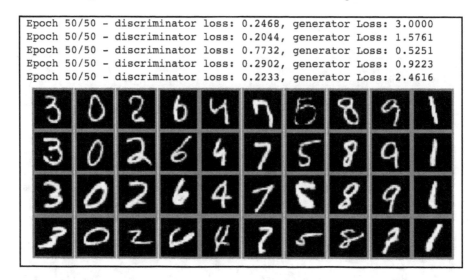

You might have noticed that the generated images are not in the order of 0 to 9. Did we do anything wrong? Fortunately, no. Recall that conditional variable c is unknown in advance to the model and is inferred during training. Label **0** does not necessarily mean digit 0 to the model. But the model acquires the knowledge that category **0** is different than any other category. Hence, the labels from **0** to **9** only represent 10 different categories. It turns out that categories **0** to **9** in our case represent digits **3**, **0**, **2**, **6**, **4**, **7**, **5**, **8**, **9**, **1**. How about the continuous variable? We can see that the rotation of generated images is different row by row, especially **0**, **7**, **8**, **9**, and **1**. The first row (the first 10 images with the input continuous value -3) shows a counterclockwise 20 degree rotation from the vertical axis. The last row (the last 10 images with the input continuous value 3) shows a clockwise 20 degree rotation from the vertical axis.

With InfoGANs, we have extended control over properties such as the width or rotation, besides the category of images we generate.

Summary

We just accomplished an important part of our learning journey regarding deep learning architectures—GANs! Throughout this chapter, we got more familiar with GANs and their variants. We started with what GANs are; the evolution paths of GANs; and how they became so popular in data synthesis, such as image generation, audio, and video generation. We also explored four GAN architectures, that is, vanilla GANs, deep convolutional GANs, conditional GANs, and the information-maximizing GANs. We implemented each individual GAN model from scratch and used them to generate digital images that appear to be real.

GANs are a great invention of deep learning that's been made in recent years. In the next chapter, we will talk about other recent advancements in deep learning, including **Bayesian neural networks**, **capsule networks**, and **meta-learning**.

5

Section 5: The Future of Deep Learning and Advanced Artificial Intelligence

In this section, we would like to talk about a few ideas in deep learning that we found impactful this year and that should be more prominent in the future.

The following chapters will be covered in this section:

- Chapter 8, *New Trends of Deep Learning*

New Trends of Deep Learning 8

In the first seven chapters of this book, deep neural networks with varied architectures have demonstrated their ability to learn from image, text, and transactional data. Even though deep learning has been developing rapidly over recent years, its evolution doesn't seem to be decelerating anytime soon. We are seeing new deep learning architectures being proposed almost every month, and new solutions becoming state-of-the-art every now and then. Hence, in this last chapter, we would like to talk about a few ideas in deep learning that we found to be impactful this year and that should be more prominent in the future.

In this chapter, we will look at the following topics:

- Bayesian neural networks
- Limitation of deep learning models
- Implementation of Bayesian neural networks
- Capsule networks
- Limitation of **convolutional neural network (CNNs)**
- Meta-learning
- Challenges in deep learning
- Implementation of meta-learning models

New trends in deep learning

There are many other interesting deep learning models and architectures that are difficult to classify, other than the ones we mentioned in previous chapters, and at the same time, they are the new trends in deep learning and will have a huge impact in years to come. In NLP, **BERT** (which stands for **Bidirectional Encoder Representations from Transformers**) became the state-of-the-art language model (for more details, refer to the following paper, which was published by Google: `https://arxiv.org/pdf/1810.04805.pdf`). As for computer vision, GANs continue to gain popularity and improve. Their inventor, Ian Goodfellow, proposed Attention Generative Adversarial Networks for generating images in finer detail, which includes three new trends, as follows:

- Bayesian neural networks
- Capsule networks
- Meta-learning

Bayesian neural networks

Bayesian deep learning combines the merits of both Bayesian learning and deep learning. It provides a deep learning framework that can achieve state-of-the-art performance and at the same time capture and model uncertainty. Let's first start with understanding what uncertainty means, and then we can move on to how Bayesian deep learning looks at things from the perspective of uncertainty.

What our deep learning models don't know – uncertainty

Uncertainty is the state of not being able to exactly describe the future outcome(s) due to limited knowledge. In the context of machine learning or deep learning, it is about the ambiguity of the predictive outcome(s), or about subjective definitions and concepts by humans, instead of objective facts of nature. Uncertainty is important as it provides us with information about how confident the predictions are—if they are under-confident or falsely over-confident, we might reject our predictions.

Our deep learning models are usually unable to estimate this uncertainty. They generate the predictions and blindly accept that they are accurate. You may argue that the last sigmoid or softmax layer provides the probability of a predictive outcome. Isn't it confidence? The higher the probability, the higher the confidence? Unfortunately, it isn't confidence, because the probability describes one outcome **relative to** others, which does not explain the overall confidence.

Not knowing uncertainty can be problematic in many cases. For example, an AI-assisted vehicle crashed in May 2016 as it failed to recognize a white tractor trailer under a bright sky. Back in 2016, the image classification system in Google Photos tagged two Africans as gorillas. If uncertainty in incorporated in algorithms, false decisions are likely avoided as predictions with low confidence will be rejected.

How we can obtain uncertainty information – Bayesian neural networks

Bayesian deep learning associates predictions with uncertainty information. Let's see how it works.

In our conventional deep learning models, parameters including weights w and bias b are optimized via **maximum likelihood estimation** (**MLE**):

$$w = argmax_w \, logP(x,y \,|\, w)$$

After the model has been trained, each coefficient of the parameters (such as $w_1, w_2, \ldots b_1, b_2, \ldots$) is a scalar, for example, $w_1 = 1$, $w_2 = 3$.

On the contrary, in Bayesian learning, each coefficient is associated with a distribution. For example, they can be in a Gaussian distribution, $w_1 \sim N(1,1), w_2 \sim N(3,2)$, as displayed in the following plots:

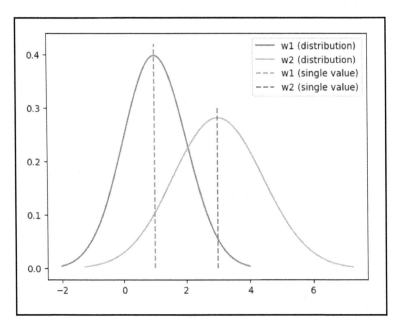

The good thing about having a distribution over a single value is that it provides a measure of how confident the predictions are. If consistent predictions are generated using different sets of parameters that have been sampled from their distributions, we can say that the predictions are of a high confidence. On the contrary, we can say that the predictions are of low confidence if the predictions are inconsistent over various samples.

Estimating the distributions of parameters is equivalent to a maximum a posteriori estimate (MAP) of the parameters:

$$w = argmax_w \, logP(w \mid x,y)$$

According to the Bayesian rule, $P(w \mid x, y)$ can be computed as follows:

$$P(w|x,y) = \frac{P(x,y|w)P(w)}{\int P(y|x,w)P(w)dw}$$

The difficult part is calculating the denominator, which is the evidence. This requires integrating over all possible values of w. Fortunately, it can be approximated using techniques such as **Monte Carlo**, or **Variational Inference**. We will not provide details on these techniques here as they are outside the scope of this book. Instead, we will implement Bayesian neural networks using TensorFlow and demonstrate the power of having uncertainty information.

Edward (http://edwardlib.org/) is the library we will be utilizing to realize Bayesian inference. It is built on top of TensorFlow and designed for probabilistic modeling and inference, including Variational Inference and Monte Carlo. At the time of writing (the end of 2018), Edward is only compatible with TensorFlow 1.7. Hence, we will have to uninstall our current version of TensorFlow and install version 1.7 before installing Edward:

```
pip uninstall tensorflow
pip install tensorflow==1.7.0.
pip install edward
```

Don't forget to install the latest version of TensorFlow after this section. Now, we can perform the following steps to implement a Bayesian neural network:

1. Let's import the necessary packages:

```
>>> import numpy as np
>>> import tensorflow as tf
>>> from edward.models import Categorical, Normal
>>> import edward as ed
```

2. Load the training and testing data. We will be using the MNIST dataset in our example:

```
>>> def load_dataset():
...     (x_train, y_train), (x_test, y_test) =
                tf.keras.datasets.mnist.load_data('./mnist_data')
...     x_train = x_train / 255.
...     x_train = x_train.reshape([-1, 28 * 28])
...     x_test = x_test / 255.
...     x_test = x_test.reshape([-1, 28 * 28])
...     return (x_train, y_train), (x_test, y_test)
>>> (x_train, y_train), (x_test, y_test) = load_dataset()
```

3. Define some placeholders and variables:

```
>>> batch_size = 100
>>> n_features = 28 * 28
>>> n_classes = 10
>>> x = tf.placeholder(tf.float32, [None, n_features])
>>> y_ph = tf.placeholder(tf.int32, [batch_size])
```

4. For simplicity, we will use a neural network with only one hidden layer, and w and b. We set up the prior for the weights and biases with Gaussian distribution, respectively:

```
>>> w = Normal(loc=tf.zeros([n_features, n_classes]),
               scale=tf.ones([n_features, n_classes]))
>>> b = Normal(loc=tf.zeros(n_classes), scale=tf.ones(n_classes))
```

5. The `loc` parameter specifies the mean of the distribution, and the scale parameter specifies the standard deviation. Then, we can compute the prediction outputs:

```
>>> y = Categorical(tf.matmul(x, w) + b)
```

Because the parameters of the model are distributions as opposed to single values, the outputs should also be of a distribution—specially categorical distribution.

6. As we mentioned previously, we use Variational Inference to approximate the posterior of w and b. We set up the approximating distributions, *Q(w)* and *Q(b)*, which will be optimized to match the true posterior distributions of w and b. The dissimilarity between two sets of distributions is measured by **Kullback-Leibler** (**KL**) divergence, which we try to minimize.

Again, the approximating distributions, *Q(w)* and *Q(b)*, are also Gaussian distributions, but with random initial positions:

```
>>> qw = Normal(loc=tf.Variable(tf.random_normal(
            [n_features, n_classes])), scale=tf.nn.softplus(
            tf.Variable(tf.random_normal([n_features, n_classes])))))
>>> qb = Normal(loc=tf.Variable(tf.random_normal([n_classes])),
                scale=tf.nn.softplus(tf.Variable(
                tf.random_normal([n_classes])))))
```

7. Next, we define and initialize a variational inference with the KL divergence:

```
>>> inference = ed.KLqp({w: qw, b: qb}, data={y: y_ph})
>>> inference.initialize(n_iter=100, scale=
                    {y: float(x_train.shape[0]) / batch_size})
```

The variational inference comes with 100 iterations.

8. Don't forget to start a TensorFlow session and initialize all variables for the session:

```
>>> sess = tf.InteractiveSession()
>>> tf.global_variables_initializer().run()
```

9. Now, we can start training the Bayesian network model in a mini-batch manner, where we reuse the batch generation function we defined in Chapter 7, *Generative Adversarial Networks*:

```
>>> def gen_batches_label(x_data, y_data, batch_size,
shuffle=True):
...         """
...         Generate batches including label for training
...         @param x_data: training data
...         @param y_data: training label
...         @param batch_size: batch size
...         @param shuffle: shuffle the data or not
...         @return: batches generator
...         """
...         n_data = x_data.shape[0]
...         if shuffle:
...             idx = np.arange(n_data)
...             np.random.shuffle(idx)
...             x_data = x_data[idx]
...             y_data = y_data[idx]
...         for i in range(0, n_data - batch_size, batch_size):
...             x_batch = x_data[i:i + batch_size]
...             y_batch = y_data[i:i + batch_size]
...             yield x_batch, y_batch

>>> for _ in range(inference.n_iter):
...     for X_batch, Y_batch in gen_batches_label(
                        x_train, y_train, batch_size):
...         inference.update(feed_dict={x: X_batch, y_ph: Y_batch})
```

10. After training is done, we evaluate our model (the optimized approximating distributions *Q(w)* and *Q(b)*) on the testing set. Because they are distributions, we can sample various sets of *w* and *b* and compute the corresponding predictions. We train the sample 30 times, but in general, the more training, the better:

```
>>> n_samples = 30
>>> pred_samples = []
>>> for _ in range(n_samples):
...        w_sample = qw.sample()
...        b_sample = qb.sample()
...        prob = tf.nn.softmax(
                    tf.matmul(x_test.astype(np.float32), w_sample)
                            + b_sample)
...        pred = np.argmax(prob.eval(), axis=1).astype(np.float32)
...        pred_samples.append(pred)
```

11. The predictions from each sampled parameter is recorded in `pred_samples`. Now, we can compute the accuracy for each set of predictions:

```
>>> acc_samples = []
>>> for pred in pred_samples:
...        acc = (pred == y_test).mean() * 100
...        acc_samples.append(acc)
```

The accuracies for the 30 sets of predictions are as follows:

```
>>> print('The classification accuracy for each sample of w and
b:',
            acc_samples)
The classification accuracy for each sample of w and b:
[90.86999999999999, 90.86, 91.84, 90.88000000000001, 91.33,
91.14999999999999, 90.42, 90.59, 91.36, 91.18, 90.25, 91.22, 89.36,
90.99000000000001, 90.99000000000001, 91.33, 91.2, 91.38, 90.56,
90.75, 90.75, 91.01, 90.96, 91.17, 91.29, 91.03, 91.12, 91.64,
91.44, 90.71000000000001]
```

The accuracies for individual samples are very consistent, around 91%. This indicates that the model predicts with high confidence. We can also take a closer look at an image example to verify this. We need to take the first testing image (that is, label 7) and display it:

```
>>> image_test_ind = 0
>>> image_test = x_test[image_test_ind]
>>> label_test = y_test[image_test_ind]
>>> print('The label of the image is:', label_test)
The label of the image is: 7
>>> import matplotlib.pyplot as plt
```

```
>>> plt.imshow(image_test.reshape((28, 28)),cmap='Blues')
>>> plt.show()
```

Refer to the following screenshot for the end result:

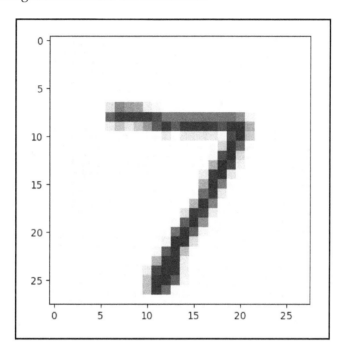

The predictions for this example are as follows:

```
>>> pred_samples_test = [pred[image_test_ind] for pred in pred_samples]
>>> print('The predictions for the example are:', pred_samples_test)
The predictions for the example are: [7.0, 7.0, 7.0, 7.0, 7.0, 7.0, 7.0,
7.0, 7.0, 7.0, 7.0, 7.0, 7.0, 7.0, 7.0, 7.0, 7.0, 7.0, 7.0, 7.0, 7.0, 7.0,
7.0, 7.0, 7.0, 7.0, 7.0, 7.0, 7.0, 7.0]
```

We also make a histogram of the predictions to visualize them better:

```
>>> plt.hist(pred_samples_test, bins=range(10))
>>> plt.xticks(np.arange(0,10))
>>> plt.xlim(0, 10)
>>> plt.xlabel("Predictions for the example")
>>> plt.ylabel("Frequency")
>>> plt.show()
```

Refer to the following screenshot for the end result:

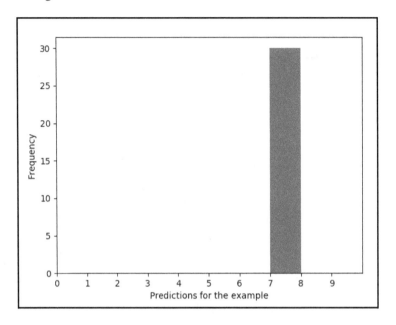

The predictions are consistent and of confidence. What will the predictions look like if they are inconsistent? We can see this by using the *notMNIST* dataset. The *notMNIST* dataset contains 529,119 28 x 28 grayscale images of letters from **A** to **J**. Refer to the following screenshot for the dataset:

We can download the dataset from `http://yaroslavvb.com/upload/notMNIST/`. Click the link for `MNIST_small.tar.gz` (`http://yaroslavvb.com/upload/notMNIST/notMNIST_small.tar.gz`), which contains a small subset of the dataset, and unzip the file. Take one example and display it:

```
>>> from scipy import ndimage
>>> image_file = 'notMNIST_small/A/MDRiXzA4LnR0Zg==.png'
>>> image_not = ndimage.imread(image_file).astype(float)
>>> plt.imshow(image_not, cmap='Blues')
>>> plt.show()
```

Refer to the following screenshot for the end result:

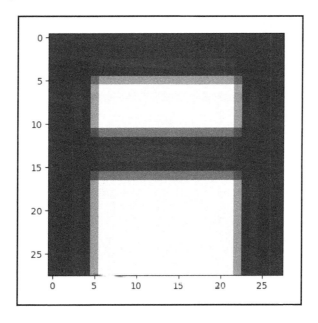

Preprocess the image, like we did previously:

```
>>> image_not = image_not / 255.
>>> image_not = image_not.reshape([-1, 28 * 28])
```

Similarly, we sample over the trained model and make predictions using each set of sampled parameters:

```
>>> pred_samples_not = []
>>> for _ in range(n_samples):
...     w_sample = qw.sample()
...     b_sample = qb.sample()
...     prob = tf.nn.softmax(tf.matmul(
                 image_not.astype(np.float32),w_sample) + b_sample)
...     pred = np.argmax(prob.eval(), axis=1).astype(np.float32)
...     pred_samples_not.append(pred[0])
```

The predictions of this notMNIST example (an **A**) are as follows:

```
>>> print('The predictions for the notMNIST example are:',
                                        pred_samples_not)
The predictions for the notMNIST example are: [2.0, 5.0, 2.0, 2.0, 2.0,
2.0, 2.0, 3.0, 5.0, 5.0, 8.0, 2.0, 5.0, 5.0, 5.0, 3.0, 2.0, 5.0, 6.0, 2.0,
2.0, 5.0, 2.0, 2.0, 2.0, 2.0, 3.0, 3.0, 8.0, 2.0]
```

Again, we make a histogram of the predictions to better visualize them:

```
>>> plt.hist(pred_samples_not, bins=range(10))
>>> plt.xticks(np.arange(0,10))
>>> plt.xlim(0,10)
>>> plt.xlabel("Predictions for the notMNIST example")
>>> plt.ylabel("Frequency")
>>> plt.show()
```

Refer to the following screenshot for the end result:

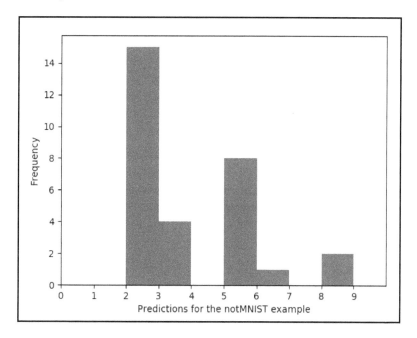

The predictions are very inconsistent. As we can see, **2**, **3**, **5**, **6**, and **8** are all over the place. This is what we expected as the ground truth is an **A**, which is not any of the 10 classes (**0** to **9**) the model knows. In Bayesian learning, the predictions are of high uncertainty, and it we will reject our predictions. In conventional learning, the model will give a prediction that provides no information of confidence or certainty.

Capsule networks

Capsule networks are a new type of deep neural network. They process visual information in a similar way to 3D computer graphics. They preserve hierarchical relationships between objects, which CNNs fail to do. Although CNNs are still the go-to solutions for most computer vision tasks, they are still facing some challenges. Let's talk about how Capsule networks came to the rescue.

What convolutional neural networks fail to do

Don't get me wrong—CNNs are great and still the dominant solution for most computer vision problems nowadays. By looking back at what we studied in the previous chapters, CNNs are good at detecting effective features from pixels that are activated by convolutional filters, thus simulating human visual system process images. They detect low-level features such as edges and lines in early layers, and high-level features such as contour and shape in later layers. However, it has a fundamental limitation—it has a lack of spatial hierarchies.

Let's say we are working on a face detection project using a CNN model. Some convolutions of the well-trained network may *recognize* eyes, but some may be triggered by noses, and some ears or mouths. The fully connected layer(s) may recognize a face as long as we have all components, including two eyes and ears, one nose, and one mouth, regardless of their relative positions. That's right! So, the following two images, A and B, will both pass the CNN face detector:

Image A:

Image B:

Obviously image B is not a face, since it has its eyes, nose, mouth, and ears all over the place. But because CNN merely cares about the presence of certain components, and not the relative positions of these components and their orientations, it is classified as a face. Capsule networks were invented by Geoffrey Hinton (*Dynamic Routing Between Capsules*, https://arxiv.org/abs/1710.09829) to incorporate information that's of relative spatial relationships between components and their orientations.

Capsule networks – incorporating oriental and relative spatial relationships

The invention of capsule networks was inspired by computer graphics, where an image is constructed from the internal geometric information of objects. This data is stored as arrays of the geometric objects and matrices that represent the hierarchical and relative positions of these objects, as well as their orientation.

In CNNs, a neuron outputs a scalar. In capsule networks, a neuron outputs a vector, which encodes all important geometric information in the following ways:

- The length of the vector indicates how likely an object (for example, an eye, ear, and nose, or a certain shape) is detected
- The direction of the vector encodes the orientation of the object

The following example of detecting a skyscraper can help you understand the vector better:

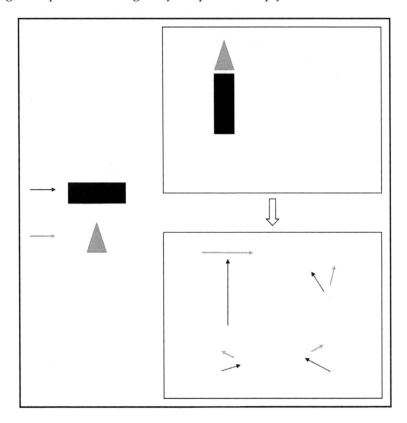

In this simplified example, two vectors (black and blue) represent the horizontal rectangle and triangle. We can observe this in the resulting vector representation map: the top-left region with the presence of skyscraper has the longest vectors, and their orientation matches that of the skyscraper; regions without the skyscraper have short vectors, and their orientation is different from the skyscraper's.

The beauty of such a representation is that the model is able to detect objects from all different view angles. Let's say we have a vector for detecting the horizontal rectangle of skyscraper with a length of 0.8. If we change the viewpoint of the skyscraper in the image, the vector will rotate accordingly as the state of the detected object changes. However, the length of the vector remains 0.8 because the object is still detected. This property of Capsule networks is called **activities equivariance** or **invariance**, which can't be achieved by CNNs with pooling.

Using vectors instead of scales as the outputs of neurons, capsule networks extend CNNs by encoding hierarchical and geometric relationships between features that have been extracted from different layers. Features are no longer in flat two dimensions, but in a three-dimensional space, similar to images in computer graphics. Now, you may be wondering how a vector is consumed and produced by a capsule. Let's compare and summarize the computation in a capsule and that found in a traditional neuron in the following tables:

Traditional neuron		
Input	Scalar x	
Computation	Weighted sum	$z = w * x + b$
	Activation	$a = f(z)$
Output	Scalar a	

Capsule		
Input	Vector $\boldsymbol{u}$	
Computation	Affine transformation	$\hat{\boldsymbol{u}} = w * \boldsymbol{u}$
	Weighted sum	$s = c * \hat{\boldsymbol{u}}$
	Activation	$\boldsymbol{v} = \dfrac{\|s\|^2}{1 + \|s\|^2} \cdot \dfrac{s}{\|s\|^2}$
Output	Vector v	

Rather than going through a weighted sum directly, a capsule first runs a matrix multiplication in order to obtain higher-level features. Let's reuse our skyscraper detection

example and assume that we have an input vector, u_1, for detecting the rectangle and u_2 for detecting the triangle. These two vectors are then multiplied by the corresponding weight vectors from the affine transformation matrix **W**. A weight vector might encode a relative position between the rectangle and skyscraper, while another weight vector might try to learn the orientation of the relationship between the triangle and the skyscraper. After affine transformation, we can obtain higher-level features, $\hat{u}_1$ and $\hat{u}_2$, which represent where and how the skyscraper should be according to the positions and orientation of the triangle and rectangle.

After this, the next step is to perform a weighted sum, which sounds quite familiar. In a traditional neuron, weights are optimized and computed via backpropagation. However, weights are learned using **dynamic routing** in a capture. The main idea of dynamic routing is to use a majority vote to determine what the most likely object should like. Weight c for vectors that are close to true predictions should be of a high value and weight c corresponding to vectors that are far from correct predictions should be of a low value.

Finally, the activation function in a capsule is also something new. Recall that in a traditional neuron, typical activation functions include sigmoid, tanh, and ReLU, whose main purpose is adding non-linearity and rescaling the input. Similarly, for a capsule, the second half of the activation function converts the length of the input vector to 1, but doesn't alter its direction; the first half of the activation function, which is called **squashing**, further scales the length so that it won't be equal to 1 and at the same time adds some non-linearity.

That is how computation in a capsule works. To conclude, capsule networks employ powerful representations—vectors—to encode important hierarchical information of features across different layers, which is not available in traditional CNNs using scalars. Last but not least, if you are interested in implementing capsule networks on your own, feel free to check out the following links about Keras and the CapsLayer:

- https://github.com/XifengGuo/CapsNet-Keras
- https://github.com/naturomics/CapsLayer

Meta-learning

Meta-learning is another exciting trend of research in deep learning. It goes beyond training on a huge dataset for a specific task, like traditional learning does. It tries to mimic a humans' learning process by leveraging a past experience that has been learned from a distribution of tasks. It can achieve good performance, even with just a handful of training samples. However, conventional deep learning methods are not able to do so.

One big challenge in deep learning – training data

You might have seen the following plot, comparing the performance between deep learning and traditional machine learning algorithms given various amount of training data:

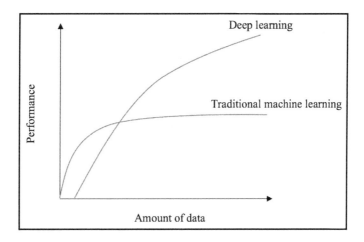

With only a small amount of training data available, deep learning algorithms usually don't work or perform worse than traditional machine learning algorithms. With enough data, deep learning starts to beat traditional learning. And as the amount of data increases, its impact on the performance gap grows. The clear message here is that deep learning in general needs a sufficient amount of training data to achieve good performance.

The reason why deep learning needs a huge dataset to succeed is that it trains the model (or some critical parts of the model) from scratch using this dataset. Do you see the problem here? Obviously, conventional deep learning algorithms can't learn fast from a handful of data samples, unlike us humans, who can pick up on this quickly by leveraging past experiences. We can summarize the weaknesses of how **machine learning** (ML)/ **deep learning** (DL) learns compared to how humans learn from the following two aspects:

- **Sample efficiency**: Deep learning has low sample efficiency as it needs sufficient samples from individual classes for classification tasks, and with enough variations for regression tasks. For instance, we usually train a handwritten digit recognizer on thousands of samples per digit.
- **Transferability**: For a specific task, deep learning doesn't learn from previous experience or leverage learned knowledge from the same task. You may argue that transfer learning is exactly like utilizing a previous experience, but remember that the transferred knowledge is acquired from a different task and that we still need to fine-tune critical parts of the model using a huge dataset.

So, how can we make deep learning learn close to how humans do—learn to learn? How can it still learn efficiently when we don't have enough training data? The answer is meta-learning.

Meta-learning – learning to learn

Meta-learning is a modern subfield in machine learning. It uses metadata about machine learning experiments to automatically solve new learning problems with similar properties. In meta-learning, training is limited to samples from a single distribution, and is not jeopardized by a small training size. This is just like how kids can tell apart cats and dogs after seeing them only a few times. On the other hand, meta-learning goes beyond one single task; it learns about distributions over tasks so that it still works for a task that's never been presented before. Like kids, with the knowledge that they've learned from cats and dogs, they can tell apart tigers and wolves without seeing any tigers or wolves before. In short, meta-learning **learns to learn**. It tries to build on knowledge (metadata) of how to solve tasks.

In meta-learning, a model is trained over a variety of tasks. Each learning task is associated with a dataset which contains both input features and a target variable. The goal of learning is to optimize the model for the least loss on a distribution of these tasks. Note that the model here means a high-level optimizer, which updates the weights of a low-level model. That is, the high-level model is trained to learn the low-level model. And one dataset of a task is considered one data sample in the whole process.

There are many different approaches to meta-learning since *meta-learning* is still a loose term and a relatively new concept. Popular ones include the following:

- **Model-learning based meta learning**: It is a sequential model that can update its parameters with just a few steps. A typical model-learning architecture can be found in the **Memory-Augmented Neural Networks (MANN)**, as depicted in the following diagram, which looks similar to an RNN. In a MANN, the last step of the model takes in a sample to be predicted. Before that, each step takes in a training sample and the label of the sample is fed in the previous step. With such an explicit storage buffer (also called **one step offset**), the network is motivated to memorize the learning experience, which goes beyond simple mapping from features to labels. Moreover, we will worry less about the limited training size under this setup, since we can easily generate a large number of training cases by randomly selecting different training data points (X, Y) and shuffling their orders. An example of model-based meta learning is depicted in the following diagram:

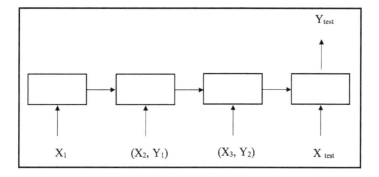

- Metric-based learning, which we will be discussing in detail in the following section.

Metric-based meta-learning

Given a limited amount of training data, what we should do is extract the most important information and not overdo this. Metric-based meta-learning tries to achieve the same goal. It extracts features at the right level by utilizing a metric or distance function.

A typical metric-based learning model is the **Siamese Neural Network**. As shown in the architecture in the following diagram, it is composed of two identical networks which share the same weights and parameters to extract features from two inputs, respectively:

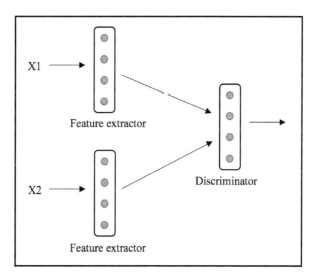

The extracted features from the twin networks are then fed into a discriminator to determine whether the two input data samples belong to the same class or not. The discriminator first computes the distance (such as L1-distance, L2-distance, cosine similarity) between the pair of features. The distance will then be passed to a fully connected layer with sigmoid activation to generate a probability of two inputs being from the same class.

In one word, the twin networks try to learn efficient features so that the relationship between two inputs is unveiled. To help better understand this metric-based network, we are going to implement it and apply it to a face recognition project with a limited amount of data.

A standard face recognition system should be able to recognize an individual's identity with just several pictures of that person in the system. Obviously, it can't be forced to take hundreds of pictures of a person in order to accumulate enough training data. Even though it is a multi-class classification problem, CNNs can't really work on a small training set in this case, where there are a lot more classes than samples per class. Moreover, if we go the typical multi-class classification route, the model will have to be retrained every time a new user enrols in the system, which is rather impractical. Fortunately, Siamese Neural Networks are good at dealing with this **few-shot learning** problem.

We will use the face database from AT&T (www.cl.cam.ac.uk/research/dtg/attarchive/facedatabase.html, also called the **ORL Database of Faces**) as an example. Download the dataset from http://www.cl.cam.ac.uk/Research/DTG/attarchive/pub/data/att_faces.tar.Z and unzip it. The extracted folder has 40 subfolders, ranging from s1 to s40, which represent 40 subjects. Each subfolder contains 10 image files, 1.pgm, 2.pgm, ..., 10.pgm. So, in total, there are only 400 image samples, from 40 individuals. Again, it would be almost impossible to get a typical CNN classifier to work with just 400 training samples.

Each image is of size 92 * 112 and has 256 grey levels. The image files are in PGM format. Let's start by reading and displaying one sample using the PIL package. **PIL** stands for **Python Imaging Library**, and can installed with the following command, if you haven't got it already:

```
pip install Pillow
```

Now, read and display one image sample:

```
>>> from PIL import Image
>>> img = Image.open('./orl_faces/s1/1.pgm')
>>> print(img.size)
(92, 112)
>>> img.show()
```

First, we write a function to load all the images, along with their subject IDs, into a dictionary where key is the subject ID and value is a list of 10 images:

```
>>> image_size = [92, 112, 1]
>>> def load_images_ids(path='./orl_faces'):
...         id_image = {}
...         for id in range(1, 41):
...             id_image[id] = []
...             for image_id in range(1, 11):
...                 img = Image.open('{}/s{}/{}.pgm'.format(
                                                        path, id, image_id))
...                 img = np.array(img).reshape(image_size)
...                 id_image[id].append(img)
...         return id_image
```

 Note that each image matrix is reshaped into the dimension [92, 112, 1].

Now, load all the images and their subject IDs:

```
>>> id_image = load_images_ids()
```

The way we work around this project with only 400 samples is to convert it from a multi-class classification to a binary classification problem. Rather than directly predicting which one out of the 40 subjects an image belongs to, we predict the probabilities of the image belonging to individual subjects, and the one with the highest probability becomes the final result. The probability of the image belonging to a subject is derived from the distance between the image and a sample from the subject. The following diagram illustrates the prediction process:

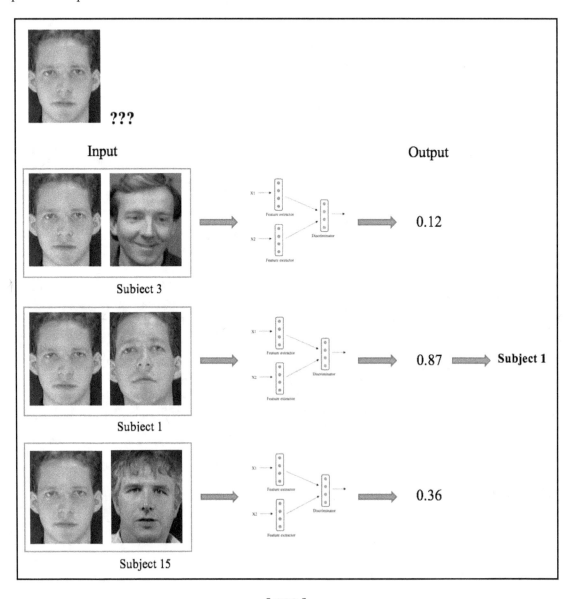

Given an image from an unknown subject, we compare it with each image from three subjects, respectively (assuming there are only three subjects in the system). We feed each pair of images to the Siamese Neural Network and obtain the probability scores. The pair with an image from subject 1 achieves the highest probability. Hence, the query image is most likely to be from subject 1. Using this strategy, we will be able to generate a lot more training samples (or, to be specific, pairs) out of 400 images in order to fit the Siamese Neural Network. For example, we can create 10 * 9 / 2 = 45 unique positive pairs per subject at most, or 45 * 40 = 1800 unique positive pairs for all 40 subjects in total. Similarly, we can form 10 * 10 = 100 unique negative pairs per pair of subjects, or 100 * (40 * 39 / 2) = 78,000 unique negative pairs for all possible pairs of subjects in total. At the end, we are able to obtain hundreds more training samples, which really boosts face recognition performance.

Now, let's build the Siamese Neural Network in Keras by performing the following steps:

1. First, import all the modules that are needed:

```
>>> from keras import backend as K
>>> from keras.layers import Activation
>>> from keras.layers import Input, Lambda, Dense, Dropout,
        Convolution2D, MaxPooling2D, Flatten
>>> from keras.models import Sequential, Model
```

2. Our Siamese Network is composed of a convolutional layer, since we are working with images, a max pooling layer, and a fully connected layer. Siamese Networks of such an architecture are called **Convolutional Siamese Neural Networks**:

```
>>> def siamese_network():
...     seq = Sequential()
...     nb_filter = 16
...     kernel_size = 6
...     # Convolution layer
...     seq.add(Convolution2D(nb_filter, (kernel_size,
kernel_size),
                input_shape=image_size, border_mode='valid'))
...     seq.add(Activation('relu'))
...     seq.add(MaxPooling2D(pool_size=(2, 2)))
...     seq.add(Dropout(.25))
...     # flatten
...     seq.add(Flatten())
...     seq.add(Dense(50, activation='relu'))
...     seq.add(Dropout(0.1))
...     return seq
```

3. Then, we can define input placeholders, two images, and pass them to the Siamese Network:

```
>>> img_1 = Input(shape=image_size)
>>> img_2 = Input(shape=image_size)
>>> base_network = siamese_network()
>>> feature_1 = base_network(img_1)
>>> feature_2 = base_network(img_2)
```

4. Then, we need to compute the distance (we are using L1-distance) between these two resulting feature vectors and map the result to a probability output:

```
>>> distance_function = lambda x: K.abs(x[0] - x[1])
>>> distance = Lambda(distance_function, output_shape=
                            lambda x: x[0])([feature_1, feature_2])
>>> prediction = Dense(1, activation='sigmoid')(distance)
```

5. Finally, we need to wrap up the Keras model with input and output placeholders and compile it with an Adam-based optimizer and cross entropy as the loss function:

```
>>> model = Model(input=[img_1, img_2], output=prediction)
>>> from keras.losses import binary_crossentropy
>>> from keras.optimizers import Adam
>>> optimizer = Adam(lr=0.001)
>>> model.compile(loss=binary_crossentropy, optimizer=optimizer)
```

6. Now that the model is ready to train, we need to construct the training set using the following function, where positive pairs are randomly selected from individual subjects and negative pairs are randomly chosen from pairs of two different subjects. The positive and negative ratio is kept at 50:50:

```
>>> np.random.seed(42)
>>> def gen_train_data(n, id_image):
...         X_1, X_2 = [], []
...         Y = [1] * (n // 2) + [0] * (n // 2)
...         # generate positive samples
...         ids = np.random.choice(range(1, 41), n // 2)
...         for id in ids:
...             two_image_ids = np.random.choice(range(10), 2, False)
...             X_1.append(id_image[id][two_image_ids[0]])
...             X_2.append(id_image[id][two_image_ids[1]])
...         # generate negative samples, by randomly selecting two
                    images from two ids
...         for _ in range(n // 2):
...             two_ids = np.random.choice(range(1, 41), 2, False)
...             two_image_ids = np.random.randint(0, 10, 2)
```

```
...             X_1.append(id_image[two_ids[0]][two_image_ids[0]])
...             X_2.append(id_image[two_ids[1]][two_image_ids[1]])
...         X_1 = np.array(X_1).reshape([n] + image_size) / 255
...         X_2 = np.array(X_2).reshape([n] + image_size) / 255
...         Y = np.array(Y)
...         return [X_1, X_2], Y
```

We obtain 8,000 training samples:

```
>>> X_train, Y_train = gen_train_data(8000, id_image)
```

7. Now, we can fit the model on the training set with 10 epochs and a 10% data split for validation:

```
>>> epochs = 10
>>> model.fit(X_train, Y_train, validation_split=0.1,
batch_size=64, verbose=1, epochs=epochs)
Epoch 1/10
7200/7200 [==============================] - 71s 10ms/step - loss:
0.5168 - val_loss: 0.3305
Epoch 2/10
7200/7200 [==============================] - 62s 9ms/step - loss:
0.3259 - val_loss: 0.2210
Epoch 3/10
7200/7200 [==============================] - 59s 8ms/step - loss:
0.2467 - val_loss: 0.2219
Epoch 4/10
7200/7200 [==============================] - 59s 8ms/step - loss:
0.2089 - val_loss: 0.1669
Epoch 5/10
7200/7200 [==============================] - 60s 8ms/step - loss:
0.1920 - val_loss: 0.1521
Epoch 6/10
7200/7200 [==============================] - 59s 8ms/step - loss:
0.1534 - val_loss: 0.1441
Epoch 7/10
7200/7200 [==============================] - 59s 8ms/step - loss:
0.1509 - val_loss: 0.1124
Epoch 8/10
7200/7200 [==============================] - 58s 8ms/step - loss:
0.1408 - val_loss: 0.1323
Epoch 9/10
7200/7200 [==============================] - 59s 8ms/step - loss:
0.1281 - val_loss: 0.1360
Epoch 10/10
7200/7200 [==============================] - 58s 8ms/step - loss:
0.1215 - val_loss: 0.1736
```

Training and validation loss both look good, but we still need to test this in a real setting. Assuming there are *n* subjects, there will be *n* samples in one test case. Among these *n* samples, one sample is the ground truth pair, which is composed of the query image and an image from the same subject; other *n*-1 samples are composed of the query image and an image from other subjects. For instance, suppose we have four subjects, *A, B, C* and *D,* and their images *a, b, c,* and *d.* Given an unknown image, *x,* one test case can be *[x, a], [x,b], [x, c],* and *[x, d].* In meta-learning, such a task is called **four-way learning**, or **n-way learning,** given *n* unique classes.

First, let's define a function that generates a test case:

```
>>> def gen_test_case(n_way):
...     ids = np.random.choice(range(1, 41), n_way)
...     id_1 = ids[0]
...     image_1 = np.random.randint(0, 10, 1)[0]
...     image_2 = np.random.randint(image_1 + 1, 9 + image_1, 1)[0] % 10
...     X_1 = [id_image[id_1][image_1]]
...     X_2 = [id_image[id_1][image_2]]
...     for id_2 in ids[1:]:
...         image_2 = np.random.randint(0, 10, 1)[0]
...         X_1.append(id_image[id_1][image_1])
...         X_2.append(id_image[id_2][image_2])
...     X_1 = np.array(X_1).reshape([n_way] + image_size) / 255
...     X_2 = np.array(X_2).reshape([n_way] + image_size) / 255
...     return [X_1, X_2]
```

Note that, for convenience, we put the ground truth sample in the first place and the wrong samples in the rest.

We will be evaluating our model in a 4-, 9-, 16-, 25-, 36-, and 40-way learning manners. In each learning manner, we repeat the experiment 1,000 times and calculate the accuracy rate. For comparison purposes, we compute the recognition performance using **K nearest neighbors (KNN)** as a baseline model, which we define as follows:

```
>>> def knn(X):
...     distances = [np.linalg.norm(x_1 - x_2)
...                     for x_1, x_2 in zip(X[0], X[1])]
...     pred = np.argmin(distances)
...     return pred
```

Finally, we kickstart our testing:

```
>>> n_experiment = 1000
>>> for n_way in [4, 9, 16, 25, 36, 40]:
...     n_correct_snn = 0
...     n_correct_knn = 0
...     for _ in range(n_experiment):
...         X_test = gen_test_case(n_way)
...         pred = model.predict(X_test)
...         pred_id = np.argmax(pred)
...         if pred_id == 0:
...             n_correct_snn += 1
...         if knn(X_test) == 0:
...             n_correct_knn += 1
...     print('{}-way few shot learning accuracy: {}'.format(
                         n_way, n_correct_snn / n_experiment))
...     print('Baseline accuracy with knn: {}\n'.format(
                         n_correct_knn / n_experiment))
4-way few shot learning accuracy: 0.963
Baseline accuracy with knn: 0.876

9-way few shot learning accuracy: 0.931
Baseline accuracy with knn: 0.752

16-way few shot learning accuracy: 0.845
Baseline accuracy with knn: 0.663

25-way few shot learning accuracy: 0.767
Baseline accuracy with knn: 0.55

36-way few shot learning accuracy: 0.679
Baseline accuracy with knn: 0.497

40-way few shot learning accuracy: 0.659
Baseline accuracy with knn: 0.478
```

Our Siamese meta-learning model largely outperforms the baseline. We can also observe that, the higher the n, the more possible classes to consider, and hence the harder it is to predict the correct one.

Summary

This is the last stop of our DL architectures and new trends in DL journey. In this chapter, we learned that Bayesian deep learning combines the merits of both Bayesian learning and deep learning. It models uncertainty, which in a way tells us how much we trust the predictions. Capsule networks capture oriental and relative spatial relationships between objects. We believe they will become more mature and popular in the future.

Meta-learning, that is, learning to learn, is an exciting topic in the DL research community. We have implemented a meta-learning model, that is, Siamese Neural Networks with Keras, and applied it to a face recognition problem. In fact, there are many other interesting things going on in DL that are worth looking into, such as deep reinforcement learning, active learning, and automated machine learning. Are there any other new trends you noticed while you were reading this book?

Other Books You May Enjoy

If you enjoyed this book, you may be interested in these other books by Packt:

Python Deep Learning Projects
Rahul Kumar, Matthew Lamons, Et al

ISBN: 978-1-78899-709-6

- Set up a deep learning development environment on Amazon Web Services (AWS)
- Apply GPU-powered instances as well as the deep learning AMI
- Implement seq-to-seq networks for modeling natural language processing (NLP)
- Develop an end-to-end speech recognition system
- Build a system for pixel-wise semantic labeling of an image
- Create a system that generates images and their regions

Python Deep Learning - Second Edition

Gianmario Spacagna, Daniel Slater, Et al

ISBN: 978-1-78934-846-0

- Grasp the mathematical theory behind neural networks and deep learning processes
- Investigate and resolve computer vision challenges using convolutional networks and capsule networks
- Solve generative tasks using variational autoencoders and Generative Adversarial Networks
- Implement complex NLP tasks using recurrent networks (LSTM and GRU) and attention models
- Explore reinforcement learning and understand how agents behave in a complex environment
- Get up to date with applications of deep learning in autonomous vehicles

Leave a review - let other readers know what you think

Please share your thoughts on this book with others by leaving a review on the site that you bought it from. If you purchased the book from Amazon, please leave us an honest review on this book's Amazon page. This is vital so that other potential readers can see and use your unbiased opinion to make purchasing decisions, we can understand what our customers think about our products, and our authors can see your feedback on the title that they have worked with Packt to create. It will only take a few minutes of your time, but is valuable to other potential customers, our authors, and Packt. Thank you!

Index

www.ingramcontent.com/pod-product-compliance
Lightning Source LLC
LaVergne TN
LVHW081516050326
832903LV00025B/1516